The Physiology of New York Boarding-Houses

The Physiology of New York Boarding-Houses

THOMAS BUTLER GUNN

EDITED AND WITH AN INTRODUCTION BY DAVID FAFLIK

RUTGERS UNIVERSITY PRESS
NEW BRUNSWICK, NEW JERSEY, AND LONDON

Library of Congress Cataloging-in-Publication Data

Gunn, Thomas Butler.
The physiology of New York boarding-houses / Thomas Butler Gunn ; edited and with an introduction by David Faflik.
p. cm.
Originally published: New York : Mason Brothers, 1857.
Includes bibliographical references.
ISBN 978-0-8135-4439-7 (hardcover : alk. paper) — ISBN 978-0-8135-4440-3 (pbk. : alk. paper)
1. Lodging-houses—New York (State)—New York—19th century.
2. Boardinghouses—New York (State)—New York—19th century. 3. New York (N.Y.)—Social life and customs—19th century. I. Faflik, David, 1972– II. Title.
HD7288.U4G86 2009
647.9409747'109034—dc22

2008019780

A British Cataloging-in-Publication record for this book is available from the British Library.

The Physiology of New York Boarding-Houses was first published by Mason Brothers in 1857.

Visit our Web site: http://rutgerspress.rutgers.edu

Manufactured in the United States of America

For the cities in our midst

CONTENTS

ACKNOWLEDGMENTS

Like the city it surveys, this book has been a collaborative creation, and many years in the making. Its foundations trace to my time in graduate school at Chapel Hill. With the support of a Gilder Lehrman Dissertation Fellowship in the summer 2004, I first encountered Gunn's *Physiology* at the New York Public Library (NYPL); that institution's crumbling copy, so precariously preserved, at once captured my imagination, and aroused my concern for the fate of a text that begs to be read. Soon I would learn that *Physiology* has retained its admirers, among them the historians John F. Kasson and William J. Rorabaugh. Both scholars have encouraged my work from the start, and remain friends and mentors to this day. I thank them for their support and belief.

No less supportive have been the libraries and their respective staff who aided me in my research and editorial work. These include the Humanities and Social Sciences Library of the NYPL, both Special Collections and the Microforms Division at the University of Chicago's Regenstein Library, and the Interlibrary Loan Office at the University of Washington's Suzzalo Library, in Seattle. The Missouri Historical Society, in St. Louis, has shared Gunn's insightful personal diary in true collegial spirit. And special mention belongs to Autumn L. Mather, senior library assistant in Reference Services at The Newberry Library. Her timely, generous intervention saved me months in preparing my final manuscript.

The entire team at Rutgers University Press has been prompt in its responses to my many queries, and patient in all matters large and small. I could not have asked for more able helpers. My wife, Kari, the ablest helper of all, knows best what went into the making of this volume. She is my final authority in all things, and the collaborator who matters most.

INTRODUCTION

In the early spring of 1842, a twenty-two-year-old New York journalist named Walt Whitman pronounced "the universal Yankee nation" a "boarding people." Resorting to comic elaboration rather than sober explanation, the young newspaper editor would go on to amplify a point for readers that well may have needed none. He writes, "Married men and single men, old women and pretty girls; milliners and masons; cobblers, colonels, and counter-jumpers; tailors and teachers; lieutenants, loafers, ladies, lackbrains, and lawyers; printers and parsons—'black spirits and white, blue spirits and gay'—all 'go out to board'" ("New York Boardinghouses," 22–23).[1]

Whitman was right to assume that his contemporaries already were familiar with "boarding out," as the domestic practice to which he refers then was known. An unprecedented urban turn during the middle decades of the nineteenth century had seen tens of thousands of Americans migrate to or toward the nearest metropolis in search of work and leisure. Meeting them there were an equal number of foreign immigrants arriving mostly from northern and western Europe. And attending them all were the rising real estate prices and severe housing shortages that constituted the commercial, communal logic behind boarding. Formerly a sporadic pastime practiced among sailors, settlers, and apprentices in both the colonial Old and New Worlds, boarding out had emerged in America in the 1830s and 1840s as a widespread ritual that saw masses of men and (to a lesser extent) women, in most instances strangers, come together under a common roof to partake of food, shelter, and upkeep for an agreed-upon weekly or monthly fee. Practically, those commodities otherwise would have been hard to find or afford under rapidly urbanizing circumstances, all the more so along the country's crowded Atlantic seaboard. Symbolically, in the pitch from which Whitman writes, it thus should come as no surprise that he proposes boarding as a behavior by which U.S. citizens everywhere might be identified. From the vantage point of the metropolitan West's unrivaled boardinghouse capital, New York, all America must have looked as if it had gone "to board."

Whitman was right in another sense as well. Given the frequent commentary that boarding had inspired in the sidewalks, streets, and parlors of an urbanizing United States, he correctly assumed that his observations on boarding were less than original; hence the poetic license he claims as he enlivens an otherwise mundane inventory of the city's boardinghouse population with a little playful alliteration. What Whitman might not have known, however, was just how accurately his words captured his country's overall cultural condition. It was not just New Yorkers who boarded. Americans of Whitman's day truly were a "boarding people" writ large. They were drawn to boardinghouses in ever-growing numbers, even among the scattered cities and towns of the nation's interior. And, perhaps more important, increasingly they had become conditioned to the itinerant lifestyle that awaited them back at their provisional homes. No doubt the vast majority of U.S. residents still favored the stand-alone dwelling, assuming they could secure one (Martin, 148).[2] Yet the author of America's first free-verse rhapsody, *Leaves of Grass* (1855), did not exaggerate boarding's broad implications when he later related a startling (if marginally inflated) demographic fact. As of 1856, he could write that fully three-quarters of Manhattan's adult population had lived or then were living in boardinghouses ("Wicked Architecture," 95).[3] That number confirms recent estimates of the boardinghouse's central place in the United States before the Civil War; it likewise suggests the extent of a nationwide trend that saw cities across the country approximate without duplicating New York's leading example. Quite simply, if Whitman is wrong, then our picture of a not-too-distant national past is wrong. If Whitman is right, then it seems incumbent upon us, a former "boarding people," to ask what a boardinghouse is, or was, and how it became a habitual habitation for our antebellum ancestors.

Cultural historians, no less than interested observers of American life and letters, might find ready answers to these and related questions in Thomas Butler Gunn's classic catalogue of all things boarding, *The Physiology of New York Boarding-Houses* (1857). A minor commercial and critical success when it first appeared, Gunn's *Physiology* has suffered a fate not unlike its ostensible subject: marked changes in the country's residential landscape since the time of its writing have all but made his book as obscure in the present tense as boarding itself now would appear to be. That is not to suggest that *Physiology* lacks relevance today. On the contrary, and on the one hand, if "boarding out" in the strictest sense of that phrase has been all but forgotten, it nevertheless persists in modified form in a range of improvised living arrangements that continue to characterize the modern metropolis. The myriad compromises and curtailments in time, space, and shelter that define our lives—not least for the many millions of Americans who reside in or near some sizeable city—trace back in no small part to what remains the pressing necessity of collective domestication. Lease-makers, overnight-stayers, and restaurant diners might testify that the basics of boarding out are with us still.

On the other hand, not only does boarding continue to exist as a social practice, albeit one that has been eclipsed by more self-evident housing situations; it also survives, even less obviously, as a *literary* phenomenon. For, if boarding out began as a way to domesticate under what must have seemed the inhospitable conditions of the big American city, then it quickly evolved an alternate capacity in its *verbal* functions as well—that is to say, as a vehicle through which city dwellers could express with words, *boarding*house words, whether and how they had adjusted to the special temporal, spatial, and cognitive demands of the metropolis. The boardinghouse, in short, formerly provided basic domestic shelter for many Americans. But it also, and simultaneously, yielded a unique fund of practical knowledge that in turn translated for not a few boarders into a conceptual, and rhetorical, means by which the first true generation of U.S. city-dwellers might register their urban experiences. Readers, writers, and talkers today may take for granted the by now-familiar renters' laments, tales of urban flight, and pleas of suburban ennui that at least in part provide articulate testimony to our postmodern existence. Preceding these by more than a century were an abundance of boardinghouse sketches, stories, poems, and plays—to list but several of boarding's storytelling *forms*—at whose narrative heart resides a restless urban American people whose interests, anxieties, and general discursive response to the city anticipate our own.

Physiology epitomizes the boardinghouse *as literature*. In it we receive a representative sampling of the kinds of finished literary products that were informed by boarding, and that regularly appeared in period broadsides, newspapers, magazines, and books, no less than as a popular spectacle on the dramatic stage. We find in *Physiology* as well a reliable template for the unique literary conventions and authorial strategies that developed in tandem with boarding out over the course of its mid-nineteenth-century career. There is, first, an emphatic first-person authority in this study that characterizes much of boarding *as a genre*. Literary boarding need not, and did not, restrict itself to the privileged point of view of an egotistical "I" reporter, necessarily. But, at a time when a writer for *Harper's Weekly* magazine could state that "every body," at least among New Yorkers, "has had, has, or will have" a close encounter with "one of the most striking institutions of this metropolitan city," the boardinghouse, it was essential that accounts such as Gunn's reward readers with a personal interpretive payoff that they might be unable to achieve on their own ("Wanted," 652).

Physiology's author was well-equipped for this task. A native of Banbury, England, Gunn began life on February 15, 1826, in a rural Oxfordshire town—far from boarding, but not far to the southeast of England's "Second City," Birmingham.[4] It nevertheless was to Oxford, and then London, that a young Gunn moved with his family during his childhood to mark his initiation into the transatlantic metropolis. At age fifteen he signed as draughtsman's apprentice to the noted architect Samuel Beazley, who maintained an office in central London's Soho Square. Here he developed a capacity for drawing that led him not into his expected profession, but into the emerging world of print periodicals. He illustrated for several English magazines, including the widely read journal *Punch*, before deciding in 1849 to try his hand, literally, in the thriving New York literary scene across the Atlantic. A skilled caricaturist, cartoonist, and observer of urban life, Gunn soon won a place in Manhattan's semi-underground of journalistic satire; steady work followed with an assortment of the city's typically short-lived periodicals, including the humorous *New York Picayune*, *Nick-nax*, *The Lantern*, and *Yankee Notions* (*NYHSD*, 280). By trying his hand at authorship as well, he combined pen with pencil to launch what would prove to be a rather successful, if low-paying, career among the growing ranks of literary men and women who earned their living piecemeal. Writing and drawing on demand for the metropolitan press, Gunn stood little chance of ensuring economic profit in the long term. What he and his associates had obtained was the chance to enjoy the urban intensity of their life's work—and an all but inevitable encounter with boarding.

In step with the rest of his peers in this proto-Bohemia, Gunn labored like he boarded, with vigor. He "settled"—for a spell, at any rate—upon his New York arrival in a boardinghouse at 132 Bleecker Street. Locals would have recognized this lower Manhattan address as fertile boarders' ground; single young male migrants, in particular, regularly looked to these precincts for housing that at once was affordable and within close proximity to the area's various employers. Among the latter were any number of surrounding mercantile establishments and retail stores, where the city's swelling army of clerks and Whitman's "counter-jumpers" dutifully spent daytime hours climbing their way into the more comfortable reaches of the middle classes. Less conspicuous were the artistic types like Gunn, members (or else would-be members) of a nascent culture industry that lacked the high profile of everyday trade, yet required an adequate supply of writers, painters, engravers, reporters, musicians, and stage performers in order to keep its alternative brand of production in motion. Thrice daily mealtimes recalled many of these downtown-dwellers to their respective boarding establishments nearby. Most likely also in attendance were a minority constituency of shop girls, female teachers, and seamstresses, who broke bread in common with the men; it was but one of boarding's democratic tendencies. Leisure hours sent boarders in different directions, depending on individual preferences. There were lyceum lectures and lending libraries for those seeking self-improvement. Theaters, museums, art galleries, and concert halls blended "high" and "low" entertainments. Saloons, oyster cellars, and brothels sold less innocent pleasures. And before and afterward were the boardinghouses, a metropolitan base from which work and pleasure both were within easy reach of occupants.

This was Gunn's boardinghouse world, the foundation for his *Physiology*. Fittingly for this milieu, he led a peripatetic existence during the early years of the 1850s. Journalistic assignments into the U.S. heartland—with visits to the Great Lakes region, New Orleans, and Kentucky, plus places in between—removed him on occasion from his chosen New York environs. A subsequent return trip to London, and then Paris, in 1854, additionally kept him in the Old World for upwards of a year. By 1855, however, he was back in Manhattan, still relatively unsettled in the customary boardinghouse fashion—"unwilling to pause," he later writes, "ever jostling onward" (*Physiology*, chapter I). Yet he found focus in a regular research routine, which he began conducting on behalf of a book that records for contemporaries and posterity alike the conditions faced by many a mid-nineteenth-century boarder.

Of course, by conventional standards, certain aspects of the boardinghouse life that followed next for Gunn *defied* convention, and so must be seen as emblematic of something other than a mass average. It was not your everyday boarder, for instance, who joined the "Bohemian Club" at Pfaff's Broadway tavern, where late-night eating, drinking, and smoking sessions brought together a select group of the city's *artistes*—Gunn among them—in self-conscious imitation of European-style creative talk. Not every boarder, like him, belonged to a literary circle that included celebrity author Fanny Fern, her biographer husband James Parton, newspaperman-poet Walt Whitman, and the nationally known editor Horace Greeley. Nor did the run-of-the-mill boardinghouse denizen spend mornings, as did Gunn, reading widely, writing rapidly, and drawing for fun or for dollars, while canvassing periodical offices and publishers come afternoons in search of the next paid engagement (Gunn, diaries).[5] But, apart from a few eccentricities and an abiding English accent, *Physiology*'s prospective author otherwise boarded out in the accepted fashion of a mainstream American bourgeoisie. His fellow magazinist, Thomas Dunn English, recalled him decades afterward as no Grub Street loafer, but as "a correct, upright, and decorous gentleman" who would have graced any workplace (English, 202). Worldly, well-groomed, and mild-mannered, Gunn by extension also would have qualified as an ideal messmate for the city's respectable middle classes. For it was not only New York's aspiring classes who boarded. Newlywed couples, cost-cutting families, bachelors, spinsters, and widows all boarded out with much of the rest of Manhattan, although they often opted for more genteel quarters farther uptown if the higher cost of finer accommodations was not prohibitive. His own straitened finances permitting, Gunn might have been but one of the boarders staring back at them from across their boardinghouse table.

He had seen many such tables by the time his *Physiology* reached bookstores in 1857. True to boardinghouse form, Gunn adopts the first-person "I" from the start of his work when he dedicates it "To All Inmates of Metropolitan Boarding-Houses, . . . By an Ex-Member of the Fraternity." The author in other words opens with an assurance that he has composed by a process that depends upon something other than mere imagination. He himself has boarded, rather. And, despite now having exchanged Manhattan boarding for home-ownership in the more affordable borough of Brooklyn, across the East River, he has returned with a fresh perspective on a topic that many readers might have thought exhausted. Yet *Physiology* is full of surprises, informed as it is by a wealth of engaging anecdotes acquired firsthand "By an Ex-Member of the Fraternity." The author's housing history had been as varied as his potential audience's, whose habitats comprised all the different domiciles on offer in Manhattan. Boarding was the language that author and audience spoke in common, and in Gunn readers met a man who has mastered the idiom. He imparts his wisdom, as it were, with his volume, and so fulfills a traditional purpose of all literatures, instruction. Thus on one level, his work reads as a wholesale compilation of boardinghouse options for a people who might have deemed any such statement redundant. On another level, his comments were colorful enough to warrant public attention: *Physiology*'s first edition sold out less than one month after it had been printed.[6]

One suspects it was not the matter but the manner of *Physiology* that attracted readers initially. Friend Fanny Fern wrote a glowing review of the book for the *New York Ledger* story paper (Bonner, 4; Fern, "A Social Nuisance").[7] Local actor Edwin Forrest, a favorite with working-class crowds from the city's Bowery district, likewise owned a copy.[8] At the opposite end of the class spectrum, meanwhile, and some blocks farther uptown, the prosperous Manhattan attorney George Templeton Strong also bought and read the book, praising it highly in his diary as "a very clever and funny treatise" (Strong, II, 349). Indeed, so thorough is Gunn's examination of urban America's domestic predicament that the work in its final form possesses certain encyclopedic qualities that Strong is right to recognize. "Exceedingly comprehensive" is how a columnist for the *Democratic Review* described *Physiology*'s overall effect ("Our Book Table," 192). But Gunn, like other boardinghouse authors of the age (as we will see, there were scores of such writers), did not rest content with straightforward reportage. He indulges, rather, an aesthetic of overwhelm that transcends the mechanical accumulation of housing data, and imparts to his writing a tone at once elevated and elevat*ing*. If he was not given to bombast—and *Physiology*'s author communicates with civility, courtesy, subtlety, and charm throughout his book—he does write with all of his senses attuned to extremes. As a result, much of *Physiology* reads in the superlative degree. Gunn repeatedly hunts and finds the biggest, smallest, best, and worst of boarding; having found them, he gleefully shares these specimen examples with readers, the rules of conversational propriety notwithstanding. He writes *what* he wants, *how* he wants, and in the process achieves with words the literary equivalent of graphic caricature, at which he excelled. More to the point, he would have us read his various boardinghouse rarities as anything but—which is to say that Gunn, in the timeless tradition of satire, locates representativeness in the anomalous, and asks that we do the same. What might strike some readers as silly distortions are in truth for him something else: the odd, the unusual, the exotic, the over-elaborate figure in *Physiology* as richly suggestive *types* of the peoples, places, and faces that one was likely to find in Manhattan. Gunn's assumption is that the metropolis itself is something extraordinary, and its boardinghouses both a cause and an effect, a magnet and a maker, of an urban American version of the strange. Judging from *Physiology*'s impressive early sales figures, many a New York reader agreed.

As with Whitman's whimsical alliterativeness, and like the poet's slight statistical inflation, Gunn pushes hard facts toward embellished fiction in tacit acknowledgment of the inherent limitations of his literary field. Because there were few who knew nothing of boarding, domestic exaggeration had developed into a discursive norm for authors who would add value, or at least interest, to material that otherwise was so pedestrian as to obviate further remark. Too obvious for understatement, the boardinghouse in literature invited rhetorical flourish instead. *Physiology* follows suit, and a reader for the *Democratic Review* regretted the net result by saying the text "strained a little," calling it "flippant . . . and rather staggery in some of its more pretentious passages" ("Our Book Table," 191). But a reviewer for *Frank Leslie's Illustrated Newspaper* had the exact opposite reaction, one that seems to have been shared across the city. Endorsing what his *Democratic* counterpart deplores, this particular writer extends his praise in words at least as hyperbolic as Gunn's. He has read the work in question "with infinite amusement." "It will meet with an unprecedented sale," as "tens of thousands feel a keen and undying interest in the subject." Not only that, but the book's "power" resides in the author's ability to record "the poisonous truth" of urban domestication generally, and New York specifically—to wit, that city-residence breeds "peculiar idiosyncrasies" in the men and women who endure it, insofar as modern metropolitan residence itself was an exceptional cultural condition. Conclusion: "*The Physiology of New York Boarding-Houses* is undoubtedly one of the striking books of the season" (*Frank Leslie's*, 95). What proved most "striking" for this reader, as for many more besides, was the apparent realization that the volume's word-drawings were so recognizably real not despite being exaggerated, but *because* they were exaggerated.

The very title of the work suggests in part the nature of its excesses. This book is a "Physiology" for sure, inasmuch as the sweeping comprehensiveness of Gunn's survey becomes, through the simple act of sustained narration, a veritable *anatomy* of residential Manhattan that promises in these pages revelations for even seasoned urban Americans. The author duly delivers an exhaustive taxonomy of type after type of boardinghouse. Individual chapters bring us such mainstays as the "'Hand-to-Mouth' Boarding-House," the "Cheap Boarding-House on a Large Scale," and the "Fashionable Boarding-House Where You Don't Get Enough to Eat." More specialized offerings include the "Artists' Boarding-House," the "Theatrical Boarding-House," the "Medical Students' Boarding-House," and the "'Serious' Boarding-House." There is even a "Vegetarian Boarding-House" for those with a taste for food reform, and a "Boarding-House

Where the Landlady Drinks" for those craving tragicomedy. The list goes on and on. Gunn has seen them all, in accordance with the first-person demands of the boardinghouse genre. But, in seeming contradiction of those demands, he likewise employs the patented gratuitous gestures than won for boarding in its literary guise so many eager readers. More is not just more here. Total inclusion is not simply a numbers game won at the expense of discriminating *ex*clusion; it is also the principle upon which the author tells his tale, in the belief that by stretching and "straining" the images on which his text rests, he might achieve more accurate mimetic effects. If the *Physiology* is no novel, then, if it does not quite qualify as an extended, fanciful prose narrative, it doubtless does manage to say something new. Its sheer staggering multiplicity, in tandem with its mock-serious celebration of strangeness, achieves for *Physiology* a specific kind of novelty, one that recalls the dynamic, historical urban context from which it was raised.

Gunn thereby ensures that *Physiology* both instructs *and* diverts. Regardless how they rated his book, readers from the late 1850s agreed in classifying it as a work of humor. *Physiology* was fun—fun to read, and fun to look at as well. The author's proclivity for lists, to begin, functions as a repeated punch line upon reading, or, rather, as a punch line whose comedic intent inheres in the very act of repetition. Gunn runs readers in circles, and we cannot help but laugh in visiting boardinghouse establishments which, if markedly different, yet somehow feel the same. No less funny is the crazy content of what gets repeated. Whether one encounters them in quick succession, or else at intervals of intervening chapters, boardinghouses such as those "Where There Are Marriageable Daughters," "Where You're Expected to Make Love to the Landlady," or "Whose Landlady Likes to Be Ill-Used" induce in us smiling assent to the comically familiar and a knowing nod at the preposterous. It is not the houses we are laughing at in these instances; it is what scholars call the "emerging metropolitan manners" that boarders' behavior typifies. Coupled with the author's self-deprecating, deadpan delivery, the cumulative effect of this lengthy behavioral record is "a comic typology" no less readable for being risible (Day and Haggerty, 15). Then there is what historian Wendy Gamber aptly has termed "boarder's beef" (Gamber, 79). The chronic complaints voiced by boarders about everything from dining room fare to household cleanliness (or a lack thereof) comprise a recurring source of humor for the genre as a whole. Gunn has his share of grievances, as do the boarders who enter into his account. And what they all hold in common is a nineteenth-century tendency toward what David S. Reynolds names "the grotesque posture"—a subversive willingness to sport with words, to push language to its outer limits (Reynolds, 441–483). Among boarders, such sportiveness often involved self-conscious contests to bemoan the most their individually experienced domestic shortcomings, but that was but one of the forms that verbal play might take. As Gunn suggests, tall tales and improbable puns, no less than immoderate "boasts," "over-quoted drollery," and "burlesque phrases applied to aught that may be supposed serious" reinforced literary boarding's version of verisimilitude (*Physiology*, chapter XII); already a forum for exaggeration, the boardinghouse in literature imagined a wild reality commensurate with the heady excitement of a city that the author ultimately defines as "an indiscriminately-got-together community" (298). Both the collective domicile and the metropolis it figured in miniature are for him an arbitrarily assembled site of "multifarious" urban pluralism (16), whether on a small or large scale. Thus out of the mouths of his boarders pour words that make a mockery of quiet modesty, his own included.

Complementing *Physiology*'s verbal antics are an entire portfolio's worth of cartoon-like *visual* images, which, in the aggregate, transform our conception of the city according to their creators' illustrative wit. Gunn the artist was reared, we will remember, in the English satirical tradition of the London journal *Punch*, to which periodical he contributed before sailing for the United States at the close of the 1840s. In *Punch* readers on both sides of the Atlantic encountered a savvy response to urban society; its tongue-in-cheek commentary on municipal politics, class privilege, and the curbside transactions of street life captured the bemused attitude that many contemporaries had taken to the cities in their midst. In *Punch* Gunn likewise entered into a related tradition of urban caricature whose impact it would be difficult to overstate—that of the great English author Charles Dickens, whose work he invokes repeatedly in his text. The printers and publishers involved with *Punch* for a time brought out after 1842 a number of Dickens's novels, following their serialization in both English and American magazines. Dickens all but perfected in these volumes the rendering of urban "types" that Gunn with so many others incorporate into their own work.[9] More telling with respect to Dickens's influence on our author is the Cruikshank connection, as in George Cruikshank. It was Cruikshank who, as Dickens's artistic collaborator, set the standard for caricature illustration during the years of Gunn's apprenticeship. Cruikshank's drawings gave Victorian readers a visual corollary for the Dickensian narrative, which in effect consisted of overlapping pedestrian traffic in interconnected peoples. Like many of the era's illustrators, *Physiology*'s author followed the Cruikshank model; unlike others, he emulates without imitating Cruikshank's high aesthetic standards. Conceived and sketched in the city, his drawings retain a striking sign of the urban about them, and so impart to his artwork a graphic metropolitanism that arguably is its signature trait. Whether flustered, funny, and quirky, cosmopolitan and composed, or simply going about their business, his caricatured city-dwellers possess an air that suggests they would be out of place amid any setting other than that of the metropolis (figure 1). We often see Gunn's images and laugh, but we just as well may respond by thinking "cities."

He did not draw alone. Helping him illustrate his *Physiology* were three of his countrymen, also itinerant artists, who like him were living and working in Bohemian New York exile from England. One of these men was famous. Born in

Figure 1. Thomas Butler Gunn's wood engraving of Walt Whitman, which the Englishman Gunn clipped from the contemporary New York periodical in which it first appeared, and then pasted into his American diary. The set of squiggles by his left shoulder, and the set of squiggles and the post on his right, as well as the name below were all added in ink by Gunn after publication. From the Thomas Butler Gunn Diaries, April 12, 1856 to end of October 1857, p. 11 (June 1856). Missouri History Museum Archives. NS 37500. Scan © 2008, Missouri History Museum.

India, and then raised in England and France, Frank Bellew came to the United States less than a year after Gunn, and in short order saw his comical book and magazine illustrations—signed in the geographic shape of his pen name, "The Triangle"—meet with much favor. Gunn was especially fortunate to have Bellew involved in his project, and the two would come to share a camaraderie enhanced by their common interest in boarding and fellow membership in Pfaff's (Starr, 3–7; Stylus, 64–65).[10] Alfred Waud's fame was still to come when the newly arrived Londoner set to work on *Physiology*. He toured the U.S. South and West for *Harper's Weekly* magazine during and after the Civil War, contributing by correspondence drawings and sketches that gave many Northern readers a glimpse of a regional American life previously unknown to them. Finally, of the four, English craftsman John Andrew offered a variation on the other three's repeated theme: he came to Manhattan by way of Boston, and was the engraver who readied for the printing press his fellow artists' pen and pencil drawings (*NYHSD*, 10, 43, 666). He did so with some success, if we are to believe our enthusiastic reviewer for *Frank Leslie's*. The "comic illustrations" of *Physiology*, he predicts, "will satisfy every one" (*Frank Leslie's*, 95). Or, as the *Democratic Review* decided, the book's "pictures" were "excellent and full of life"—*boardinghouse* life, the writer specifies, of which "who has *not*, at some time or other," partaken, he asks ("Our Book Table," 191–192).

It was more than a rhetorical question, as Whitman's introductory remarks show. For, despite the levity behind *Physiology*, boarding out was serious business for the "universal Yankee nation," and we would be wrong to interpret our author's comedic treatment of his materials as an indication that he somehow deemed them trivial. In Gunn's day, as in ours, boarding both as a social practice and as a channel for literary expression intersected in decisive ways with the core issues of race, class, gender, and ethnicity that today have become touchstones of American cultural studies. We might laugh at *Physiology*'s contents. But the book asks us to think critically as well, about the conflicting attributes of U.S. identity in age that now seems multicultural by default, and furthermore increasingly, inescapably urban.

Like the nation that contained it, Gunn's metropolis is as heterogeneous as we would expect it to be, considering that Manhattan became the first city in the United States to cross the half-million mark in population at the start of the decade in which he wrote. Sheer demographic fact had made New York a case study in diversity by at least 1850, if not earlier. The city accordingly served from that moment forward as a kind of testing ground for the problems and possibilities of a democratic brand of pluralism into which the outsider Gunn, foreign-born as he was, might offer special insight. To board with him, moreover, is to enter into an operative domestic metaphor that equates the macrocosm of country with the microcosm of house, *boarding*house. Writing from what he calls "the capital of the Western World"—as pertains, "at least, on this side of the Atlantic," he says—the author trains his gaze on the national "character" and "present peculiarities" of an American people whom he labels "aborigines." What he concludes after only a preliminary investigation is this: "we conceive that no better place for sketching these ["peculiarities"] can be selected than out substitutes for homes—Boarding-Houses" (*Physiology*, chapter I).

Of course, boarding was not unique to the United States. Europeans boarded, too, or, as was often the case in expanding urban centers overseas, they lodged in single-room "communal" quarters without partaking of the boardinghouse's shared meals. Yet, if it was not monopolized by the New World, boarding was resorted to by urban Americans at higher rates, in greater numbers, and with a more pronounced cultural prominence than it was anywhere else outside U.S. borders. Gunn stops short of citing a "national institution of boardinghouses," as would another Englishman visiting America only a few years later (Grattan, 109–115). But he proceeds from the premise that American boardinghouses as such "contain types of a large portion of the population" (*Physiology*, chapter I).

Not all of *Physiology*'s chapters unfold neatly on a "type" by "type" basis, of course, but still much of the book's interest and momentum—its "plot," if you will—inhere in the author's urge to categorize all of the peoples he meets and places where he stays. Sorting boarders, and boarding establishments, into a scheme of class hierarchies is but one of Gunn's tactics in his endeavor to achieve order. And yet, although writing from what must seem the "safe" side of the genteel class divide, our ex-boarder turned author takes pains in his *Physiology* to underscore the unstable nature of *distinct* class hierarchies among metropolitan boarders. What he labels the "Tip-Top Boarding-House," for example, provides amenities to match its high asking price for board; French-influenced cuisine, spotless white linen, and dining-room decorum are the luxuries here afforded the well-to-do and ambitious middle classes. At least hypothetically, however, even the finest household was run on an open-door policy. Any boarder who could provide personal references, and then make, or else perennially defer, scheduled rent payments might have access to all of the above perquisites, maybe more.

It nevertheless was the middle mass toward which most boarders and boardinghouses tended, and where the lines between classes sometimes blurred. The antebellum period stands out historically for promoting a domestic ideology in which the autonomous, well-run middle-class household was believed to act as a moral buffer against the dislocations of a volatile market economy and competitive society. American urbanization tested this belief, and in boarding domesticity met a qualifying condition that not even the most optimistic of contemporary domestic advice manuals on cooking, cleaning, and child-rearing could ignore. Residing within the restrictive limits of the city, boarders were notorious for cutting corners, for having to make do with communal, semipublic space rather than pursue an elusive middle-class ideal of private domestic sanctuary. Thus shabbiness and gentility often shared space under the same urban roof, as evidenced by *Physiology*'s many disgruntled boarders. Disparate household standards reappeared outside, too. Promiscuous city-blocks not infrequently saw what the author calls "Mean" or "Cheap" boardinghouses set but several paces apart from "respectable" domiciles, like his rare "Boarding-House Which Gives Satisfaction to Every Body." Even a casual glance at outward domestic appearances could relay much about the class conditions of boarders within. But, perhaps most important for readers of *Physiology* is the class mixing that occurs *inside* the covers of this book. Gunn's habit of juxtaposing any one household description with another in a seemingly random sequence of chapters reads as something of an arbitrary jumble in the end. And with good reason: as with his domestic exaggerations, the author's employing class overlap as a narrative strategy is a decision that belongs as much to the unfettered growth of the city as it does to his own idiosyncrasies. Gunn's attempt to recall New York's expansion on page, and in print, marks but another instance of the implications for an urban version of literary realism. The book's disjointedness, in other words, is the city's.

Similarly, his systematic crossing of apparent class boundaries puts the lie to the idyllic visions of domesticity that were then current in popular literature, not least in full-fledged boardinghouse novels such as Sarah Josepha Hale's *Boarding Out* (1845) and Fanny Fern's *Ruth Hall* (1854).[11] Each of these comparable works interrogates normative domestic dreams in its way; especially pronounced is the skepticism with which they regard boarding's middle-class pretensions. Yet with Gunn the impetus toward what we might call "undoing the domestic" is at once unrelenting and unforgiving in a way that it is not for his peers. He leaves little room for ambivalence when he concludes *Physiology* with the following: "a Boarding-House is, emphatically, NOT a home" (*Physiology*, chapter XXXIV). His is also an unmistakably male perspective that both helps to qualify a female-dominated discourse on "home," and reflexively exposes the masculine bias that at times clouds his household vision. *The Physiology of New York Boarding-Houses* is, in short, the seldom-told story of an urban America not hurting from homelessness per se; serious consideration of social pathologies of that magnitude would reach the reading public at a later date, and by a different route. Rather, Gunn writes with a national "average" in mind—whether that "average" be real or imagined—when he holds urban America accountable for failing in its larger middle-class mission: a freedom conceived as having and holding a home of one's own.

All of which begs the question of Manhattan's sizeable "other half," those area wage laborers, migrants, immigrants, and proto-bohemians, like Gunn, for whom the boardinghouse was seldom a stopping point en route to the privileged householder status that the author himself would go on to enjoy. For far too many metropolitans, the boardinghouse remained either a precarious, low-rent foothold in a city offering basic employment opportunities, or else a dead-end domestic shelter whose connotations of downward mobility rendered lives already obscure all the more so. Gunn, we know, had firsthand knowledge of the down-and-out domestic experience that awaited many of the city's marginal groups. His effectiveness as narrator rested in part on his ability to document that very experience, which he does, in part.

Herein lies a major interpretive impasse in his work—for the author and, by extension, for the reader. Gunn can relate the residentially compounded struggles of those local artists for whom the boardinghouse often became a barren, garret-like reminder of professional hardship and domestic privation because he had survived such a state but recently. His input was and is personal, and we are inclined to listen to him as a result. But because he was an "Ex-Member of the Fraternity," and an Anglo-American middle-class male at that, Gunn's capacity for sympathy, let alone empathy, must have its limits. *Physiology* in consequence violates at least one of the unspoken rules of the boardinghouse report. Not having certain facts at his command, facts that derived from racial, ethnic, and socioeconomic experiences that were naturally unavailable to him, the author relies instead on secondhand information to complete his account of New York's rainbow assortment of residences. More accurately, he imagines, without quite fictionalizing, short-term stays at a collection of actual metropolitan boardinghouse "types" from which conventional renters' etiquette would have barred him by virtue of his "Britishness," bourgeois "whiteness," or both. It is with some caution, then, that readers should receive Gunn's "firsthand" accounts of having kept company with a range of recent ethnic "other" arrivals, whether at "The German 'Gasthaus,'" "The Irish Immigrant Boarding-House," "The Chinese Boarding-House," or even among symbolically black "tars" at "The Sailors' Boarding-House"—each of which locales receives chapter-length treatment (*Physiology*, chapter XXXI). Whether *Physiology* moves us beyond boarding's middle-class mainstream is not the question. The book indeed does lead us in such directions, for Gunn has captured at its antebellum beginning the disturbing *spirit* of an urban American underworld of low-end housing that remains intact today. If the author's end is admirable, however, his means are less than reliable. A not wholly trustworthy out-of-body experience grants him temporary narrative access to boardinghouse places to which he did not belong. Having gained that access, he in turn resorts to the use of persistent stereotypes for Celtic "Paddies," "squint-eyed" Asians, and improvident, hard-drinking sailors to draw a composite picture of America that ultimately feels less faithful than one of his clever caricatures (chapters XXIX, XXX, and XXXI).

If Gunn could be culturally insensitive, he also held certain views that were progressive by comparison with those of many Americans in his day. The author was particularly alert to the nation's contradictory stance on race, and he returned to his forte, firsthand reportage, when from 1861 to 1863 he served as a Southern Civil War correspondent for the estimable *New York Tribune* newspaper—and in the process came into direct contact with African American slavery. That experience lay several years ahead of him at the time when he wrote *Physiology*. Meanwhile, he was content to recognize the glaring absence of blacks at most U.S. boardinghouses, save in their capacity as occupants of low-end racially segregated establishments, or else as (poorly) paid domestic servants at "white" ones. African Americans make a few cameo appearances here: there is the "colored boy" at one residence, whose rigid disciplining reminds Gunn of nothing so much as a " 'hand' on a slave plantation" (*Physiology*, chapter V); and there is the entire staff at "The Boarding-House Whose Landlady is a Southerner." Though limited in scope and duration, these scenes give some indication of the author's own views on American race relations, views that he made plain in the diary he kept during his years in New York. There, he candidly declares slavery "the sum of all villainies," and Americans who condone it complicit in support of an "unchristian sham republic" (Gunn, diaries, May 23, 1858). *Physiology*'s narrator is far too diffident for confrontational statements of this kind, his liberal ways with language notwithstanding. *Physiology*'s author was less likely to remain silent when it came to matters of consequence. Acknowledging, then, at least a small discrepancy between the respective voices of Gunn the writer and Gunn the "Physiologist," we might conclude that both the personal and comical qualities of *Physiology* do not prevent the book's giving at least oblique consideration to American matters racial and political.

Nor does *Physiology* avoid another fundamental aspect of boarding, one that touches on larger issues of national belonging—gender. Gunn's attitudes toward women could be quite conservative, both inside and outside of print. He took a moral position, mainly, believing as he did that a woman's "proper" role was by her husband's side, to be seen but seldom heard when in mixed company (Gunn, diaries, December 27, 1856). So, it is little surprise that he failed to maintain cordial relations with the unconventional author Fanny Fern for longer than he did, the twice-divorced Fern being guilty in his eyes of any number of feminine indiscretions. As he writes in his diary:

> She dresses immodestly, exposing her bosom, more than women generally do in ball costume. She makes smutty jokes. She compliments (!) male visitors by supposing them to have begotten illegitimate children. . . . She will call attention to her feet, to other portions and the least intellectual ones, of her body. She hung up one of her shoes, near the gas, in the room I occupied one night,[12] I suppose to set me regaling my mind with speculations about it. (I grinned, got a book and never looked at the shoe.). . . She openly hints at her sexual desires.—All of which is less harmful than her writings (Gunn diaries, vol. 10, May 1, 1859).

Clearly these are not the comments of a man who is prepared to have women enjoy equal membership in modern urban America. But, notwithstanding such remarks, and the mindset that permitted Gunn to make them, *Physiology* reads in many ways as a "woman's" book, from beginning to end.

Its being so is more a byproduct of boarding than any "feminist" intention of the author's. Historically, the majority of boardinghouse keepers were widows struggling to make ends meet without the income of a breadwinning husband. Because landladies enjoyed at least a modicum of social respect through their status as small proprietors, many a bereft wife could halt an unwelcome slide into the working classes by accepting boarders into her own home after converting and furnishing it for that purpose. Leasing premises from an absentee owner, and in turn renting rooms to boarders, was an alternative option for women as well. In either case, boarding out at once met the necessity of self-support, even as it satisfied middle-class domestic expectations by keeping working women—which is what landladies were, after all—exactly where much of America expected them to be, in the home. That is also where *Physiology* unfolds, of course, the author by design having written a determinedly *interior* drama in his house-by-house inspection of the city. Antebellum boarders by and large might have been men, then, but boardinghouses predominantly were conceived as a "female" space. That space was *social*, as Gunn reminds us when he highlights the distinction between "*keeping*, instead of *boarding*" (*Physiology*, chapter XXXIII). It was also *narrative*, as the author perhaps unwittingly concedes by granting so much of *Physiology*'s incident and action to women. And it was above all *ironic*, in that the starring role in these pages arguably goes not to the pervasive first-person male narrator, but to the female boardinghouse keepers whose parts prove in the final analysis less supportive than indispensable. Through boarding women did, apparently, belong.

If boarding was socially significant, and culturally inclusive, finally, it left maybe its greatest legacy in the realm of American literature. The list of U.S. authors from the young republic and antebellum nation who boarded out at some stage in their careers includes not only hundreds, perhaps thousands, of rank-and-file writers but also dozens of eminent names that we might not automatically associate with the American metropolis. Early Romantics Charles Brockden Brown and William Cullen Bryant boarded out in New York, as did Whitman, Fern, Edgar Allan Poe, Harriet Jacobs, and Herman Melville after them. The prolific George Lippard boarded out in Philadelphia before his publishing breakthrough in the early 1840s, while literary New England boarded throughout the period in and around Boston. Phillis Wheatley, Ralph Waldo Emerson, Henry David Thoreau, Nathaniel Hawthorne, Oliver Wendell Holmes, and Emily Dickinson all had been to the boardinghouse.

Not satisfied to domesticate with the rest of urban America, U.S. writers also converted their experiences into poetry and prose on more occasions than many of us might realize. It is not only the obvious instances of literary boarding that should arrest our attention: the opening chapters of Melville's whaling epic *Moby-Dick* (1851), for instance, plus select passages from Hawthorne's reform novel *The Blithedale Romance* (1852) and Holmes's classic boardinghouse monologue *The Autocrat of the Breakfast Table* (1858). Rather, the very language, themes, settings, and images of a wide range of period literature make frequent use of boardinghouse frames—literal and figurative—to invoke the cities in writers' midst. Gunn in other words kept double company when boarding out. Many an American author had experimented with communal living; just as many more converted that phase of their lives into imagining the metropolis anew.

To read for boarding as a literary form is often as easy as locating those written landscapes that take the city as their subject. The boardinghouse frequently figures as a landmark of such landscapes, or else as an inconspicuous vantage point on them. That inconspicuousness is key, for Gunn like other writers from his era effectively rendered boarders' world visible for readers by making themselves *in*visible inside their metropolitan texts. We might consider it another boardinghouse irony: in order to permit us to see the city on a manageable scale—bounded by boardinghouse walls, and with a roof on top—the ever-present, tell-tale "I" featured in works like *Physiology* becomes all "eyes" in the end. It is not a bodily presence that guides us through Gunn's houses, for example. It is not a physical person who leads readers, but a perceptual capacity bestowed by the very act of boardinghouse narration that allows uninvited guests to step across the thresholds of urban residences whose inner workings recall the larger city out of doors.

Gunn did not invent the disappearing urban narrator. One would need to return to Europe to trace the development of this literary device. The mythical devil figure Asmodeus from sixteenth-century Spanish legend would be the consensus choice of origins, as our author no doubt knows. He invokes Asmodean "supernatural powers" in his work's epigraph, powers that enable him to lift the city's rooftops and so grant us unimpeded visual access to a domestic indoors otherwise off limits (*Physiology*, t.p.). He likewise follows a related urban narrative tradition in Englishmen Joseph Addison's and Richard Steele's *Spectator* essays from the early eighteenth century, with their similar promise of ocular empowerment to readers trained to *see* the city with proper sophistication. Most important, Gunn in addition writes with full knowledge of his own era's quintessential city-dweller, the flâneur of literary Paris. The flâneur as he (there are few instances of female flâneurs) appears in contemporary print combined dilettante newspaper reportage and theater criticism with his true vocation, sidewalk connoisseurship (Wolff, 141–156). In wandering through the commercial city, exploring its arcades, boulevards, and architecture, its citizens and of course its hotels and boardinghouses, the leisured, somewhat lazy, and financially secure flâneur lost himself in the urban crowd. Yet for the flâneur and the readers of his *feuilletons*, or printed newspaper sketches—as well as in *feuilletons* bound and published in book form as *physiologies*—the paradoxically pleasurable threat of losing one's urban self was offset by an alternate urge to organize, and, yes, in the manner of Gunn, to *categorize* a confusing modern metropolis. Whether in this or any other, the flâneur's *physiology* takes as its primary purpose boarding's reason for being: to make the city habitable as a home, and available as a conceptual category by which to ground oneself in environs that must have seemed perpetually in motion. In the flâneur metropolitan habitation thus met urban meditation. In flanerie the city became a site to "settle" in both senses of the word. It was an area for roving city-strollers to occupy, and an arena for those so inclined to enjoy unhurried reflection on the sights, sounds, and sensations of the urban.

Physiology's example alone suggests the shared transatlantic dimensions of flanerie as a means for "seeing" and "reading" the city. Indeed, the figure of the flâneur displayed in these pages followed a number of different routes from the Old to the New World, in Gunn's day most recently (though not exclusively) through the novels of Frenchman Honoré de Balzac, and in more fugitive form through Charles Dickens's popular "Boz" sketches of the early 1830s (Brand, *Spectator*).[13] Both Balzac and "Boz" found fruitful overlap in flanerie and boarding, with Balzac's boardinghouse novel *Le Père Goriot* (1835) and Dickens's tale "The Boarding House" (1836) both anticipating Gunn's labors some two decades later.[14] But by whatever door he entered the country, by the boardinghouse or some other, the flâneur as a modern embodiment for an urban literary form had inspired by mid-century many American admirers and imitators—not a few of them boarder-authors like Gunn, if not all of them so migratory as he in their transcontinental travels and geographic habits.

Decidedly *of* the city, the flâneur nevertheless sought to observe his urban surroundings from a safe critical distance. Gunn replicates that perceptual position, we recall, in being an "Ex-Member of the Fraternity," which is to say, a former boarder. But however he achieved it—say, from some boardinghouse window several stories above street-level—the flâneur primarily saw his visual prerogative in opportunistic terms: to find personal urban space where it sometimes seemed there was none, to be at home in cities that forever had changed the meaning of "home," and to merge with the metropolitan crowd without the total sacrifice of self-hood. These were the modern problems that boarders and flâneurs alike confronted in real metropolitan life, much as they did in a complicatedly "realistic" boardinghouse literature.

Yet they did so with a difference in the United States. In an urbanizing nation west of Paris, "American" boarder-flâneurs like Gunn tended to resist the temptations of passive spectatorship that many of their European counterparts found so attractive. Americans' boardinghouse narrative posture was on the contrary active. Boarder-flâneurs created States-side an aesthetic mechanism for drawing closer to, rather than farther from, whatever city loomed largest on their horizon. In boarding, accordingly, many an American reader and writer of the nineteenth century discovered a metaphor actually to inhabit, a trope that could stand on the strength of its basis in sociological fact, and a conduit for racial, ethnic, class, and gender commentary, however indirect. The next century would bring twin sagas of inner-city decline and suburban flight. Meanwhile, literary boarding helped turn the nation's collective attention toward the new urban paradigm that defined so many citizens' lives. At a cultural moment when it mattered most, then, works like *The Physiology of New York Boarding-Houses* served to remind many Americans of what they already knew—that the U.S. city was here to stay.

Thomas Butler Gunn proved less permanent. In April 1863, some three years into his work as a Southern Civil War correspondent, *Physiology*'s author returned to England as the *New York Tribune* newspaper's London correspondent. He held that position for a number of years before retracing the steps that had taken him from his native Banbury, near Birmingham, decades earlier. "Home" at last in the nearby village of Upper Wardington, he thereafter contributed articles and essays to the local *Banbury Guardian*, most notably a series of architectural pieces on the area's churches. Gunn died in Birmingham in the spring of 1904. An obituary in the *Guardian* mourned his passing, with a staff writer praising his lost colleague's "geniality and sincerity" ("Veteran Journalist," *Banbury Guardian*). The personal and personable likewise describe Gunn's *Physiology*, as any reader today can attest.

NOTES

1. Whitman made these remarks as the newly hired editor of the New York penny-newspaper the *Aurora*.

2. Historian Edgar W. Martin writes that in 1860, four-fifths of the American population remained rural—this after the most intensive period of urbanization in the nation's history. Rural Americans likewise, says Martin, continued to opt whenever and wherever possible for the single-family home.

3. From a series on "Wicked Architecture" that Whitman completed for another New York periodical, *Life Illustrated*.

4. Unless indicated otherwise, much of the biographical background on Gunn that appears here comes from his obituary, "Death of Mr. Thomas Butler Gunn, A Veteran Journalist," *The Banbury Guardian* [Great Britain], Thursday, April 14, 1904.

5. While living in the United States, Gunn kept a diary in which he recorded his day-to-day activities, as well as his innermost thoughts on New York's literary world. All twenty-one volumes of this diary today reside at the Missouri Historical Society, in St. Louis, Missouri.

6. Through his connections with sometime friends James Parton and Fanny Fern, Gunn managed to place his manuscript for *Physiology* with Mason Brothers publishers. Although the firm specialized in publishing sheet music and music-related books, it produced fiction and nonfiction as well. A first-edition printing for a hardback work such as Gunn's normally would have been two thousand copies; at a time when the average New York laborer earned only a dollar a day, and when a new, leather-bound book cost about the same, *Physiology* achieved a profitable rate of return when its first run sold out in less than a month (Zboray, 74).

7. Gunn had a falling out with the paper's owner and editor, Robert Bonner, and so Fern's review never appeared in print. It is worth noting that the author's relationship with friends James Parton and Fanny Fern also strained, in part because of his troubles with Bonner—to whom Fern and her husband were close. The *New York Ledger* itself was an over-sized, eight-page periodical that contained an array of reading materials for families; it specialized in serial fiction. At six cents per copy, the *Ledger* enjoyed a wide circulation during the middle to latter half of the nineteenth century.

8. Forrest's copy of *Physiology* now resides in the Rare Books Library of the University of Pennsylvania.

9. In addition to his artwork and journalism, Gunn also experimented in writing fiction during the 1850s. He contributed stories to both the American magazine *Harper's* and the English journal that Dickens himself edited and published, *Household Words.*

10. Before they worked together on *Physiology*, Gunn and Bellew both had contributed boardinghouse caricatures to the New York periodical *The Lantern*. Gunn's drawing "A New Berth" appeared in volume one of the journal's 1852 edition (p. 180), while Bellew's "Fancy Sketch" appeared in the very next number, volume two (p. 195).

11. As editor of the famed women's magazine *Godey's Lady's Book*, Sarah Josepha Hale played an especially prominent role in defining middle-class domestic standards for women in the nineteenth-century United States.

12. Gunn's friendship with Fern and her husband, James Parton, ended around the time of this diary entry. Up until then, Gunn had been a frequent overnight guest in Fern and Parton's Brooklyn home.

13. In his revisionist account of flanerie, scholar Dana Brand argues, first, that the flâneur has a seventeenth-century English origin, and not, as is commonly thought, a nineteenth-century French one. Second, Brand's flâneur made his way to America via the popular periodical essays of Addison and Steele and then through the sketches and novels of Charles Dickens. The timing of this latter claim is essential: the flâneur was available to American writers, says Brand, at that exact moment when the city increasingly became a central subject in their works.

14. Published initially in French, Balzac's novels were appearing in English translation in the United States by the mid-1840s. His works thereafter were much in vogue with American readers.

WORKS CITED

Balzac, Honoré de. *Le Père Goriot* [1835]. Trans. Burton Raffel. New York: W. W. Norton & Company, 1994.

Bonner, Robert. "Property and Temper Both Lost—The Wrath of Mr. McElrath." *New York Ledger* (May 7, 1859): 4.

Brand, Dana. *The Spectator and the City in Nineteenth-Century American Literature*. New York: Cambridge University Press, 1991.

Day, Jared N., and Timothy J. Haggerty. "The Bachelor and the Landlady: A Tale of Gotham." *Seaport: New York's History Magazine* (Winter 2005): 14–21.

"Death of Mr. Thomas Butler Gunn, A Veteran Journalist." *The Banbury Guardian* [Great Britain], Thursday, April 14, 1904.

Dickens, Charles. "The Boarding House." From *Sketches by Boz* [1836; tale originally appeared in the *Monthly Magazine* in two installments, May and August 1834], in *Dickens' Journalism: Sketches by Boz and Other Early Papers, 1833–39*, edited by Michael Slater, 273–305. London: Phoenix Giants, 1994.

English, Thomas Dunn. "The Club at Pfaff's." *The Literary World* (June 12, 1886): 202.

Fern, Fanny. *Ruth Hall: A Domestic Tale of the Present Time* [1854]. In *Ruth Hall and Other Writings by Fanny Fern*, edited by Joyce W. Warren. New Brunswick: Rutgers University Press, 2002.

———. "A Social Nuisance." *New York Ledger* (May 7, 1859): 3.

Frank Leslie's Illustrated Newspaper (July 11, 1857): 95.

Gamber, Wendy. *The Boardinghouse in Nineteenth-Century America*. Baltimore: Johns Hopkins University Press, 2007.

Grattan, Thomas. *Civilized America*. Vol. 1 [1859]. Rept. New York: Johnson Reprint Corp., 1969, 109–115.

Groce, George C., and David H. Wallace. *The New York Historical Society's Dictionary of Artists in America, 1564–1860* [*NYHSD*]. New Haven: Yale University Press, 1957, 10, 43, 280, 666.

Gunn, Thomas Butler. Manuscript diaries, July 17, 1849–April 7, 1863, 21 vols.

Hale, Sarah Josepha. *"Boarding Out." A Tale of Domestic Life*. New York: Harper & Brothers, 1846.

Hawthorne, Nathaniel. *The Blithedale Romance* [1852], vol. 3 (1964) in *The Centenary Edition of the Works of Nathaniel Hawthorne*, edited by William Charvat, Roy Harvey Pearce, and Claude M. Simpson. Columbus: Ohio State University Press, 1964–.

Holmes, Oliver Wendell. *The Autocrat of the Breakfast Table*. Boston: Phillips, Sampson, and Company, 1858.

Martin, Edgar W. *The Standard of Living in 1860: American Consumption Levels on the Eve of the Civil War*. Chicago: University of Chicago Press, 1942, 148.

Melville, Herman. *Moby Dick, or The Whale* [1851], 150th anniversary edition of the Northwestern-Newberry volume, edited by Harrison Hayford, Hershel Parker, and G. Thomas Tanselle. Evanston: Northwestern University Press, 2001.

"Our Book Table." *Democratic Review* (August 1857): 192.

Reynolds, David S. *Beneath the American Renaissance: The Subversive Imagination in the Age of Emerson and Melville*. Cambridge, Mass.: Harvard University Press, 1988, 441–483.

Starr, Louis Morris. *Bohemian Brigade: Civil War Newsmen in Action*. New York: Knopf, 1954, 3–7.

Strong, George Templeton. *The Diary of George Templeton Strong: The Turbulent Fifties, 1850–1859*, edited by Allan Nevins and Milton Halsey Thomas. New York: Macmillan, 1952, July 14, 1857, II, 349.

Stylus. "Our New York Letter." *The Literary World* (February 20, 1886): 64–65.

"Wanted—a Boarding-House." *Harper's Weekly* (October 10, 1857): 652.

Whitman, Walt. "New York Boardinghouses" (March 18, 1842), from *Walt Whitman of the New York Aurora*, edited by Joseph Jay Rubin and Charles H. Brown. State College, Pa.: Bald Eagle Press, 1950, 22–23.

———. "Wicked Architecture." *Life Illustrated* (July 19, 1856), from *New York Dissected: A Sheaf of Recently Discovered Newspaper Articles by the Author of Leaves of Grass*, edited by Emory Holloway and Ralph Adimari. New York: Rufus Rockwell Wilson, Inc., 1936, 95.

Wolff, Janet. "The Invisible Flâneuse: Women and the Literature of Modernity," in *The Problems of Modernity: Adorno and Benjamin*, edited by Andrew Benjamin. London: Routledge, 1989, 141–156.

Zboray, Ronald J. "Antebellum Reading and the Ironies of Technological Innovation." *American Quarterly* 40, no. 1, Special Issue: Reading America (March 1988): 65–82.

A NOTE ON THE TEXT

The text of *Physiology* that appears here is the original Mason Brothers edition of 1857, the one and only version that exists. No major modifications of substance, grammar, or punctuation have been made to the book's content in these pages. I have corrected for occasional printers' and spelling errors, however. As to the latter, Gunn could be especially careless with respect to the spelling of surnames. These have been altered in the main text only if their misspelling invites confusion; corrections otherwise appear in the explanatory notes. I have followed a similar practice regarding Gunn's frequent use of French words: although I preserve Gunn's spelling in the main text, I provide the more generally accepted spellings in the explanatory notes. Spellings in the author's British English have been maintained, moreover, except in those few instances when his meaning might be unclear. *Physiology*, finally, is a visual as well as verbal work. For the sake of space, this Rutgers University Press edition does not include all of the original's many illustrations, but only single standout images from individual chapters.

The Physiology of New York Boarding-Houses

THOMAS BUTLER GUNN

WITH ILLUSTRATIONS ON WOOD,
DESIGNED AND DRAWN BY
THE "TRIANGLE," A. R. WAUD, AND THE AUTHOR,
AND ENGRAVED BY JOHN ANDREW

"Je vais, par mon pouvoir diabolique, enlever les toits des maisons; et le dedans, va se découvrir à vos yeux."
Le Diable Boiteux.[1]

(I am about, by my supernatural powers, to take away the roofs from the houses, and to reveal to your eyes whatever is doing within them.)

To
All Inmates of Metropolitan Boarding-Houses,
Especially Single Young Men,
This Book
Is Respectfully Dedicated
By an Ex-Member of the Fraternity.

Preface

The Bedouins—so we are informed by Layard[1]—set any member of a tribe who is unable to sleep to watch the camels. With the like practical philosophy the Author of this volume, having had considerable experience of New York Boarding-Houses, resolved to devote that not-altogether-agreeably-acquired knowledge to the formation of a book. He hopes his readers will approve the performance. He thinks some of them may recognize more or less particulars as the counterpart of those familiar to their own personal observation. Perhaps it were indicative of a too sanguine disposition to express expectations of securing the approbation of the proprietors and proprietresses of the Establishments treated of. He trusts, however, they will read his "Physiology." They may derive profit from it—if not pleasure.

May he suggest that a more judicious present from a Boarder or Boarders to a Landlady than this volume—especially if a leaf or so be turned down in appropriate places—could scarcely be imagined?

And, further, may he here record his very sincere thanks to Messrs. Frank Bellew, Alfred R. Waud, and John Andrew, for their valuable and indispensable assistance on the illustrations?

T. B. G.

Contents

CHAPTER I

Introductory, Metropolitan, and Anticipatory

Individually, we haven't the slightest doubt of the necessity for this work; but being very much alive to the responsibility of emulating Le Sage's *Diable Boiteux* in unroofing houses, and unveiling to our readers the peculiarities of the Establishments whose generic title we have assumed, we shall offer a preliminary word or so in justification of our task.

More than half a million of human beings are said to be resident in this capital of the Western World. Now each individual of them has, is, or may become subject to Boarding-House domiciliation. Like death, no class is exempt from it—a topic of more universal interest, commending itself equally to author-craft and the public, could scarcely be hoped for. Is it not, then, remarkable that ours should be the first attempt to grapple with it in a fitting and comprehensive manner?

A volume such as we can conceive rather than produce—penned with profound and philosophic knowledge of the subject, scrupulous veracity, and delectable wit and wisdom—would needs be priceless. We wish we could cast such a one on the restless waters of the sea of life around us. To the lips of the student of human nature a chalice, fraught with instruction and delight, should be freely offered; to the alien and stranger a book of good counsel and comfort; and to mankind in general, we, like the serpent in Eden—yet possessing, withal, no latent guile—would proffer knowledge. In default of this much-to-be-desired volume, we respectfully tender ours. The remark of a sage Gascon (who must have been the Tupper of his day), "that there's scarcely any place where so much can be seen as in the world," may, certainly, in a minor degree, be applied to this metropolis.[1] It has no equal—at least, on this side of the Atlantic. It is the most free and easy place conceivable. The right to do "as you d—n please"—to quote the democratic phraseology of the aborigines—is nowhere so universally recognized, or less curbed by authority. Individual character, therefore, whether of men or social institutions, is apt to be forcibly developed, and to present peculiarities worth noting. And we conceive that no better place for sketching these can be selected than our substitutes for homes—Boarding-Houses. Our *Physiology* should contain types of a large portion of the population.

There is another, though a secondary reason, for our book's existence. The present is a mutable generation, possessing but little of the conservative element, unwilling to pause, ever jostling onward, considering nothing final. Does it not behoove us, then, to leave record of what has been for the benefit of that illustrious personage—Posterity? It is true that he may (or may not) have the privilege of turning over with indifferent hand certain dusty files of newspapers, there to rake among embers and ashes which blaze briskly enough now. But being a great philosopher (which must certainly be the case if he avail himself of only half the books bequeathed to him), he may cogitate *à la* Carlyle's *Past and Present*,[2] thus: "Life *was* a fact with my great-great-grandfather. He went to bed of nights, and got up of mornings, even as I do. He attired himself (after a very absurd and ungainly fashion, to be sure, compared with the present mode), and was hungry two or three times a day. I should like to know, in detail, how the old boy existed. Here are advertisements respecting Boarding-Houses. Perhaps he lived at one? I wonder what they were!"

In anticipation of this, and for other equally good reasons, we take pen in hand. And as the doughtiest of heroes, the mightiest of achievements, pass away when unchronicled, so—did we not undertake to embalm them in printer's ink—might the various characteristics of New York Boarding-Houses. Cheops, king of Egypt, to secure this sort of immortality, erected a pyramid—and that's all we know about him. He'd much better have kept a diary. We might, then, have known what he had for breakfast. A few sheets of perishable *papyri* pinned to Time's wing makes us cotemporary with Cleopatra.

It may be, then, that a thousand years hence, some student, curious in antiquarian knowledge, will, in some future Astor Library,[3] turn over our pages, diligent intent on the past and this Physiology of New York Boarding-Houses. Let us hope so.

CHAPTER II

Of Looking Out for a Boarding-House

The Establishments of which we purpose to speak are many and multifarious, possessing their own idiocracies, and but seldom amenable to other rules and regulations than those of their proprietors. As *Gow Chrom*, in Scott's novel, fought "for his own hand,"[1] so each tenement may be described as *sui generis*, irrespective of others. They have some general characteristics, but not enough of particular ones to suggest order in their enumeration. Classification, therefore, becomes impossible. We shall only endeavor to place them under appropriate titles.

Where, now, to begin? As one who for the first time enters upon Boarding-House existence is desirous of discovering the abode of all others most suited to his necessities and inclinations, so, here, we experience a temporary difficulty of choice. The subject is so vast, so comprehensive. "The world" (of Boarding-Houses) "is all before us—where to choose." We will take advantage of our simile and commence by describing the proceedings of the seeker for a Boarding-House.

He either inserts in the *Herald*, *Tribune*, or *Times*,[2] an advertisement specifying his particular requirements, or consults those addressed to humanity in general through the medium of their columns—perhaps adopts both measures. In the former case, the next morning puts him in possession of a vast amount of correspondence, from the daintily-penned and delicately-enveloped *billets* of uptowndom to the ill-spelled, penciled-scrawled notes of Greenwich and Hudson streets.[3] It matters not that he has indicated any definite locality; sanguine householders in remote Brooklyn districts clutch at him, Hoboken residents yearn toward him, and the writer of a stray Williamsburg epistle is "confident

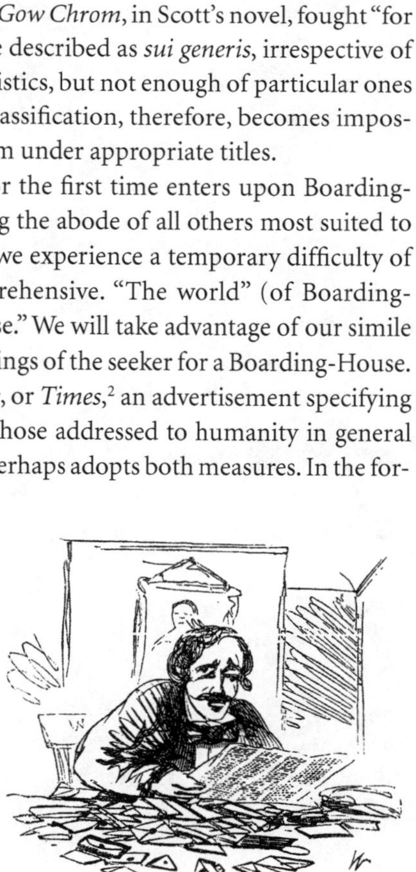

that an arrangement can be made" if he will favor *her* with a visit.[4] After laying aside as ineligible as many letters as there are *Smiths* in a New York Directory, he devotes a morning to the purposes of inspection and selection.

He becomes acquainted with strange localities and bell-handles. He scrutinizes informatory scraps of paper wafered up beside doorways. He endures tedious waitings at thresholds—it being a curious fact in connection with Boarding-Houses that a single application for admission through the usual medium never procures it. And according as his quest be high or low, so will his experience vary.

If the former, he may expect to be ushered into spacious and luxuriously-furnished parlors, where, seated in comfortably-padded rocking-chairs, and contemplating marble tables, on which gorgeously-bound volumes are artistically arranged, thousand-dollar piano-fortes, and mirrors capable of abashing a modest man to utter speechlessness, he will tarry the advent of stately dames, whose dresses rustle as with conscious opulence. He will precede them—they being scrupulous as to exposure of ankles—up broad staircases to handsome apartments; and listen with bland satisfaction to the enumeration of "all the modern improvements" which their mansions comprise; nor, perhaps, be startled at the "figure" for which they may be enjoyed. If "money be no object," he will not have to seek far, or fare badly.

But the researches of him whose aspirations are circumscribed by a shallow purse will produce different results. By Irish girls, with unkempt hair and uncleanly physiognomy, he will be inducted into sitting-rooms where the Venetian blinds are kept scrupulously closed, for the double purpose of excluding flies and preventing a too close scrutiny of the upholstery. He will have interviews with landladies of various appearance, ages and characteristics—landladies dubious and dingy, landladies severe and suspicious (inflexible as to "references *or* payments in advance"), landladies calm and confiding, landladies chatty and conciliatory—the majority being widows. He will survey innumerable rooms—generally under that peculiarly cheerful aspect attendant on unmade beds and un-emptied washing-basins—and, if of sanatory principles,[5] examine the construction of windows in order to ascertain whether they be asphyxiative or movable. He will find occasion to admire how apartments may be indifferently ventilated by half-windows, and attics constructed so that standing erect within them is only practicable in one spot. How a three-feet-by-sixteen inches strip of thread-bare carpet, a twelve-and-a-half-cents-Chatham-square mirror, and a disjointed chair may, in the lively imagination of Boarding-House proprietresses, be considered *furniture*. How double, triple, and even quintuple beds in single rooms, and closets into which he only succeeds in effecting entrance by dint of violent compression between the "cot" and wall, are esteemed highly eligible accommodations for single gentlemen. How partitions (of a purely nominal character) may in no wise prevent the occupants of adjoining rooms from holding conversations one with the other, becoming cognizant of neighboring snores, or turnings in bed. He will observe that lavatory arrangements are mostly of an imperfect description, generally comprising a frail and rickety washing-stand—which has apparently existed for ages in a Niagara of soap-suds, a ewer and basin of limited capacity, and a cottony, web-like towel, about as well calculated for its purpose as a similar-sized sheet of blotting paper would be. In rooms which have not recently submitted to the purifying brush of the white-washer, he will notice the mortal remains of mosquitoes (not to mention more odoriferous and objectionable insects) ornamenting ceilings and walls, where they have encountered Destiny in the shape of the slippers or boot-soles of former occupants. All this and much more will be revealed to the individual in search of a cheap Boarding-House.

We have foreshadowed the extremes of our subject, or as nearly so as we propose to touch upon. For, though it affords such ample scope as to include the most magnificent of our palace hotels—which are *but* Boarding-Houses, temporary or permanent—equally with the squalid tenements of the Five Points and Cow Bay,[6] yet there are heights to which we shall not care to soar, depths to which we will not descend. We intend to be neither statistical nor subterranean. Nor, unattractive as our sketch of the characteristics of cheap Boarding-Houses appears, are we unconscious of the existence of Establishments where moderate prices may procure a fair average amount of comfort and cleanliness. Such will find honorable mention in our Physiology. But as in life they are infrequent, a proportionately small space will be here accorded to them.

CHAPTER III

Of Boarding with a Private Family

Very often, when circumstances compel an individual to find eating, drinking, and sleeping accommodation among strangers, he compromises the Boarding-House question by securing lodgings with a private family. Probably he entertains a wholesome distrust of the Establishments to which our book is devoted, perhaps hopes for a nearer approach to domestic felicity for eschewing them. If prudent, however, he will religiously avoid such tenements as put forth advertisements offering "all the comforts of a home" at low, or indeed any prices. For, as few persons receive boarders from inclination, it logically follows that the resources of those who are unable to cater for more than one must be very limited, and it is more than probable that they are simply cannibals, desirous of securing *somebody to feed upon*. You may in such houses find yourself a dish for an entire family; served up regularly at breakfast, dinner, and supper, and also fleeced to supply clothing for a brood of juvenile ogres. Domestic economy of this kind can be as easily imagined as described, and for this reason, as well as to shun the charge of invidiousness in selection, we shall not go into detail about it. We prefer, rather, a household of better quality—of which you have some preceding knowledge, and where you consent to become "one of the family."

Your landlord Brown—we choose that name as comparatively clear of libelous application—has, then, a wife and small family of three—we will not take unfair advantage by supposing more. Perhaps business relations and mutual convenience have induced you to become his boarder. Mrs. B. is a prettyish woman, amiable, and well-meaning; her children; a boy, a girl, and a baby. You possess that repugnance to and dread of all infants of tender years natural to unmarried men—except *very* mildly-developed ones, who, we verily believe, *do* succeed in getting up a timid sort of interest in them—but, apart from this, anticipate a reasonable amount of comfort in your new quarters, and, for a short time, are not disappointed. Mrs. B. is anxious to please and be pleased, her husband, a good-humored, every-day-kind-of-man, and you popular with both. But, presently, certain disadvantages incidental to your position begin to disclose themselves.

Being treated "exactly as one of the family," it is tacitly expected that you will let pass, without comment or objection, whatever may conflict with your own tastes and inclinations. Mrs. B.'s cookery is not worse than that of the majority of young wives married from Boarding-Houses—which is to say she knows nothing at all about it—and the Celt conducts herself according to her natural ignorance and proclivity to dirt—you must "take things as they are," and make the best of them. Little irregularities as to meal hours—always common where there is a baby who is apt to intimate his particular wants in a not-to-be-choked-off manner—family make-shifts and expedients, you can not suppose will be dropped or amended in consequence of *your* presence. Brown is used to them; you must become so.

When breakfast is delayed for half an hour—you fidgeting all the time with thoughts of the store, work-shop, or office—you can't be brutal enough to complain when you learn that "poor Mrs. B. didn't get a wink of sleep all night, the child cried so," nor would you be guilty of the discourtesy of commencing the meal in her absence. If *you* come down later than usual, and find reserved for you a mug-full of coffee, black, bitter as aloes, and boiling on the stove, a fragment of overcooked steak adhering to its plate through the medium of congealed grease, a patch of liquefying butter peppered with flies, and a sodden biscuit—why "you can't expect the things to be about all day." Eat your breakfast in silence, and show your appreciation of "the comforts of a home" by not disturbing Bridget, who's "washing up."

Mrs. B., too, and her husband, have the occasional tiffs and differences natural to the married state on unimportant questions, at table or elsewhere, when they appeal to your judgment. You are gallant and side with the wife, upon which Brown thinks you a humbug, and hints as much. Venture on the opposite line of conduct, with ever so guarded a proviso, Mrs. B. is "disappointed in you, as she thought you had a better opinion of the ladies." So you hold your tongue, are considered sulky, and the boy and girl told not to go near you.

These innocents, also, are scarcely a source of unmixed gratification to yourself and those about them. For the boy surreptitiously borrows your knife, breaks the smaller blade short off in endeavoring to whittle out a boat, and cuts his fingers severely—in consequence of which you get into disgrace with his mother. And the girl addresses you by an abbreviation of your Christian name—having heard her father do so—favors you with "sharp" answers, and announces the calls of your friends in a shrill yell up the staircase. You incline toward both darlings at first, but finding their affection become so rampant as scarcely to leave you a quiet moment, and the small coins at first received as a favor, soon clamorously demanded as a right, you endeavor gradually to break off—upon which they turn spiteful, and persuade Mrs. B. that you are an undeveloped Herod.[1] She would like to know what the "poor children" have done to displease you.

Nor is this all. The Browns are sociable people, and give little parties. Mrs. B. has unmarried sisters, and young lady acquaintances. You enjoy yourself very much, and do not object "to see the girls home," even though the distance be considerable. Perhaps exhilarated by their pleasant society, and willfully unmindful of the fact that there is *another* young lady who claims the monopoly of such attentions, you propose stepping into Taylor's for an ice-cream or so.[2] *She* hears of it, be sure, and you are tartly informed that if you go out for walks with Miss —s,' *she* shall retaliate in company with Mr. Smith. (Smith is your rival, and you have a suspicion that his whiskers are more *distingué*-looking than yours.)

Or, on rainy nights, the young ladies accept their brother-in-law's proffered hospitality; when, in consequence of limited accommodation, you give up your room to them, and sleep on the sofa. Bachelors' apartments are not proverbially tidy, and it is just possible that you have left certain unsealed letters, from *her*, in drawers, or the pockets of the old coat which serves you for a dressing gown. Of course you wouldn't for the world suspect the young ladies of reading them. Yet you think of Madame *Bluebeard* in the story,[3] and are haunted with a lively recollection of particular passages in the said letters, wherein the Misses —s' personal appearance and demeanor are commented very severely upon, and such epithets as "forward minxes," "bold-faced hussies," applied to them. These reflections, combined with the hardness of the sofa, are quite sufficient to keep you in a vivacious state of unrest till the morning, when you make your toilet in the back kitchen among dirty plates, household utensils, and irruptions from Bridget. And, innocent as "the girls" look when you bid them good-morning, you could swear they have counted the number of your dickeys, and know that your socks are awfully in need of darning.

Brown, too, has his friends who sometimes stop all night, and, *of course*, share *your* bed. Perhaps they get to sleep first, and snore. Perhaps they never can do either, in a strange couch, and so lie tumbling, tossing, and kicking, till you become equally incapable of repose. We have had bed-fellows who couldn't partake of "the balmy" unless in strange positions, such as on their backs, with their knees making a pyramid of the bed-clothes. We have also known them to moan all night like broken-hearted ring-doves.*

Mrs. B. returns her sisters' visits, and occasionally stays a day or two with her mother. (Nobody could be hard-hearted enough to wish to keep her *always* at home.) During such absences, Brown and yourself are turned over to the tender mercies of Bridget, who don't make the beds till the evening. Perhaps, by special order, she institutes a general clean up. In which case, on returning home, you find the floor of your apartment damp from a recent inundation, your hat in the

* On such occasions—and indeed on others, such as snoring, snorting, grunting, etc.—we have found *whistling* an efficacious check. It probably disturbs the unconscious serenaders into abandoning their involuntary accompaniment. We, therefore, advise suffering wives, when their lords commence nasal melody, to sit up in bed and whistle like so many insane keyholes. Of course the counsel is unnecessary to husbands—ladies *never* snore.

shower-bath, your boots hung near the ceiling, your pipes, hair-brush, and tobacco-jar jumbled among your shirt-collars, and the rest of your property carefully put away in equally appropriate localities. You may, however, discover this in *progress*, and have the gratification of carrying the furniture from the passage into your room. Of Bridget's cookery we shall say nothing, having already intimated that she is an Irishwoman, and therefore but one degree above the Hottentot *zero* of the culinary thermometer.[4]

You are also liable to the performance of the part of cavalier to Mrs. B., in accompanying her to theaters, fetching her home from balls, etc., when Brown—it's just like him—won't. This, of itself, would be no great hardship, but there's "your" young lady who wonders married women (with an emphasis on the adjective) "are not really ashamed of themselves" to be seen at such places with gentlemen, and "hopes their husbands' eyes will soon be opened." Your refusal, though veiled under never so ingenious a pretext, is perceived and resented by Mrs. B., perhaps by her husband. Or, on the other hand, you—having no *tendresse* elsewhere[5]—accord these attentions so readily as to excite his jealousy. Between these two stools you will need to be a dexterous moral acrobat not to come to the ground. We remember an instance in which a husband's feelings were so wrought upon by the fact of a boarder's esquiring his wife from a party—which he himself had expressly declined doing—that they instigated him to taking his revenge on the *hat* of the offender. He was discovered, subsequent to their return, kicking it about the passage in a most vindictive manner.

Now and then you may be weak enough to suffer yourself to be inveigled into assisting at Mrs. B.'s Saturday evening marketings—the inducement, "choosing something you like" for Sunday's dinner; the result—carrying the basket. Indeed, if you are of easy nature, there's no knowing what may be required of you. Whitewashing, putting up beds, conveying orders to trades-people, acting as proxy in disputing their "little bills"—and occasionally advancing the money to pay them—hearing the children's lessons, keeping the garden in order—for all these tasks, and many more, you are available. If a May-day moving be in contemplation, you'd better, at the outset, dispatch a doctor's certificate of sickness to your employers, for you'll have to come to it, finally, after losing a day and a half. Should your coat or pants suffer in any of these operations, Mrs. B. meets your application for repairs with a laugh, calls you an "old bachelor," and commends you to Bridget, who, in her turn, thinks you're "betther able to atthind to such matthers yerrself thin she is."

When Brown wants to smoke, he naturally uses your cigars and apartment, hence you are suspected of inoculating him with low tastes, and seducing him from the bosom of his family. Unmistakable hints are thrown out as to the necessity of taking down the window curtains and having them washed, "to get the smell out," and "poor dear baby's cough" is attributed to "that horrid tobacco." Baby, indeed, becomes a very formidable personage. If not on good terms with the mother, you can not raise your voice above a whisper, sneeze, laugh, cough, whistle, sing, open or shut the door, without disturbing it. Terrible to reflect upon are those evenings on which Mrs. B. goes out, leaving baby to the care of Bridget. Perhaps she takes her keys with her, when you and Brown sup on crackers, cheese, and beer (fetched and paid for, by yourself, from the corner grocery.) *He* doesn't remain in-doors, but you must, having to write a letter, during the composition of which baby wails incessantly. On the infantile clamor reaching a crisis suggestive of blackness in the face, protruded eyes, and generally convulsive appearance, you descend, and discover Bridget endeavoring to quiet her charge by filling its tiny mouth with lumps of pork fat. Half an hour subsequently you start, on your own responsibility, to fetch Mrs. B. home. About the time, too, that you have become so misanthropic on the subject of babies as to strongly recommend Godfrey's Cordial,[6] and other opiates—in the hope of fatal results—you are requested to act as god-father.

To detail all the minutiae of annoyances ordinarily included in Boarding with a Private Family, would far transcend our limits. Another incident—warranted genuine—and we have done. We knew a lodger, who, coming home one night keyless, and finding the street-door locked, effected an entrance—being a bit of a gymnast—into his bedroom by means of the balcony and window. Next morning, when the servant was stirring about the house, he called to her, bidding her take the key from the top of the door (where it was generally deposited to be out of the way of the dear children) and release him. She, startled at such an inscrutable occurrence, set up an appalling howl, rushed up stairs into the apartment of her master and mistress, and frightened the baby into a fit. In consequence, our friend's Brown told him at breakfast-time that this was a course of conduct he really couldn't think of putting up with, and perhaps he had better find accommodations elsewhere! Incontinently he did so.

The Boarder in a Private Family usually quits it on general grounds of discontent and incompatibility of temper. He has, in fact, been so much "one of the family," that he has lost claim to his own individuality. His entertainers' presumed *property in him* can only be repudiated by flight, and that social *hegira* takes place accordingly.[7]

CHAPTER IV

The Cheap Boarding-House on a Large Scale

PRIVATE Boarding-Houses, in which limited numbers of persons are accommodated, will rate in a work of this kind; and to them our prefatory remarks on the impossibility of classification, are especially applicable. Like their proprietors and occupants they are of all stations, and comprise every variety of social characteristic. We shall present such samples as have the greatest diversity, and afford scope for displaying our subject in its strongest lights.

Having emancipated our imaginary Boarder from the "Private Family," we at once turn him loose into the metropolitan world, nor shall we cramp our sphere of action by following individual adventures. Yet we will allow his choice to guide ours in the selection of the first Establishment claiming notice. Probably, disgusted with his recent experience, he will rush to the opposite extreme, and become an inmate of the cheap Boarding-House on a large scale.

It comprises two tenements which have been stately mansions in their day, but, like the neighborhood, have gone down in the world. Its mistress—who can recollect when there was a bridge at Canal-street, and little else beside fields north of it; when New York had but *one* omnibus, which used to call at the residences of citizens for "fares"; with much more, sounding strange and half-fabulous to the ears of the present generation—will tell you of the old Knickerbocker families resident there in the presidency of Jefferson, and how, on ball-nights, rows of carriages stood along the triangular patch of enclosed vegetation (which the aborigines of the locality insanely denominate a Park) fronting the houses. But that's fifty years ago; respectability has followed fashion up town, and the two old mansions are humiliated to the condition of a cheap Boarding-House.

Their spacious rooms have been divided and subdivided into so many apartments, that the place resembles a penitentiary, a hive, or barrack. Some contain an extra number of beds, and the minor chambers are unusually small, even for a Boarding-House. Ours—we have intimated that we intend to draw freely on personal experience in our Physiology—was eight feet by six. It was just possible to open the door to sufficient width to obtain ingress, the bed partially blockading it, and upon this we could recline, poke the fire in the stove, and touch three sides of the room with perfect facility. Many a winter's night have we lain and watched the dull red glow of a handful of anthracite glaring at us like the angry eye of a dwarf Cyclops, and once, while poking vigorously for the purpose of blinding him, we upset the stove, the pipe of which descended upon us with some violence.

A conjunction of the two staircases having been effected by breaking down the partition-wall at the second story, you were, at first, in doubt as to which house your room appertained, only arriving at the knowledge by dint of repeatedly knocking your head against a low doorway in a dark passage, and simultaneously tumbling down two steps, which, in time, impressed the locality of the boundary on your memory. Cumbrous old oaken staircases they were, too, of a fashion and solidity shaming those of the present day. Many a powdered beauty has, without question, in ante-revolutionary days, tripped down them, and many a red-coated, cocked-hatted officer of King George as escort. If such a couple could, by the pale moonlight peering in at the skylight above, and stealing solemnly down on the shabby, cracked, dirty plastered wall, revisit the scene now—!

The mistress of the establishment is a bulky Englishwoman of (certainly) five-and-fifty, in possession of a third husband, and the most perfectly developed snuffle we have ever encountered. A tradition has been handed down from former lodgers, that the union originated in the male party's running deeply in arrears for board, and honorably compounding the same by matrimony. He is a grave, quiet, and useful man, his wife's junior by ten or fifteen years. He does the marketing, carving, white-washing, and general repairing, and has a box of carpenter's tools in the front basement, the contents of which are in frequent use. Superficial observers fancy him the weaker vessel, but the Irish servant girls—who rather like him, but entertain the reverse feeling toward their mistress—say Mrs. "has got to mind," when her husband tells her. And there's an air of quiet determination about him which is corroborative. Mrs. —'s mother (a venerable but virulent old lady of three-score who keeps her chamber, and makes the girls cry when they bring her meals) is known to have predicted that her daughter "will see *this one* out and have another," but we own to doubts as to the correctness of her judgment.

When the houses possess their full complement of boarders—which they generally do, the Establishment being about as well-managed and dieted as can be expected, at the price—over fifty persons find a substitute for a home within their walls, the American element scarcely predominating over the English, Scotch, and Irish. The oldest inhabitant is an elderly Philadelphian. He has boarded there for any number of years, not without temporary desertions, much private growling against the authorities, and innumerable resolves of a final change of residence—always to be carried out next week. He considers New York an aggressive and presumptuous metropolis, every way inferior to his native city; tells you how, after the great fire of 1836,[1] the former was only too happy to borrow money of the latter; disparages the Croton by contrasting it with the Schuylkill;[2] laments the unhealthy atmosphere of the Empire State, and defers purchasing clothes (however strongly in need of them) until he has occasion to visit Philadelphia. Otherwise he is a rational man, though possessing strong prejudices, the bitterest of which are directed against the memory of Sydney Smith.[3] On Sunday morning, if breakfast is delayed, he is apt to be *wrathy*, and sometimes, after twenty minutes pacing up and down the hall, has been known to dart off to an indignant meal at Sweeney's.[4] He has become identified with the Boarding-House, will probably terminate his days there, and be buried in the back yard. Five or six years ago he lost a considerable sum of money, his box being broken open by some scoundrel then resident in the Establishment. On this occasion he quitted it—for a whole month. But, like the dove to the ark,[5] he came back again, and, to use the strong expression of a cockney boarder at that time,[6] we don't think that the combined forces of several strong men, a steam-engine, and a bull-dog, could keep him away.

In feats of in-doors pedestrianism (to which he is prone on the evenings of the working-day week, as on Sunday mornings), he is often accompanied by a long, gaunt, whitish dog, whose hair comes off when you pat him, and who is so old that he dates back to the time of the landlady's first marriage. He, too, appears part of the Establishment, and inseparable from it. He is always hungry, has no objection to mustard, and *won't be lost*. For his mistress has several times commissioned small boys to abandon him in remote localities, but *Solon* (like his Philadelphia friend) invariably returns to his old home.[7] Once, in mid-summer, the individual thus charged made him over to the city authorities for the sum of fifty cents. But on reaching the place of detention for all lawless and unmuzzled dogs, Solon was recognized, and a message dispatched to his owners, to the effect that the senders "know'd the dog was set store by, and didn't they want him agin?" A walk up-town, and the expenditure of a dollar on the part of Mr. —, redeemed him. The old dog is rather a favorite of the boarders, and will follow such as have been domiciled there for any time on Sunday afternoon rambles; at other times dozing out his existence in the sitting-room, lying in summer winking in the sunlight, and in winter, beside the stove. This, and the hall, seems to be his peculiar domain. He seldom ventures into the dining-room, and if so, there is an expression of conscious guilt about his physiognomy and tail, which denotes a lively apprehension of painful consequences.

This *tabooed* apartment is a long room at the back of the houses, with bare white-washed walls, and a row of windows on one side, like a hospital from which the beds have been removed. In lieu of them, there are two longitudinal tables, surrounded by excessively high stools; and in winter, at the further end (where the landlady sits), is a stove. Hither the boarders are summoned at the hours of 7, 2 and 6, by a large bell, the jangling dissonance of which might convert one to the Turkish opinion that those articles are an invention of the devil.[8] They troop in like a file of soldiers, each to his stool, partake of their food in silence, (mutely *stoking* themselves, as it were) and troop out again. There is little, if any, conversation. The mistress of the Establishment presides, assisted by her husband and servants, and "gets through" matters very expeditiously. As already intimated, the meals are of indifferently-good quality. We have known the beef of tougher consistency and more *veiny* construction than was desirable, and the potatoes to exhibit as many eyes as Argus;[9] but on the whole, the diet was endurable. Our chief objection applies all most universally to the *cuisine* of Boarding-Houses. The meals were uniformly served up "neither cold, nor hot"—a state St. John didn't approve of in Laodicean Christians.[10] The soups, too, might have been improved by a less liberal allowance of grease and unground pepper, of which latter there always remained a deep sediment—as of small shot—in each plate. But the boarders were not more discontented than is generally, naturally, and inevitably the case in most Establishments.

There were comparatively few lady-boarders at —'s. We remember one who was strongly suspected of stealing clothing, etc., from the rooms of other lodgers. She generally came down to meals after the usual time, and was supposed to carry off the purloined property concealed within her superfluity of *crinoline*. Finally, being one day tracked, as she walked abroad, by our quiet landlord, he, upon her taking the arm of a suspicious-looking male companion, stepped forward and suggested that perhaps she'd better not trouble herself to come back any more. Which hint she acted upon. During the excitement produced by the thefts, it was proposed to apply to a clairvoyant for the discovery of the delinquent, and a subscription got up among the boarders for that purpose. The result was hardly satisfactory, for though the gifted seer described most minutely not only the pawn-broker's shop, but the very shelf whereon the stolen property was deposited, yet unfortunately, the particulars applied equally well to some half-hundred shelves and establishments, and the few "uncles" applied to refusing to allow their stores to be overhauled—in one case threatening to "pound" the applicant—the guilty person was not thereby detected.

The sitting-room of our Boarding-House is a large, dull back-parlor, partially lighted by two long windows, which command a cheerful prospect of the exterior of the dining-room, a number of decayed barrels, and a sloppy, dirty passage-like yard, at the extremity of which is a deformed tree. Here (in the sitting-room), on winter evenings, the boarders congregate, to anathematize the stove when ill-tended, to spit upon it when red hot. The furniture comprises some chairs, many stools, a print of a stage coach which is yellow with age, and a spectral old sofa. To sit down upon the latter article is a disconcerting transaction; for though the horse-hair covering retains its fully plumped appearance, the springs and stuffing have been removed, and no sooner do you deposit yourself thereon, than an un-looked-for descent of at least six inches is the result. It is especially startling to fat old gentlemen.

Smoking being forbidden here (in deference to an ancient carpet, the pattern of which has long ago faded into invisibility), a small apartment like the interior of a deal-box, and formed by annexing a bit of the dining-room, is devoted to the lovers of the "flagrant weed."[11] We remember decorating its sides with fancy sketches and portraits of the more prominent boarders, which proceeding developed another characteristic on the part of the landlord. He came out with savagely ironical, but ungrammatically-written notices, the venom of which appeared to consist in the frequent repetition of the words "some people," and wafered them up on the inner side of the street door.

On certain days the strip of yard is transformed into a grove of wet linen, for washing is done at this Establishment. The Irish girls who perform this (and every other) species of labor, have their separate back-kitchen, which is dark, subterranean and cock-roachy, and where our landlady's snuffle is often raised in anger. Sometimes her husband acts as mediator, as also, when boarders get a little in arrear. Mrs. —, by-the-by, has an awful way of coming "down upon" defaulters. As the luckless debtor took his seat at the breakfast table, he would, in the midst of a dead silence, receive an ominously nasal intimation *that she wanted to speak with him before he went out.*

We have seen her glide, like an avenging Fury,[12] after a victim. There was always a battle-royal in the hall subsequently.[13] We shall not readily forget her fury at being denominated a "Billingsgate" on one of these occasions.[14]

It were unreasonable, however, to blame her for having a sharp eye to the main chance. Boarding-House keepers, in general, fully earn their gains, and many lodgers require looking after. Meantime our present Establishment is a thriving one, and it is whispered that our landlady and her husband have had conferences on the question of retiring to the country.

In which case what *is* to become of our Philadelphian?

CHAPTER V

The Fashionable Boarding-House Where You Don't Get Enough to Eat

This is a stylish mansion of free stone, in a patrician neighborhood, not far from the pleasant vicinity of Washington-square. Its interior decorations are of that peculiar French-New-York order which displays more of gilding than good taste, and more of plate-glass than either; its furniture is showy but fragile, and its domestic conveniences include, of course, "all the modern improvements."

Madame, the proprietress—she prefers being addressed by that title (and if you can do it with *outré* French accent so much the better)—has been a handsome woman in her day, and unwilling to relinquish pretensions to the character, now resorts to art to sustain it. She never advertises for boarders, considering it *low*, and relying entirely on her private connection. You are received, if an applicant, much after a fashion described in our second Chapter, being, however, ushered into the sitting-room by a colored boy (than whom no "hand" on a slave plantation could be more arbitrarily drilled), and his mistress generally appears in a *robe-de-chambre*, with a *blasé* look, and artificial flowers in her hair. She is particular in her inquiries as to your position, profession, and references. It always happens that there is but one room vacant—in consequence (as she incidentally informs you) of its recent occupant leaving for a tour in Europe. And in all probability her daughters will chance to drop in in the course of the interview, when you are accorded the favor of an immediate introduction. They are two dashing, showy girls, rather good-looking, and very brightly dressed—a little more so than is consistent with morning costume. Your reception is a gracious one, but the ladies presently diverge into a side conversation, evolving an awful familiarity with Knickerbocker names. It inevitably occurs that they have just returned from one of Mrs. —'s "candle receptions" on the Fifth Avenue—which fact, on a six months' repetition, is suggestive of a most melancholy state of health on the part of the lady, and a sad look-out on that of her husband. On expressing your intention of becoming an inmate of the Establishment—which *Madame* listens to with an air indicative of hope that you will prove worthy of the privilege—you learn that it has an especial boot-black, with whom you're expected to make a private arrangement; and are mildly, but firmly, requested not to bring your baggage in *a cart*.

If you're a *very* young man, you congratulate yourself on the prospect—perhaps indulge in a few roseate visions in which those brilliant young ladies especially figure—and move in accordingly. And, certainly, you will have no cause for complaint on the score of lack of courtesy or assumption of aristocratic exclusiveness. *That* pervades every thing. The arrangements are as elegant as a dish of trifle or *blanc mange*[1]—and as unsatisfactory.

Your chamber—in which you are requested "not to wash *wide*," to smoke, or to rub matches against the walls—is very neat and cleanly, and pretty well furnished, but the three chairs are of such brittle construction that you would as soon think of sitting upon them as upon spun-glass, and instinctively speculate as to what you'll have to pay for breakage. But had you as many hands as Briareus,[2] and wanted to wash them every half hour, you couldn't be better supplied with towels. There are also dainty little bits of crochet-work under the soap dish, and tumblers, and a big china slop-jar—we don't know the French equivalent, or wouldn't horrify the reader by using such a vulgar word. The bed is small and snow-white—like a snow-drift on a child's grave. In winter it has fewer blankets on than is desirable.

You are not rung to meals by a bell, as in vulgar Boarding-Houses. The colored boy taps at your door at 9 A.M., and deferentially informs you that breakfast is ready. On descending, you find the gentlemen boarders in dressing-gowns with ropes like bell-pulls, and the ladies in elegant *robes-de-chambre*, with artful contrivances of lace about their heads and busts. Severally, they accord you a gracious good-morning as you glide to the seat which *Madame's* gesture indicates, remove your napkin from its ring and spread it over your knees in preparation. The ladies are very lively and chatty, especially the younger one—so much so, indeed, that a cynic might suspect the existence of a design to keep the boarders' jaws otherwise employed than on the breakfast, which is light, tasty, and unsubstantial. There are *very* small mutton-chops, *patés*, nick-nacks, and French bread and coffee—made also *à la Française*. Each dish is extinguished under a gorgeous cover of German silver, with which material the table is generally resplendent. You can read the papers, if you like, during the progress of the meal, and that without being thought ill-bred. *Madame* is a subscriber to the *Courier* and *Enquirer*, the *Herald*, *Times*, and *Home Journal*, the two last being the favorites of the ladies.[3] The *Herald* is generally depreciated by them, but can not be dispensed with on account of its winter reports of upper-ten balls and summer correspondence from watering-places; their knowledge of the fashionable world enabling them to explain the initials, and fill up the dashes by which the names of its inhabitants are half-chronicled. *Madame* also reads the *Churchman*[4]—as a matter of duty. She is strictly orthodox, and a regular attendant at Grace Church.[5]

Lunch, consisting of pie, delicate shavings of cold meat, and coffee, is served at 1 P.M., and dinner at 6. This meal invariably comprises five courses, commencing with thin, whitey-brown soup, and concluding with dessert, of which watermelons form the staple in summer, and frosted apples in winter. The ladies now appear in *very* full-dress, and are fragrant with *eau de Cologne*, frangi-panni, *jockey-club*, or *otto of roses*;[6] while the more magnificently got-up gentlemen sport lace shirt-fronts and wristlets, resembling the ornamental paper one sees on French plum-boxes.[7] As at breakfast, the meal is seasoned by much animated conversation, the ladies doing their full share. All carving is performed at a side-table by a darkey of butler-like aspect, who produces remarkably small, thin slices, which are conveyed to your *left* side by the colored boy. If you are at all absent-minded, or not specially intent upon your plate, it (with the contents) is very apt to be whisked away by the last-mentioned youth, in obedience to strict, but privately-issued, instructions. And, considering the fascinations of the young ladies, there is great risk of this. We have seen no less than *three* successive plates reft from a hungry boarder, who lacked moral courage to remonstrate. He went out subsequently and had a porter-house steak at a Broadway restaurant.

Entrées, side-dishes, and French cookery in general, preponderate over joints, but there are plenty of artificial flowers and iced-water. The pastry is of the lightest consistency and most delicate construction, and you are helped to bits shaped like an attenuated triangle. A cup or two of green, and very weak tea, served in the adjoining parlor, after the lapse of half an hour, concludes the repast.

The boarders, like the Establishment, are eminently genteel. At the time of our sojourn they were very much as follows: Two superannuated bank clerks, a stock-broker, three or four Cubans, an old major who had been in the Canadian army, a fast young Southerner from South Carolina, a London architect, and a crockery and China merchant from Canal-street.[8] This last was an obliging individual, very much alive to the inferiority of his social position and the privilege of being admitted to such aristocratic society. He received the rallyings of the young ladies and their playful allusions to "the shop" with much humility and good-humor, and we suspect him of secretly admiring one of them. *Madame* made him useful in many ways. When it became desirable to snub any boarder, he (the crockery merchant) was put into the position of the offender, after the *flogging boy* system once pursued in the education of young princes, by which they took their flagellations by deputy. As witness the following instance. The Cubans *would* smoke in their chambers, disregarding the injunction that confined that indulgence to a balcony in the rear of the dining-room. So Mr. —, to whom the slightest whiff of tobacco was productive of great intestinal discommotion,[9] was severely cautioned "not to do that again," and informed that if he must have his horrid cigars, he'd better smoke 'em *at the store,* down town.

Each of the young ladies has her part, and admirably does she play up to it. The elder, who is one-and-twenty, affects the sentimental and literary, occasionally flavoring it by a dash of piety. She admires Longfellow, Holmes, and Tupper, and looks upon Willis as a fallen angel.[10] The younger (who is about eighteen) aspires to the character of a *fast* young lady, is particularly fond of dancing, thinks sleighing "first-rate fun," and adores Mr. Wallack Lester (which amiable weakness, by-the-by, is not uncommon with up-town young ladies).[11] She aims, too, at smartness in conversation, and brilliancy of repartee, principally at the expense of weak-minded or unguarded persons, for whom she sets little pit-falls—as thus. You hear her assert strong distaste for some book, tune, fashion, etc.—being the very reverse of former professions. You innocently express surprise, commencing with the fatal words, "I thought—." When Miss — immediately breaks in upon the sentence, exclaiming, with great vivacity, "O, Mr. —, it don't do always to trust one's thoughts! *I* thought, at first, you were very clever and amusing—*and you're not!*" Upon which you are supposed to be crushed for the rest of the evening. This lady's fascinations are brought to bear on the younger of the bachelor boarders, and two of the Cubans are desperately in love with her. Her sister devotes herself to the seniors, and we incline to the supposition that she will, in the long run—after she has sufficiently humiliated him—marry the crockery merchant.

Both the young ladies and their mother come out in great force in the evenings. She does not pretend to music, but they both play and sing, after due solicitation. Conversation turns mostly on the newest novel, fashion, or marriage, and THE OPERA. There is also another topic—next door. *Madame* has a standing feud with one of her neighbors, who attempts to depreciate her as the keeper of a Boarding-House. She will "reckon up" their origin for you with dreadful exactness, and designates them as low, stuck-up people. With respect to *her* position in life, she feelingly hints that undeserved misfortunes have reduced her to it, and says that but for the dear girls she shouldn't have thought of surviving the death of her husband.

The reader will have noticed that in our enumeration of the various boarders no ladies appear. *Madame* always avoids admitting such, unless *old*. This, we think, will be found to be *invariably* the case in all Establishments where there are unmarried daughters, and for double reasons. In the first place, it is desirable to avoid risk of counter attractions, in the second place, ladies are apt to observe each other too much and too closely. The many little dodges which to the thick sight of man are invisible, lie quite open to the quick eye of woman.

Yet we do recollect a lady-boarder, too. But she was old, *rich*, and had a son, whom the younger daughter did especially favor. He, a mild youth, addicted to playing on the flute, used to collect the rents of various tenement houses, owned by his mother (and sometimes came home with black-eyes in consequence). This lady and her son, may, with one of the elderly stock-brokers, have claimed this title of Pet-Boarders. (We shall have much to say of the species hereafter.) He was a fussy old boy of sixty, accustomed to diluting the editorials of the *Courier* and *Enquirer* and delivering them in an oracular manner as his opinions over the dinner-table. His linen was very particularly cared for, and the young ladies marked his shirts and pocket handkerchiefs with their own fair hands.

During the summer season, the blinds in the front of the house are kept scrupulously closed, and every thing done to give it an "out of town" look. If the ladies stir abroad it is at early morning, or late at night, and then so limp in figure, and disguised in aspect that you would scarcely recognize them. But, for the most part, they confine themselves to back rooms, *Madame* even discarding the basement, which is her place of business, where trades-people wait upon her, have their bills severely scrutinized, and occasionally are brought up sharp about overcharges.

The boarders' payments are monthly. You find a small billet in a delicate envelope, directed in an angular Italian hand, stuck in the looking-glass, and containing your bill—always on the morning before it is due. And, if a week elapse without payment, you discover a remarkable change in the demeanor of the young ladies toward you. They will become quite cool, absolutely Arctic. *Madame* is not accustomed to admitting arrears. She tells the crockery merchant that she never has boarders who don't pay punctually. If you would develop her displeasure still further, only spill a cup of coffee on the clean table-cloth.

A ball celebrates each anniversary of the opening of her Establishment, when there is a great display of dancing, lemonade, candies, bon-bons, ginger-wine, and artificial flowers. Most of the ladies invited are ugly, and "dear friends" of her daughters. They are recommended to you with charming cordiality, as most excellent, intellectual girls. (And, by the way, we never knew an ugly woman who wasn't excellent, or intellectual.) On these occasions the arbiter of fashion, the janitor of upper tendom, the sexton of Grace Church—in a word, the great BROWN is in the ascendant. He is a friend of *Madame's*.

And thus, in her glory, we leave her.

CHAPTER VI

The Dirty Boarding-House

WERE we simply guided by our own inclinations, it is more than probable that we should blink the responsibility of writing this Chapter. We don't affect to despise that respectable proverb which asserts that nobody can touch pitch without being defiled. But in our capacity of pen-and-ink photographist, we can not afford to ignore the existence of the Dirty Boarding-House. Our book would be incomplete without it. Having no choice, then, but to proceed, we do so—premising that the reader shall not be detained longer than is necessary within the uncleanly Establishment we select as an extreme type of a class of dwellings which are only too numerous.

It is a dingy, narrow-fronted, three-story edifice, in a mean street on the east side of the town, within two doors of one of our busiest thoroughfares. Its mistress, a lady of Irish extraction, has retained, in full perfection, that lively antipathy to soap and water characteristic of her nationality. Her husband is a policeman. And six or seven ubiquitous children impart the reverse of gladness to their mutual household.

Mrs. —'s hydrophobia is equally manifest in her person, children, and Establishment—the former being large, loose, oleaginous and black-worsted-stockinged; the second, unkempt, inodorous, and ragged; and the three emphatically dirty. Her hair is red, and *coiffe à la horsetail.* Her dress favors the spectator with glimpses of her stays. She has a generally un-tied, stringy, down-at-heel-and-go-to-bed-with-her-clothes-on aspect. No good man could look at her without a wish to put her under a pump. Which would be also his impulse with respect to the children.

Their ages range from three months to eight years, the minors being vociferous twins. Their affections are confined to dirt-pies, candies, dead cats, and the gutters of the vicinity. It is difficult to avoid treading on them as you mount the staircase, which is generally—if we may be allowed the expression—in a squirmy condition.

The premises are of peculiar construction. A little dry-goods establishment, having no connection with them, occupies the lower story; ascent to the upper rooms being gained by the narrow and excessively dirty staircase just alluded to. These extend over a boot-store in the adjacent thoroughfare, as we discovered on the first night of our sojourn in the Dirty Boarding-House. We were then inducted into a small room, very like the interior of a collapsed diving-bell. It had no particular shape, and but one window, which was hermetically fastened, and looked into a sort of shaft, covered at top by a cucumber-frame skylight for the purpose of illuminating the premises below. Opposite us, in an apartment of similar construction, we remarked that two of the window-panes had been removed—possibly for ventilation—thus allowing one of the occupants an opportunity of sticking his feet through, and going to sleep in that position. We thought of plagiarizing the idea—it was in July—but were doubtful as to the result.

Our neighbors—two rough, good-humored laboring-men, sometimes played the banjo, and sometimes fought in bed. They also sent the landlady's eldest son out for beer, and generously invited us to partake; bringing it into our chamber at midnight, in a ewer. And once they made our room-mate drunk on New England rum with tobacco in it. He was a remarkably ugly boy, the expression of whose countenance could only be compared to that of a bilious codfish attempting to swallow a cannon ball. He used to make himself ill in attempting to smoke strong cigars, and, at first, manifested an inclination to become unpleasantly confidential on the subject of his "busts." He received our advice—to confine his indulgences to pea-nuts and the Bowery pit[1]—with indignation.

Heat and insect phlebotomists—after four nights' occupancy of this apartment—effected our removal to another. This was a little room over the passage, which had been white-washed no later than three years ago; and where we had the unshared privilege of feeding myriads of creeping *carnivori*. We never saw "Red Rovers" in such profusion or of equal ferocity.[2] They would have reduced a Daniel Lambert to an anatomical preparation in the course of one summer.[3] We soon learnt why the old English poets made the devil lord of insects.[4] "Ne'er a king's son in Christendom could be better bitten." We were spotted all over like a leopard, and had to go to sleep with a lamp and matches by our bed-side; waking up, regularly, to half hourly *battues*[5]—or, rather, to explosive and inodorous cremations. Of the size of these vampires our readers may form some idea by the fact that there was an awful legend current among the boarders, that the crystal of a watch had been broken by an elderly bed-bug tumbling upon it!

If the speculative question propounded by Lowell's *Parson Wilbur*[6]—whether Noah was justified in preserving this portion of the animal tribe—had been submitted to the inmates of the Dirty Boarding-House, we are confident that a most emphatic negative would have been rendered! The opinion of the learned Italian Jesuit Giulio Cordara (so complimentary to Providence)—that insects didn't exist in Paradise, but were created subsequent, to the fall, for the especial annoyance of mankind—might have been received with favor.[7]

Bed-making was performed at any hour from 3 to 7 P.M., by a relative of the landlady's, who also officiated as cook and general attendant. One room, extending from front to rear, over the dry-goods store, served as parlor, kitchen, and dining-room. A big, white screen concealed the culinary department from general observation, behind which—judging from auricular-olfactory testimony—was a mixed-up arrangement of pots and pans, babies, crockery, cradles, cooking-stoves, and blankets. We believe the landlady, her husband, children and servant slept there. In the public half the boarders used to divert themselves by killing cock-roaches of evenings.

The diet provided at the Dirty Boarding-House was plentiful, though porky—swine's flesh forming its staple. *Porgies*[8]—purchased in their decadence from perambulatory fish-vendors—sometimes varied this anti-Hebraical peculiarity. The coffee tasted like diluted molasses, flavored with roast peas, chicory, Flanders-brick,[9] and dirt. The hashes were tallowy. The buckwheat cakes partook equally of the characteristics of flannel and gutta-percha[10]—and sometimes had insects (known as Croton-water bugs) in them. But pork was the universal dish. Every body was over-porked. Boarders had rashes brought out upon them in consequence, and we remember one consulting a doctor under the impression that he had contracted varioloid.[11]

There might have been a dozen boarders. The aristocrats of the place were a dispensary doctor (who generally fuddled himself on Monday morning, and continued in that condition until Saturday night); a dry-goods clerk from the store below; and a young man engaged in the wholesale fish-exporting business, down-town. The latter used to perfume the room with a *bouquet de salt-mackerel*. Another boarder aspired to the position of Pet, and was hated by the rest because he brought home butter of an athletic description, as an equivalent for his entertainment; also—it was said—cheating the landlady by altering the weight-mark on the top of the firkin.[12] In justice, however, be it remarked, that he could eat of it at table. He even professed to *like* it.

The "peck of dirt" assigned by an unpleasant proverb to every member of the human family, as part of his inevitable aliment, might have been disposed of in a very short time at the Dirty Boarding-House. The landlady didn't waste time in washing plates, dishes, and other gastronomic utensils, and a sediment of a week's antiquity often collected in the bottoms of the pitchers. The knives and forks were picturesque and various in size and pattern, the backs of the former having been worn into a keen edge, and most of the latter owning broken, distorted prongs, and revolving handles. Some had been repaired with putty, which came off in use. (This applies also to the plates.) The cruets stood awry, and were destitute of stoppers (which might account for the presence of hairs and crumbs in the ketchup).[13] It was advisable to scrape the surface of the salt before *chipping a bit out* for use. The table-cloth resembled a map of the United States, in consequence of the many parti-colored stains ornamenting it. We believe it was reversed—once a fortnight.

The like stoical indifference, amounting almost to sublimity, to what ordinary mortals affect to consider the decencies of daily life, exhibited itself in other particulars. In bed-making, one sheet only was changed at a time, and many of the blankets had large gaps in what ought to have been their centers—admirably adapting them to summer use. We incline to the belief that the towels (originally constructed from ancient coffee-bags) were washed but once a year, though the ingenious expedient of shifting them from room to room slightly disguised this fact, or invested it with the charm of novelty. So seldom was broom or brush used in our apartment, that on our shedding a shirt-button, it lay undisturbed beside the washing-stand until rendered invisible by the fine coating of dust which successive weeks deposited upon it. And this, too, in spite of the servant's passion for keeping windows closed. She and her mistress had as great an aversion to fresh air as to water. There was always an atmosphere of the night before last in the dining-room.

The landlord—a man with a face like a dyspeptic bull-dog—we saw very little of. He used to come home at all hours of the day and night, and generally went immediately to bed (behind the screen), though sometimes he might be observed lingering about the entry, or a low groggery at the corner of the block. On these occasions he was often accompanied by an individual possessing the most unmistakably rascally face we had ever looked upon. Let our readers picture to themselves a hybrid between an ourang-outang and a hyena, and it will give them some idea of his countenance. Subsequently we learned that the fellow was a Tombs lawyer,[14] which, in a manner, justified his physiognomy.

Boarders were expected to pay up promptly in the Dirty Establishment. We remember a row occurring at breakfast, on the occasion of a defaulter taking his seat before settling for the past week. After much verbal profanity on both sides, the policeman attempted to eject his lodger, seizing him by the hair of his head for that purpose. They tumbled down stairs together, and into a fight at the bottom. Our landlord had the worst of it, nor was he rescued from his antagonist until his wife and the servant came to his assistance. The nose of the latter young lady sustained some injury in the conflict, and resembled a damaged tomato for three days afterward.

This damsel (who was much horrified on the above occasion, by the doctor's proposition to amputate her proboscis) might have been selected as the extreme type of objectionable *Biddyness*.[15] She never took off her clothes, washed or combed herself, or went out of doors. Her intellect was not equal to the comprehension of a simple request, and repetition confused her. You might have sown potatoes in her brogue, it was so thick. She would have been perfectly contented on an exclusive diet of the skins of her national vegetable, and tobacco. She had but a limited idea of cause and effect. We have seen her fill a stove with big lumps of anthracite, and apply a solitary match to the bottom for the purpose of producing ignition: have known her to trim a lamp with vinegar—or what passed for it (diluted vitriol[16]) in the Dirty Board-House. An unfortunate partiality for smoking often brought her within danger of extempore and involuntary *Sutteeism*,[17] as she was infrequently discovered in a state of slow combustion, in consequence of the presence of unextinguished pipes in her pocket. We put her out, once, with the contents of a slop-pail. (It didn't make her dirtier.) Also she had several narrow escapes from blowing herself up with camphene,[18] which, we doubt not, she will finally effect. We shall read of it in the papers some day.

In the ceiling of the room overlooking the adjoining thoroughfare—a large one containing four beds—there was a trap-door, affording egress on to the roof. Here, on summer nights, the boarders would assemble, in their shirt-sleeves, to indulge in beer and short-pipes—occasionally varying those contemplative enjoyments by pelting the cats, with which the neighboring roofs abounded. Once they borrowed a fowling piece, which, being loaded with small shot, brought many feline flirtations to a tragic conclusion. The victims, if obtainable, were generally dropped down their owners' chimneys. This subsequently led to a discontinuance of the practice. Another amusement, introduced by the doctor, met with great favor. It consisted in standing at a window on Sunday afternoons, and dazzling the eyes of pedestrians or occupants of opposite houses, with the reflection produced by agitating a looking-glass. A gaunt carpenter and his wife (Spiritualists) actually invited a roomful of friends to witness this inscrutable phenomenon, when, unhappily, the secret was discovered in consequence of over-zeal on the part of the operators. No less than six mirrors, at an equal number of windows, were in use on that occasion. Such were the diversions, and such our experience of a Dirty Boarding-House. May the reader never have to reside in one!

CHAPTER VII

The "Hand-to-Mouth" Boarding-House

This Establishment stands in one of those shabby thoroughfares which the extension of Canal-street is rapidly improving off the face of New York.[1] It is a frame house, and like its mistress, of forlorn and pinched-up aspect, both having seen better days. Like her, too, it has sometimes made attempts to brighten up a little, and show a cheery face to the world—and looked more dismal for the failure.

Miss — is a maiden lady, so palpably past the meridian of life, that she does not attempt to deny it. Her face is thin and withered, and two long, hay-colored curls depend mournfully on either side of it. Her figure is so devoid of symmetry, that, but for her countenance, you would be in doubt as to which side of her you were standing. She does not dress herself tastefully. Every way she is a plain, unpicturesque old maid—just such a one as young ladies are prone to favor with valentines representing witch-like harridans on broomsticks,[2] or surrounded by attendant familiars, in the shapes of cats, parrots, and devils.

She has kept a Boarding-House for upward of twenty years, but it has scarcely returned the compliment. For twice that time her industry has failed to lift her above the dread of tomorrow. That she works hard, her bony hands attest—that she rises early, the Irish servant-girl often grumblingly avows—that the dietary and domestic arrangements are needlessly expensive, the boarders would indignantly deny—yet it is certain that Miss — is always a little in arrears with the world—of all creditors the most unmerciful, and the surest to take interest out of its debtors in a disagreeable manner.

Her house, described in the *Sun* (to which entertaining journal she is a subscriber[3]) as containing "genteel apartments within five minutes' walk of Broadway," comprises half-a-dozen indifferently-furnished rooms, exclusive of the parlor and kitchen. The former of these has a threadbare, but miraculously-darned carpet, a sprinkling of feeble-backed cane chairs—which are very shaky on their legs—a faded sofa, an ancestral rocking-chair (with one of those aggravating pieces of clean *crochet*-work which stick to your hair or tumble off when you sit down, spread carefully over its top) and a gaunt piano, which has not been tuned since the presidency of James K. Polk.[4] The chambers, too, are equipped in an equally poor manner, but though the sheets display so many patches as to impart a scratching sensation to the spines of recumbent boarders, no Broadway dandy's shirt-front could be more scrupulously washed.

Of course, as the Establishment is a cheap one, the quality of the meals furnished is not of the first order. Miss — (in common with the landladies of most poor Boarding-Houses, and some well-to-do ones), does her own marketing, trudging through rain or sunshine at early morning, and returning with a heavy basket laden with such provisions as her slender purse affords. Occasionally, however, she is unable to effect this without debt; and complains bitterly (or would do so, had any one the complaisance to listen to her), that butchers take advantage of this, in supplying inferior meat at increased prices. Her groceries are often purchased in small quantities, just enough for each meal, previous to which the servant may be seen hurrying from the corner store, with a loaf under each arm, and various cone-shaped parcels of coffee, tea or sugar, wrapped in that coarse straw paper peculiarly devoted to such purposes. Sometimes Miss — is necessitated to waylay you in the passage, to solicit cash advances on your week's board, upon which the quality of your dinner will depend. It is politic, as well as good-natured, to comply, as you will thereby secure a savory dish or so, as well as the good-will of your landlady.

Sooth to say, what with her landlord's regular yearly demand for higher rent and the increasing price of food, she has a hard time of it. She owes her servant money, who, consequently brow-beats and defies her, and invites muscular Irishmen into the kitchen, with scarcely a feint of the usual apologetic fiction, "Shure, it's me cousin, mum!" She is in arrears with her milkman, who absolutely lords it over her, and has, more than once, cut off the supply of lacteal fluid. Her coal merchant demurs about bringing a ton of Red Ash or Peach Orchard[5]—until paid, like a subscription to a newly-started newspaper, "punctually in advance." Nor are her cares and anxieties particularly lightened by the comments of her boarders, or their general behavior to her. Not that there is—on the part of the male boarders—any especial manifestation of want of feeling and consideration (beyond that spirit of antagonism we shall have occasion, hereafter, to remark as frequently existing between the mistresses of these Establishments and their lodgers). As is generally the case, *they* are more unthinkingly than intentionally unjust.

Half a dozen careless men (engaged in various employments, as printers, gilders, clerks, etc.), could scarcely be expected to trouble themselves with considerations of delicacy on the behalf of the lonely old maid who contracted to supply their necessities of eating, drinking, and sleeping. So they grumbled occasionally at the deficiencies at table, cut jokes at their landlady's personal appearance and presumed hopeless aspirations toward matrimony, quizzed her peculiarities, and loaned or refused her money with equal *brusquerie*. But the demeanor of the lady-boarders deserves special mention, as illustrative of the kindness of heart sometimes exhibited by woman toward the weaker of their own sex.

They were but two in number, wives of boarders. Their leisure—that is to say the whole of their time—appeared to be divided between Broadway, the novels of Mr. G. W. Reynolds,[6] and disquisitions on the characters of such persons as enjoyed the felicity of their acquaintance. When they came down late to breakfast—which they invariably did—with limp figures, hair screwed up in fragments of last week's *Police Gazette*,[7] and similar graceful *dishabille*—one couldn't help envying the happiness of their husbands, who sewed on their own shirt-buttons, the ladies declining such tasks, and, indeed, all needlework, on the standing plea of sickness. One had a child, a puny, weak little creature, afflicted with water on the brain, of which it subsequently died. And many an evening, when the be-*rouged*, be-*hooped*, and be-*flounced* mother was disporting herself at cheap public balls, did poor Miss — take care of this child. When it died its affectionate parent said, "perhaps it was a good thing for God to take it." Probably it was.

But it was not to be expected that any such simple good offices on the part of the landlady could mollify the indignation and contempt entertained by this lady and her companion toward one who had failed in that great object of female ambition (in their eyes)—catching a husband. They were perpetually, persistently, and inexorably down upon her. All her shortcomings and piteous shifts to keep up appearances were dragged into light, sneered at, and tattled about. They knew the number of her dresses, and how often they had been turned and dyed. They forbade their husbands advancing loans to her, on account of board, or still more insultingly recommended it; subsequently informing every body of the obligation. They were implacable toward little delays in the appearance of meals, assuming a clamorous indignation at their husbands being "kept away from business"—if but for ten minutes. They evinced a preternatural facility of discovering deteriorations of diet, and sometimes succeeded in setting the men grumbling. They indirectly accused her of appropriating small quantities of coal from their private stores to her own use. (This, by the way, is a fruitful source of squabbles in most Boarding-Houses. We have known a suspicious individual to sit up all night in a dark cellar in order to detect purely imaginary depredators.) They so badgered and worried the servants on the question of having their breakfasts brought up to them in bed, that Miss — declared, tearfully, "It was *impossible* to get a girl to sit up late stay with her." They invented rancorous slanders about the landlady's antecedents, and sowed them broadcast among her tradesfolks. And, finally, they affected virtuously improper surmises on her manifesting emotion at the receipt of letters directed in a masculine hand, from California. We believe they came from an only brother who hadn't behaved very well to her, and had been exported to the diggings by his sister's money. She used to cry a good deal over them, and to sit up late in the back parlor writing long answers by the light of an oil lamp, which smelt unpleasantly.

Very far from us be it to arraign the average justice accorded by the world to our lonely spinster, or to her class. The term "old maid"—ordinarily affixed like a tin-kettle to the tail of an unoffending animal, to torment its bearer and amuse lookers-on—could scarcely be rendered less ludicrous or more endurable by our championship. Yet it might be worthy of inquiry whether a too large license is not accorded to wives over their single sisters. Whether *their* whims, oddities, and eccentricities are not passed over very lightly, in comparison with those of the solitary virgin whose temper is fretted into asperities by the world's indifference or contempt. And, finally, whether some old maids are not as good, kindly and unselfish creatures as any in the world.

It is too generally assumed that unmarried women are so compulsorily. But whether this is the case or no, why should one sex be ridiculed for its voluntary or involuntary choice, while the other is allowed to consult its selfish pleasure? Listen to noble Jean Paul, "It is not always our duty to marry, but *is* always our duty to abide by right, not to purchase happiness by the loss of honor, nor to avoid unweddedness by untruthfulness."[8]

With respect to poor Miss —, we can only hope that the brother who didn't behave very well to her may have luck at the diggings, and come back to redeem his character.

CHAPTER VIII

The "Serious" Boarding-House

Is, though not within what were once considered the limits of upper-tendom—being south of Bleecker-street[1]—just on its ancient confines. A plain house of somber color, on the shady side of the way in the afternoon, the door bearing its mistress' name in black letters upon a square and brightly-polished brass plate. The steps are, even in winter, kept scrupulously clean, and the area-gate locked; tradesfolks being expected to ring a bell especially devoted to them. You will not, in general, hear of this Establishment through the medium of advertisements, neither does the landlady reply to any. "She is thankful," she tells you, "that her house is mostly full." She has been known, occasionally, to insert a few lines in the *Evangelist* newspaper.[2]

On applying for board—which, however, unless you're a mildly-developed young man, or under the coercion of severely religious parents, you are not at all likely to do—expect to be inducted into a grim front parlor. There, you will scarcely have time to observe a book-case filled with volumes of sermons and such light literature, (which is always kept locked, possibly from motives of humanity,) half a dozen strait-backed and very unaccommodating looking chairs, a cheerful lithograph, representing a number of savages engaged in knocking a missionary's brains out with big clubs, and badly executed portraits, in oil, of the landlady and her husband, when the former appears. Being, as aforesaid, a mildly-developed youth, you probably have not read Dickens' *David Copperfield*,[3] otherwise you would instinctively jump at the idea that Miss Murdstone had quarreled with her amiable brother, emigrated to New York, got married, and set up as the keeper of a Boarding-House.[4] Mrs. — might, we are persuaded, have played the part at Burton's, with immense success, on the strength of her countenance alone.[5]

She receives you with stony politeness, and at once proceeds to inform you of the rules of her establishment; characterizing it as a *quiet*, *Christian* one. Cards, latch-keys, reading in bed, Sunday papers, and smoking, are prohibited. With respect to the last-mentioned luxuries, however, she grimly concedes, that she can't prevent your indulging in them in your own room—if you find pleasure in *such things*—but, she adds, she doesn't wish a *bad example* set to her young gentlemen. As to the question of latch-keys, if any *unavoidable* occasion necessitate your being out later than eleven, "at which hour we *invariably* lock the street door," Mr. — (her husband) will sit up for you.

This gentleman—we shall fancy the reader weak enough to become a boarder—is somewhat advanced in years, and has an expression of countenance such as might be supposed would be produced by an exclusive diet of persimmons.[6] Like his wife, he is a Presbyterian—Hard-Shell denomination.[7] They entertain strong views as to creed, objecting to all Christians of other denominations, to music, dancing, books (unless *serious* ones), theatres, and any attempt at cheerfulness on Sunday. The day, by the by, is scarcely known to them by that good, old-fashioned word, the Sabbath, and "Lord's day," having usurped its place. But rigidly righteous as this may seem, their faith is entirely eclipsed by the virulent theology of Mrs. —'s mother, a formidable old lady, who wears a cap similar to that in which Hannah More is generally depicted.[8] *Her* Christianity is of the most sulphureously blue-light order. She has the liveliest belief in what a friend of ours once felicitously termed "the inherent d—nation of every body." Indeed, Pandemonium is so unpleasantly prominent in the excellent matron's creed,[9] as to excite a suspicion that it is to her religion (and that of those resembling her) what pickles are to lunch—a great zest and relish.

The boarders—especially such as differ in faith from the family—frequently come in for the benefit of the opinions of this venerable female. In common with her daughter and son-in-law, she has an especially pious aversion to Roman Catholicism—which she terms "Idolatry"—and to Episcopalianism. We remember her informing a lady of the latter persuasion, who had ventured on a mild encomium on the Church of England service for the Burial of the Dead, that it was only "a whitening of sepulchers";[10] and that if she looked for salvation in that quarter, she'd be very unpleasantly undeceived, some day. In which healthy sentiment she was abetted by another boarder, also malignantly-orthodox, according to the Calvinistic standard.[11] This lady had had three husbands, two of whom committed suicide, while the third ran away from her. She considered the world wicked enough to deserve a much worse punishment than burning up (could it be conveniently contrived) but had, individually, a great terror of quitting it. For let but a hint be dropped of the presence of any slight epidemic in the city, she instantly left town.

Three times each Sunday did she, the landlady, and landlady's mother, go to church; Mr. — sometimes accompanying them. His preparatory "grace" before dinner was longer on that day than others. If any thing detained him the boarders were expected to wait, unless one took the office upon himself. During the time of our sojourn one gentleman was particularly available for this, being a clergyman and ex-missionary, and the landlady's especial pride, glory, and bulwark of Presbyterian respectability.

He was a kindly-natured man, rather cramped by his creed, as is not uncommonly the case with his class. Too much is expected of them. If we persist in demanding an inhuman amount of perfection from our spiritual instructors, it is no wonder if some become straight-laced. And this, we think, accounts for the very general and unjust accusation of hypocrisy made against clergymen. For one can't go through life, maintaining an unpleasantly perfect altitude above fallible mortals, without risking *that*, or the sin of over-righteousness—of all sins the most abominable. Our clergyman was comparatively free from both, though a latent stratum of intolerance, underlying his piety, became eruptive on occasion. A quick-tempered, narrow-minded, conscientious, opinionated, and charitable man, he only lacked large-heartedness to become a good one.

He was a widower, without family, though fulfilling the double part of uncle and preceptor to a boy of twelve—one of the most extraordinary of juveniles.

It is a privilege to have known that moral and intellectual Phenomenon. He was a rosy-faced, dark-haired, near-sighted youth, possessing a small, flute-like voice, and preternatural glibness of speech. He never, by any chance, did a boyish action. He always descended to breakfast bursting with information as to the state of the thermometer, and was so superfluously polite as to bid you good-day whenever he met you, though it should chance twenty times in the course of a morning. He dabbled in entomology, *didn't approve of Shakespeare*, and objected to story-books, "as he had heard of persons becoming insane from the pernicious habit of novel-reading." He spoke of the simplest things with the greatest elaboration, and would inform the landlady that "owing to the negligence of the servant, some water had been spilt in the passage, which, by the action of the weather, had been converted into ice, and that he should recommend its immediate removal, in order to prevent accidents!" He addressed grown persons over the dinner-table on the political, social, or religious questions of the day, and would encourage them to enter into discussions with him. He greatly enjoyed defining his position on every possible subject, and once favored us with his "platform," which was ultra-Garrisonian.[12] He always read the newspapers. He was a staunch advocate of the Maine Law.*[13] He had a little dressing-gown, and

* Apropos of which, we find it impossible to resist indulging our readers with the insertion of the following verses—whether of the young gentleman's composition we can not positively assert, though strongly inclining to that opinion. We picked them up in MS. on the staircase and calligraphy being small, neat, skinny, and formal. They *might* have been copied from some Temperance Hymn-Book:[14]

"I'm a little Temperance boy,
Twelve years old!
And I love Temperance
Better than gold!

a special costume for gardening. At table, his appetite and choice of food were guided by those of his uncle, and, probably, had that gentleman needed castor-oil, he would have demanded a similar dose. He was insufferably affable, revoltingly polite, preternaturally precocious. Had you inquired his sentiments as to Predestination, Original Sin, or Chinese Metaphysics, we've no doubt he would have "gone in" with perfect confidence in his ability to explain those not particularly simple subjects. You could as soon have put the author of the life of P. T. Barnum out of countenance.[15] He called upon the girl who waited at table—a hard-featured, small-pox-marked, Scotch damsel, hired on account of her Protestantism and ugliness—three times as much as any grown boarder. The ladies of the Establishment admired his "excellent moral principles," petted him, and once formed an audience to a lecture of his delivering. We believe the subject was *On Sea-weed and the Moral Lessons inculcated by It.* The male boarders, to a man, detested him—which was very unkind, as he always treated them with the greatest condescension.

We used to sit opposite to him at meals, and were never tired of looking at and speculating about his future. We knew what a nice young man he *must* grow up into. We fancied the offensively virtuous life he would lead, merging all minor peccadilloes into one ineradicable cancer of spiritual self-conceit. And furthermore, when removed to a sphere worthy of his manifold perfections, we thought what an unpleasant angel he'd make. We could imagine him stepping up to Michael and glibly expressing his general approval of celestial arrangements,[16] but offering a hint or so by way of improving the Constitution.

He was not the only youthful boarder in the "Serious" Establishment. Two others, a boy and girl, owed their existence to the union of a heavy gentleman (engaged in the oil-trade) with a small, weak-eyed lady, his second wife. It was whispered (and here we may remark that there was far more than the average under-current of tattle and slander afloat in the "Serious" Boarding-House) that she had brought her husband a large fortune, and that he behaved very meanly to her—the ladies asserting "she hadn't a frock fit to put on." But he was eminently pious. Immensely so. And, by-the-by, it is worthy of observation that pious men generally marry *prudently*; and if they become widowers, scarcely ever *remain* such. Knowing that money is the root of all evil, they burn with Christian heroism to struggle with it; honoring matrimony as a divine institution, they can't have too much of it. The children of these parents had different but unpleasing idiosyncrasies. The boy was fourteen, had straight hair, a face like a bad lemon, a querulous voice, bony legs, and large feet. He used to put his arms round his mother's neck at dinner-time—toward the conclusion of the meal—

Every little boy, like me,
    The Temperance-pledge should sign,
For God loves little boys
    Who don't love wine!!!"

and whiningly solicit permission to over-eat himself. The girl was only remarkable for sulkiness, detestation of her father, and a habit of kicking her brother's shins under the table. The twain sometimes endeavored to get up a game of romps with the Prodigy, but he considered his dignity insulted by such proposals, and always kept aloof. You could not offend him more thoroughly than by treating him as *a boy*. He was very susceptible of such affronts, and never, thoroughly, forgave a boarder who once *took him up in his arms*. On another occasion, too, he was moved to such anger as to tell the landlady that he considered her behavior "beastly"—for which he subsequently apologized in words of three syllables.

The meals provided at the "Serious" Boarding-House were excellent in quality, plentiful in quantity, and not ill-served; though the entire duty of attendance fell upon the angular shoulders of the Scotch virgin. For the elect are by no means indifferent to the pleasures of the palate, not infrequently attaching over-much importance to that which might be denominated the grossest of all enjoyments. An unregenerate scoffer would say that by voluntarily debarring themselves from many innocent pleasures they are necessitated to fall back upon the most unspiritual ones. We have seen the brother and sister recently alluded to absolutely wallow in turkey and cranberry sauce. Generally there was a completed rampart of dishes encircling *that* family at dinner.

Sunday—always a dull day in Boarding-Houses—was preternaturally slow in the "Serious" one. Church-going, with intervals of feeding to repletion appeared to be the rule of conduct with the majority of its occupants. Some of the young men, however, stayed at home during the afternoon and "carried on" extensively in their chambers; beating each other with pillows and struggling upon the beds. When Mrs. — ascended, or sent up the Scotch virgin to remonstrate, they assumed a meek aspect and endeavored to criminate one another. When less actively disposed, they slept, coming down gaping and with generally foggy aspects at the sound of the supper bell. There were very few attempts at conversation, as the landlady, her mother, the malignantly-orthodox lady, and heavy gentleman disapproved of the introduction of secular topics on Sunday. On working-days we talked politics, in which the clergyman, like most of his class, took great interest, especially when of an exciting and belligerent character. We don't mention this invidiously. On the contrary, we liked him for it. Once we knew a clergyman who, during the Mexican war, would get unusually enthusiastic about feats of individual heroism and throat-cutting—why shouldn't he? It was *human*.

We recollect a lady-boarder who—being comparatively unacquainted with the rigorous piety of the Establishment—gave great offense by playing upon the piano on Sunday; as did her husband by reading the *Herald*, which paper was an abomination in the eyes of the landlady. So much so, indeed, that upon its accidental appearance on the breakfast-table one morning, Mrs. — started up with horror and astonishment depicted on her countenance, seized the obnoxious sheet, rushed to the stove and, in a frenzy of religious zeal, committed it to the flames. This little incident, in conjunction with others, probably accelerated the removal of that couple from the "Serious" Boarding-House, for they left soon afterwards.

Our landlady's "trials"—she so denominated all matters not in accordance with her wishes—were far more severe in conjunction with another boarder. Like the serpent of old, he entered into this Presbyterian Eden but to blight and destroy. He was a reporter to a daily newspaper. His behavior, while domiciled in the "Serious" Establishment, is fearful to think of. He whistled godless negro melodies while going up stairs, rang the ugly servant-girl up at unholy hours of the night and morning, and once effected a nocturnal, burglar-like entrance at a basement window. He smoked short pipes in bed, dropped Play-bills in the parlors, asked mild-young-men-boarders out to take drinks, and—horrible to relate—seduced one of them into a Model Artist exhibition.[17] He affected a passion for the malignantly-orthodox female, cut jokes on the cap of the landlady's mother, and invited both ladies to accompany him to Christy's.[18] He proclaimed his adhesion to the Mormon faith, and made jocular attempts to convert the heavy gentleman. And, finally, he devoted his energies to the perversion of the rising generation.

We don't think he had much success with the Prodigy. That immaculate youth stood poised on too high a pinnacle of conscious virtue to be knocked off by mortal aim. But with the others—the boy and the girl—he sped but too well. Discovering that they were unacquainted with the institution of pocket-money, he tempted them, by presents of small coins, to the utterance of awful words. The bony-legged boy did, in consideration of the sum of fifty cents—he refused two shillings, with the additional bonus of a large apple, as too little—actually

thrust his head into a room where three ladies sat and utter, in a small, sepulchral, but perfectly distinct voice, the fearful anathema consigning them to eternal perdition.

He didn't appear next morning. Nor did his preceptor, for that night he put a climax to his atrocities by bringing home one of the mild-young-men-boarders in—as the landlady declared—a dreadful state, in which he was subsequently discovered on the door mat. The tempter at once received instant and severe notice to quit. The fallen youth was confined to his room for a week, by his father, who took his dinners up to him, and—it was darkly whispered—administered paternal chastisement regularly, every night and morning, immediately after family prayer. We can depose to the boy's howling dismally at those periods, and that, when reinstated at the Boarding-House table, he looked remarkably sheepish.

CHAPTER IX

The Theatrical Boarding-House

To the best of our belief, this Establishment—the details and domestic economy of which were unique in their way—is extinct, we therefore speak of it in the past tense.

Like the Cheap Boarding-House on a large scale, described in Chapter Four, it consisted of two tenements, which, in this case, formed brick-and-mortar units in a street diverging eastward from Broadway, not far from the theater of that name. Whether influenced by the location, a predilection on the part of the landlady for the profession, the gregarious habits of the class, or the three reasons combined, the majority of the boarders were actors.

It was conducted on what might be termed providential principles. Receiving the scriptural injunction of "take no thought for to-morrow" in a literal sense, its mistress, a stout, unctuously-smiling widow, of Irish extraction, devoutly obeyed it. Every thing was done by shifts and expedients. "Chance governed all," as in Milton's Chaos.[1] You enjoyed the pleasing uncertainties of alternate hunger and plenty, as in savage life, with the additional advantages of social intercourse of a novel and entertaining character. There were no regular meal hours. A newly-caught boarder, of sanguine disposition, might, it is true, place credence in a mild superstition attaching gastronomic importance to certain periods of the day, but this faith—touching in its very simplicity—never outlasted a week. *Two* rendered him a confirmed infidel as to all order whatever. He either *dis*-accommodated himself into harmony with the mis-rule around—or left. We were young, and the place had its attractions. We were poor, also, and it wasn't dear. For nearly six months we lived in that Theatrical Boarding-House.

Generally, one's earliest experience was in connection with the subject of loans. As surely as rapidly, you glided into the anomalous and unnatural position of creditor to your landlady. She borrowed five or ten dollars of you on the day subsequent to your arrival, and henceforth you vainly struggled against destiny. In the language of appeals to a charitable public, "the smallest contributions were thankfully received." Solicitations for "quarters," shillings, *sixpences*, beset you; sometimes through the medium of a faded female, half-servant, half-boarder, oftener that of the landlady's daughter, a shrill and objectionable girl in pantalettes, whose hair curled the wrong way, who was horribly inquisitive, never closed doors, and appeared subject to a mysterious disease denominated "the Mumps," which necessitated the perpetual bandaging of her head in dirty handkerchiefs. Like Poe's Raven,[2] she would come "tapping, tapping at one's chamber-door," with the words "Mother says —" prefacing the inevitable message. We have sat full half-an-hour waiting breakfast while this was in operation elsewhere in order to raise money for the purchase of a mutton-chop.

Payments to the butcher partook of the general irregularity of the Establishment, wherefore he, not infrequently, waxed wroth, and supplied meat of dubious quality, or none at all. Entering at night by means of the area gate (for less than twenty minutes' pulling at the street-door bell was never known to procure admission) we have discovered injured tradesfolk sitting gloomily in back kitchens. There they would remain for hours, lying in wait for our landlady, she having unaccountably vanished, while the servants plied hither and thither among the boarders for the wherewithal to exorcise them. These girls' wages, too, were awfully in arrear. The amount of lying, dodgery, and pretense put into operation (never however effectually) in order to screen the system—or rather want of it—must have been prodigious.

The supply of linen being scant, the advent of a new boarder was invariably marked by a foray into others' chambers, in order to furnish forth the required complement of bed-furniture for the stranger. Here a pillow would be surreptitiously confiscated, there a blanket, elsewhere a coverlid. It was bitter winter weather, and loud and dire were the complaints of the victimized on the following morning, when "the stupidity of them girls" formed the staple excuse. Time, however, had taught *Us* the wisdom of the serpent. We, noting any deficiency of bed-gear, made *raids* on our own account, replacing from the couches of others those articles of which ours had been deprived. Necessity must palliate, if not justify the act. Often have we lain and listened to the anathemas of some temporary neighbor on the unknown abstractor.

Our meals—taken in a sort of white-washed school-room of limited dimensions in the rear of the premises—were mostly of a carnivorous description, from which circumstance we infer that the pie-venders of that vicinity are inexorably opposed to the credit system. Occasionally dinner was totally ignored. No bell's harmonious discord sounded the tocsin of appetite.[3] Hungry and exasperate boarders would assemble in dismal conclave, sit until expectancy palled into despair, then wrathfully disappear—the sterner spirits being, sometimes, partially mollified by homeopathic relays of steak. On such crises Mrs. — would be invisible. Our impression is that she locked herself in a subterranean cupboard or closet till the evil hour had passed.

But, as we have said, the Establishment had its pleasanter aspects. Shifty and incongruous as its arrangements were, the very absence of all order imparted a piquant zest to existence within its walls, appealing, as it did, to the vagabond side of human nature. If one day's dinner were omitted, tomorrow's plenty effaced all ireful recollection of it. And during intervals of cash or credit, you were never too late or too early for a meal. It was a true Liberty Hall, if ever such existed, and Rabelais' inscription over the gate of the Abbey of Theleme, "Do what thou wilt," might have been written on its portal.[4] Where else, we ask, should we have been allowed to sit wrapped up in blankets and bed-clothes on deathly cold winter nights, while scribbling a comic story on the edge of the washing-stand? Where, subsequently, to insert a small stove within the thirteen-inch space between our bed-foot and the wall, to extemporize a hole for the stove-pipe with a rusty knife and hammer; and finally, to char the bed-post to the extent and blackness which we assuredly did. The Theatrical Boarding-House had its advantages.

You could send out for beer at any seasonable or unseasonable hour. You could call fellow-boarders by their nick-names, cut jokes and fraternize with every body. We like actors. And in spite of all the charges which from Le Sage's day to the present have been brought against them, the world likes them, and will continue to do so. They generally have that practical wisdom which disposes to look on the cheery side of things. At our Boarding-House they punned, laughed, talked slangy and stagy, drank ale or champagne with equal good humor, and got up the jolliest of supplementary suppers.

Of one of these entertainments (given by the husband of a *tragedienne* during his temporary bachelorhood consequent on her absence while fulfilling a professional engagement at another city), we have a lively recollection. It was a good notion of a supper—a hare, chickens, oysters and champagne; whist, poker, piano-forte-playing, and singing to follow. Speeches were made also, which, as the hours drew on, increased in eloquence and pathos. We remember one gentleman pledging his honor that his wife would *die*, if desired, for the behoof of any friend he might mention. Another was moved to shed tears copiously during a burst of confidence on the subject of his early years. Choruses, too, were sung, some being of an abnormal, and even gymnastic character, as witness the following. The vocalist, suiting action to words, commenced:

"One finger and thumb keep moving—
Keep moving—
To drive dull Care away!"

Others joining in with voice and gesture on a repetition of the lines, the exhortation increased in its demands "*two* fingers and thumbs" being next in requisition, and so on, until finally, at the words,

"Two arms and two legs keep moving!"

all present were jumping up and down in an energetically ludicrous manner only conceivable in insane Shaking Quakers.[5] As this occurred at something like

2 A.M., certain boarders overhead and below were unreasonable enough to remonstrate, but our landlady's company having sanctioned the festivities during the earlier part of the evening, such complaints were treated with merited derision. We have but an indistinct idea at what hour the party broke up, having quitted it at 6 A.M., leaving cards predominant.

It was pre-eminently a masculine Establishment, and appeared the more so, as the few lady-boarders generally preferred taking their meals within the sanctity of their own apartments. They, however, sometimes congregated on wintry afternoons in a gloomy old parlor appertaining to the larger and duller of the houses, where we once surprised a select party of three engaged in the consumption of cigars and hot brandy and water. One of these, the proprietress of a rather prettyish face and a large-headed child (which latter article was periodically brought to see her), had a room immediately adjoining ours; and for some time we were in error as to the sex of the occupant, being misled by her proficiency in the art of whistling. Our undeception only occurred upon tapping at her door for the purpose of re-igniting a lamp, which we had knocked over and extinguished among the bed-clothes.

At a later period, when a slight intimacy had sprung up, she occasionally borrowed our boots on rainy evenings to walk to the theater in, receiving with great good humor any playful allusions to the (presumably) lovely limbs they were honored by encasing—and once telling us to come round to Burton's as she "played a *leg-part*." On our return from that place of popular entertainment, she was very anxious to learn "how she looked from the parquette," and "whether we heard her distinctly." She had but three lines and a monosyllable to utter during the entire performance!

But, unquestionably, the lioness of the place was the *tragedienne* before alluded to. She was a handsome, jolly woman, with a deep, rich voice, and would ask you how you did, or make an observation about the weather in such heartfelt, cordial tones as imparted quite a glow to the recipient. She had a will of her own, too, and it was popularly supposed that her husband (who played walking gentleman, and was some years her junior) knew it. She was, also, a little jealous of him—not without reason. We fancy he had an equal attachment to champagne and to his wife, and it was said the lady herself had a *penchant* for the former. With two anecdotes in which she figures, the present chapter may fitly conclude.

There was a hard-headed and generally obnoxious Scotch boarder, who, to some originally disagreeable characteristics, added the one of occasional intoxication; when he was prone to discourse about John Knox and the "Free Kirk" of his country.[6] The actors used to "sell" him by challenging his admiration for imaginary passages in non-existent novels by Walter Scott; and to excite his anger by pretending to mistake him for an Irishman; as also by addressing him as Mac Wuggles, Mac Scratcher, Mac Grits, Mac Turn'emup, and similar titles. Now he, coming home one night from an adjacent bar-room, and availing himself of the opening of the street-door by the servant of our *tragedienne* (whether impelled by antecedent whisky-skins or his natural obtuseness, we know not), followed the girl up-stairs to her lady's apartment; apologizing for his presence, when questioned, by a muttered reference to his ordinary theological topic. Mrs. —, not considering this satisfactory, shrieked for her husband, who, like his wife, was in undress, and leaping up at the summons pursued the invader to our chamber door, where overtaking him, he, with his lady's assistance, administered severe fistical chastisement. Upon our issuing forth, lamp in hand, an eminently dramatic tableau was visible. The howling Caledonian,[7] with the sanguine stream of life gushing from his nose, and his countenance further ornamented by feminine talons, lay writhing in the grasp of the infuriate actor, whose left whisker he was holding on to in a peculiarly painful manner, while above and around hovered a Lady Macbeth-like figure, awful in white flannel.[8] Other boarders appearing, a separation was effected, and the Scotchman persuaded to go down stairs, where he armed himself with a carving-knife, swore revenge on every body, very nearly assassinated the landlady who repaired to him with pacific intentions, and finally went to sleep with his head in a coal-scuttle. But "with the morning calm reflection came"; by dinner-time the three had exchanged apologies, shaken hands, and despite the victim's discolored eyes, swollen nose, and face scarified *à la* gridiron, were hob-nobbing one with the other most cordially—an edifying and Christian spectacle.

Our remaining anecdote is trite, but has a spice of the ridiculous which may justify its narration. A brother actor of our *tragedienne's* husband having borrowed a pair of nether habiliments from him for "light comedy" purposes, was, by the lady, encountered in the passage and ordered back to his apartment, there to immediately disendue himself of them, she not approving of the loan. And the voice which we had over-night heard in Juliet's love-impassioned speech was exalted in wrath, even to letting dwellers on the upper floors know that "Bill— shouldn't have them pants—they had been purchased with *her* money, and she'd burn 'em ere his request should be granted!"

CHAPTER X

The Boarding-House Wherein "Spiritualism" Becomes Predominant

A HANDSOME up-town edifice within five minutes' walk of Fifth Avenue, and of such height that scaling its staircase (midway up which a foggy aroma of dinners always hovers) is involuntarily suggestive of Jacob's ladder.[1] In outward appearance it is aristocratic, in inner arrangements unexceptionable, its dinner-hour fashionably late. In no particular, therefore, would it differ from many similar Establishments, but for the peculiarities of its inmates, which fairly entitle it to a place in our Physiology.

The reader, if a New Yorker, has doubtless often noticed in Broadway the tall, spare figure of an elderly gentleman attired in a suit of black of the cut and fashion of the past century. Who has not turned to gaze on that venerable-looking person? on the long, gray hair straggling over his shoulders and back; on the three-cornered cocked-hat, the breeches and knee-buckles of '76? Such an aspect might have graced the council-board of William Penn or the Pilgrim Fathers.[2] That, reader, is the Doctor, and he being the arch-priest and grand exponent of Spiritualism at the house of which we speak, it becomes necessary to pay our respects to him.[3]

Were he to write his auto-biography (as we trust he will, some day), it would doubtless prove a deeply interesting volume. Far be it from our hasty pen to anticipate such a task, or to risk the displeasure of a conscientious seeker after truth by the attempt. Yet we have heard that in his pursuit of that celestial maid, he, in common with other of her admirers, has occasionally got *garroted* by certain of the pestilent heresies which are wont to assume her likeness—sometimes releasing himself with extreme difficulty. Enough of that. Suffice it to say, that after considerable theological experience—rivaling, indeed, that of Orestes

Brownson,[4] though starting from the very point at which *he* has rested—the Doctor now enjoys a lucrative medical practice, believes strongly in the Maine Law, and is equally ardent in his advocacy of Spiritualism. We have been told of singular and startling phenomena as the immediate agents in producing his conversion to the latter—how the spirit of a defunct relative not only shook, slapped, pinched, and tweaked the Doctor nocturnally, but was accustomed to lift him from his bed and treat him to rides round the room (how he looked during the operation let our artist's pencil portray), always finally restoring him to his resting-place, and considerately tucking him up—how, desirous of accommodating himself to these celestial visitations, he studied music, and learned to play upon the guitar and harmonicon—with much more of retrospective matter which we dismiss as irrelevant—turning at once to the Boarding-House, and his proselytizing therein.

Within the Establishment are many lady-boarders of Eastern origin, who, though past the age of girlhood, have retained the simplicity of heart and trustfulness of nature proper to the morning of life. Now from Eve's time downwards the sex has exhibited a *penchant* for knowledge, even when acquired at the risk of danger; and it would seem that the minds of old maids are, from the fact of so much of their nature lying, as it were, fallow, peculiarly subject to become the recipients of such stray tares as, sown broadcast by imposition and credulity, are producing every day such plentiful crops of misery and insanity. Any way our Doctor (whom, of course, we acquit of disingenuity) experienced great success in his advocacy of Spiritualism among the lady-boarders.

In the first place, Physiological classes were formed, and the Doctor commenced a series of lectures on Anatomy—which, however, came to a sudden termination in consequence of the uncalled-for squeamishness of all but one of the virgin auditory. These being abandoned, the discovery of "Mediums," formation of "Circles," and procuring of "Manifestations," became the order of the day—or rather evening, for at such time, after the labors of the day, did the Doctor vouchsafe to act as spiritual hierophant.[5] Here every thing progressed admirably. Little supernatural *soirees* were got up, and the ladies had the satisfaction of being astonished, frightened, and mystified in the most delightful manner. Nothing could be pleasanter—but, unfortunately, there existed among the inmates of the establishment one or two skeptics of the sterner sex, and especially one individual whom we shall designate as the Incredulous Boarder.

He was the Doctor's moral antipodes in every thing, appearance, characteristics, and opinions. The former never had his hair cut, and shaved only his upper lip; the latter was bald, and scrupulously-razored, with the exception of a moustache. The former attired himself in a style particularly calculated to attract notice; the latter's costume was simple and unpretentious. The former possessed unlimited faith in the supernatural, the latter unbounded skepticism. Being, therefore, of such radically opposite natures, how could they fail to antagonize?

The Doctor denounced his adversary as a rhinoceros-hided infidel, and furthermore informed him that he was possessed by Seven Devils. It might have been this baleful influence which impelled him to devote himself to the production of utter confusion and dismay in the ranks of the faithful—to assail the Doctor's opinions on all subjects—to charge the reverend person with profaning the Sabbath by the performance of *valses, polkas*, and the like secular compositions—to speak of the Maine Law with derision, of Spiritualism as humbug—and finally to characterize its professors as ghostly Peter Funks.[6] These abominable opinions he *would* express on all possible occasions.

Great, therefore, was the exultation, when, one evening, a whisper passed round that the Incredulous One had experienced a softening of the heart, and petitioned to be allowed to make one in a "Circle." In the hope of his conversion it was granted, though the Doctor retired to his room in dudgeon, as mistrusting the sincerity of the neophyte. Notwithstanding which, remarkable and unexampled success followed. Tabular gyrations and knockings occurred almost immediately, and presently, after performing a spiritual *Schottische*,[7] zig-zagging in a very startling manner into corners, and once descending heavily on the corns of a male believer, the supernaturally-stirred mahogany penned one of the ladies in a corner, and nearly cut her in twain, against the wall. This was naturally regarded as a great triumph, and the Doctor descended to share it. His presence apparently induced greater manifestations from the spirit-world. The fire-irons rattled, and groans were heard as proceeding from the heart of the chandelier. In compliance with the general request, the Doctor mounted a chair for the purpose of investigation. Solemnly, and at regular intervals, the lugubrious sounds were repeated. Questions were put and responded to—by groans. It was unanimously concluded that some unhappy spirit was present, but unable, from unexplained circumstances, to definitely communicate his sorrows. And thus to the awe and satisfaction of the community, the proceedings of the evening terminated.

Nor was the faith of believers shaken by the assertions of the still Incredulous Boarder, on the following morning—that *he*, and he alone, contrived to produce the movements of the table, and that a little inquiry had reduced the groaning spirit to the simple origin of a loose plank in the flooring overhead, upon which a girl chanced to be seated in a rocking-chair, while nursing a baby. He was considered a ribald outcast from truth, one given over to unbelief, a conscious blasphemer of the mysteries of Spiritualism! The ladies held fast to their faith, and the skirts of the Doctor. Far be it from us to desire to dislodge them!

We have recently heard that he is organizing *Spiritual Dancing-classes*.

CHAPTER XI

The Mean Boarding-House

Mean Boarding-Houses, like mean people, are, unfortunately, not uncommon or peculiar to any rank or locality. We have already had occasion to speak of one Establishment in which a stratum of aristocratic pretense overlays this characteristic, we now turn to another in humbler life.

It is a clean-looking frame building, in a quietish street, some twenty minutes' walk from Chatham Square,[1] and midway between East Broadway and the river.[2] If the broken and puddley sidewalks of the vicinity had been especially sown with an intention of producing a crop of old barrels, boxes, disabled kettles and contused saucepans, they could not be more plentiful. There are more private dwellings than shops, one or two Dutch or Irish grocery stores, a disused pump, a few street-lamps, and some trees. Our Boarding-House is a corner one, standing some little distance to the rear of the street-front. You reach its stoop by an ascent of half a dozen wooden steps.

Its landlady claims England as the land of her nativity, in defiance of the richest of brogues and most Milesian of appellations.[3] She is a widow, with three daughters. The eldest has a husband, the second expects to obtain one, and the third is a girl of eight. Between the two latter a species of guerilla warfare unceasingly rages, the grown-up young lady having apparently made up her mind to regard her sister's existence as a personal insult, which conviction she expresses through the medium of slaps, and stray epithets, on all possible occasions; while the younger revenges herself by trying on her oppressor's bonnets, and indulging in fugitive performances on the piano, which generally terminate in a grand *finale* of screams and spankings.

The old lady, her mother (she owns to five-and-fifty, and her wig is innocent of all deception) has West Indian antecedents, and talks much of "Jamaiky," in connection with her late husband. According to her representations he was a species of marital phoenix—never known to swear, to smoke, to partake of any stronger liquor than ginger-beer, or to *find fault with his meals*. (She is particular in dwelling on this last point for the benefit of boarders.) There is extant a book of travels in Ireland, containing marginal notes in the hand-writing of the defunct, which denounce its author as "a meen man," and inform you that "he tells lice" when not eulogistic of the country. We infer that the commentator was a patriotic, but imperfectly-educated Irishman.

His relict has been one and the mistress of her Establishment for eight years.[4] She frequently alludes to the "novelty" of her employment, by way of indirectly apologizing for all deficiencies. There are plenty of them. It is, emphatically, a Mean Boarding-House.

If we knew any body with an unappeasable appetite for salt fish and sheep's liver, we would give him Mrs. —'s address. Those dainties always predominate at her table. They formed the staple meal at least thrice a week, and underwent no end of revivification—if we may be allowed the expression in connection with cookery. A piscine odor permeated the entire Establishment—the very window-curtains smelt of it. It was a singular and beautiful study to observe the many transformations a single dish endured. In the breakfast steak of today you might recognize the corned beef of yesterday's dinner, and reasonably anticipate encountering it in tomorrow's meat-pie, and the next day's hash. We got to dating from the advent of certain portions of animal food—reckoning upon our fingers the lapse of days by them.

All meats—whether pork, veal, mutton, or beef—are, in a double sense, exceedingly rare in the Mean Boarding-House—probably being served up in that state that the difficulties of mastication may prevent any considerable consumption; not to hint at the desirability of punishing with indigestion and nightmare such brutal boarders whose appetites will NOT be deterred. The joints always present fine anatomical displays of bone, and great difficulties to the carver. But joints are of seldom occurrence. Liver and salt fish predominate. And—for a treat—an occasional bullock's-heart on Sunday.

The vegetables are worthy of notice. Potatoes tasting like something between yellow soap and bad artichokes, carrots out of which all flavor has been boiled, and large, rank, greasy cabbages. (There is always a suggestion of these latter, by-the-bye, flavoring the piscine odor before alluded to.) Mrs. — prides herself on her pastry. It is of solid construction, and damp, putty-like material. We should suppose that dripping, saleratus,[5] and potato-starch enter largely into the ingredients. With the home-made bread—produced as a luxury—it partakes of a highly dyspeptic character. The tea is so weak that you wouldn't suppose it had strength to drown a fly, or dissolve sugar. The coffee tastes of horse-beans, and is invariably concocted over night (why, we know not) being re-warmed for the morning's consumption.

Mrs. — dispenses these delicacies to her boarders in person, with much indirect discourse as to the superiority of "good, plain livings" over "kickshaws,"[6] and many reminiscences of her husband's culinary predilections. It invariably happens that he would have preferred the meal in progress to all others. Besides being a marital phoenix, he is a defunct *Mrs. Harris*, to be invoked on all possible occasions.[7]

The economy observable in dietary arrangements, is also carried out in other matters. The scanty stair-carpet—confined to its place by a limited allowance of rods—dwindles into shabby drugget on turning the first landing-place,[8] and disappears altogether at the second story. Cheap calico window-curtains—on which are landscapes of gorgeous colors, but more than Chinese contempt for perspective—supply the place of sun-blinds. And the various chambers have but little other furniture than beds, washing-stands, and little mirrors, chairs being infrequent. Our apartment contained but half a window, an unpainted pine-partition separating it from the adjoining room, and dividing the casement equally between them. It was, too, rather a screen than partition, as it did not reach the ceiling by two feet, which afforded opportunity for interchange of small courtesies, such as brushes, matches, etc., with our neighbor. (On one occasion he smashed our looking-glass with an injudiciously thrown blacking-box.) Our bedstead, also, did not possess its full complement of *slats* or cross-pieces, and we tumbled through—twice a night on the average—until we contrived extemporaneous repairs with an old drawing-board, and fragmentary easel.

The boarders at the time of our sojourn, were about twelve in number, the sexes being pretty equally represented. We will briefly enumerate them. A married Tipperarian,[9] who had greatly distinguished himself in the Smith O'Brien campaign of '48,[10] by demolishing a drum with the British arms upon it; and was, in consequence, greatly beloved by his compatriots. A widow, with two daughters, the elder acknowledging to a husband in California, but refusing to

recognize him in a hairy and intoxicated individual, who, one night, attempted to force an entrance into the house, and demanded speech with "Betsy." An ex-sailor, temporarily reduced—or advanced—to the position of a policeman, addicted to interlarding his speech with proverbs, and to going to sleep on duty, in which condition he once had his *star* stolen from him. His wife and children. A red-haired dry-goods clerk, who found favor in the eyes of the landlady's daughter, and propitiated the mother and married sister by presents of ribbons. A hatter, an attorney's clerk, and a japanner or dealer in ornamental furniture, complete the list. The last-mentioned individual was our neighbor, on the other side of the partition, and had a shop in the vicinity.

Combining the foregoing particulars of board and boarders, our reader's fancy will easily supply the detail, of existence within the walls of the Mean Boarding-House. Our landlady had but one characteristic in addition to those already chronicled. She generally vanished immediately after dinner, and did not turn up till supper-time, when she always groaned a good deal, and, in response to the inquiries of lady-boarders, said she "felt better." The Tipperarian declared, privately, that she was in the habit of "mugging herself" with spirits; going to bed with her clothes on, and a black-bottle, for that purpose.

Our sojourn would scarcely have been a protracted one under any circumstances, but was brought to a speedier close than we had anticipated. A few weeks' residence in any Boarding-House generally reveals to the observer a strong under-current of slander, in which more or less of the inhabitants love to dabble privately, sprinkling each other's characters as with diabolic benediction. (Had we cared to descant on the topic we might have added a considerable *addendum*, especially treating of it, to each chapter.) In the Mean Establishment, this amiable weakness flourished in great force, and presently blossomed into results. The landlady's daughter didn't like the policeman, considering his calling *low*; and the California widow objected to his wife, accusing her of smuggling bottles of Charles's *Cordial Gin* into the house, and, what was worse, not inviting other ladies to partake of them.[11] The attorney's clerk—an every-way unpleasant individual, and the "funny man" of the house—originated floating libels to the effect that the japanner's wardrobe consisted of but one shirt, two dickeys, one pair of socks and a collar, and that he washed 'em himself, and dried them by suspension from his chamber window. The dry-goods man privately solicited attention to the hatter's appetite, and was sure that the husband of the landlady's married daughter didn't talk so much with the California widow for nothing. Finally rows took place at table, boarder squabbling with boarder and with the authorities.

The ex-sailor, provoked by the undisguised scorn of the landlady's daughter, publicly informed every body that there was a blamed sight more Boarding-Houses than parish-churches in New York, and that he didn't care a rotten piece of junk for the whole bilin' of 'em, subsequently offering to fight the landlady's son-in-law (which was declined). He then left with his family. The japanner followed, and his departure subsequently influenced ours.

We did not join in the general chorus of depreciation which pursued our late neighbor, and in consequence were looked upon as one disaffected to the ruling powers, and persecuted accordingly. Our being "at home" was denied to visitors, our letters were refused, or performed quarantine in the landlady's pocket before reaching us, private intimations of "dinner's ready" were given to other boarders in advance of the bell (in order that we might arrive at a disadvantage), an especially uncomfortable chair with a *caving-in* seat and rickety back was assigned to us, our plate, knife and fork were violently hurled at us, our ewer was unfilled, our towel removed, our soap sequestered. Finally we were talked *at*, over the dinner table. *We* left, and making common cause with the japanner determined on "humors of revenge."

A neatly-worded advertisement to the effect that Mrs. — was desirous of accommodating Irish and German families with board at the rate of $1.50 per head, weekly, presently appeared in the leading daily papers. Emigration was in full vigor, and plenty of applicants responded to the invitation, the average being—as we were informed by the policeman, whose beat lay in that quarter (and who took a fiendish pleasure in directing inquirers to Mrs. —'s) about ten families, daily. Some came with bag and baggage, and were slow to admit the possibility of a hoax, attempting to effect lodgments in the passage, and claiming the proprietress as their country-woman. There was, also, much difficulty in explaining the matter to the Germans in consequence of their general ignorance of the English language.

The landlady made her son-in-law write ungrammatically-indignant letters to the papers denouncing the authors of the advertisement as malignant and evil-disposed ex-boarders. But the series of events were not destined to end thus quietly. The Tipperarian fell into disfavor, being suspected of intimacy with the conspirators. He was therefore not only subjected to a series of petty persecutions similar to those which had effected our removal, but an additional one was originated for his especial annoyance. Knowing that he went to bed early, the attorney's clerk stimulated other male boarders to the nocturnal performance of negro choruses, interspersed with howls, under his window, at the back of the house. On the second of these *charivari* the wrathful Celt descended in great fury and undress, made so fierce an attack on the party that he utterly routed them, pursued the landlady's son-in-law into the street, and for the space of several blocks, finally giving him in charge of our friend the policeman and ex-boarder, who promptly conveyed him to the station-house. Next morning, as might be expected, the Tipperarian received notice to quit. Before doing so, however, he, learning from his wife that another musical entertainment—and one of some pretensions—was projected on a particular evening, resolved on an attempt at reciprocity.

With this view (after making arrangements for his wife's removal), he engaged three barrel-organs, a trombone, and five drums; laid in a supply of whisky, tobacco and sausages; and perpetrated the most unique *soiree musicale* we ever had the pleasure of attending, The company were mainly Irishmen, but included one German (to play the trombone), and the japanner (who took a drum). All arrived at 8 P.M.—much about the time that the more genteel party assembled below—and until the notes of a harp and violin gave the signal, quiet was observed, broken by the performance of a grand overture by the entire strength of the company (with the exception of one big drum which, proving too large to be got through the doorway, had been burst in the endeavor). We despair of conveying to our readers any idea of the effect. With the exception of the German, no performer had the slightest practical knowledge of music. The barrel organs went off at different tunes, the four impromptu drummers attempted a *demoniac reveillé*, and the German played any thing he pleased—all uniting in one common sentiment, that of endeavoring to make as much noise as possible. A pause for refreshment, in the shape of pipes and whisky, encouraged the opposition to a feeble attempt at rivalry with a guitar and flute—our drums soon silenced it. The subsequent performance of "Ben Bolt" (that melody was just then at the height of its popularity),[12] by the combined aids of one barrel-organ, the trombone, and an extemporaneous accompaniment formed by shaking cents together in a washing-basin, was voted less effective, and the drums insisted on coming into play again. Ten minutes more produced an envoy from below, in the shape of the attorney's clerk, who, looking very pale and excited—but got-up, with respect to costume generally, and shirt-collar in particular, in a gorgeous manner—wished to know (with Mrs. —'s compliments) "the meaning of all this." The Tipperarian replied by explaining that "a little music" was in progress, and proffered hospitality, in the shape of a pipe, sausages, and whisky. Rejecting these with ireful dignity, the envoy waxed wroth, and stimulated by the consciousness that the company below were listening to the colloquy, began to talk loudly and fiercely. In all probability a fight would have ensued, but for an unlooked-for accident which very nearly induced a tragic termination to the absurdities of the night.

In the excitement incidental to the occasion, the opposition party had quitted their room for the stair-case, or crowded about the doorway, thus establishing a thorough draught of air from the open window, which wafted the light gauzy curtain to a recently-ignited lamp. It was on fire in a moment. The alarm was given, women screamed, men swore, fire-bells tolled, engines arrived and a posse of red shirts and a dense mob blockaded the streets, as the Tipperarian was lugged off by the police—his guests escaping in the confusion.

He was fined ten dollars next day, and discharged from custody. We received an industriously greased and ill-spelt *challenge* from the attorney's clerk for our presumed participation in the concert, and disgusted him exceedingly by an expression of readiness for a pugilistic encounter—which, however, never came off. And since then we have heard nothing of the Mean Boarding-House, or of its occupants. Nor are we particularly desirous of information.

CHAPTER XII

The Boarding-House Where There Are Marriageable Daughters

This Establishment has some few characteristics akin to those detailed in connection with the aristocratic one described in Chapter Five, yet as it is every way a broader and stronger type of a very numerous class, we at once recognize its claims to a place in our Physiology.

It is situate in a street north of Canal (no matter for its name)—one of those which intersect Broadway, the blocks adjacent to which are more stylishly built than those farther on, where they degenerate into very common-place and mean-looking tenements. Our present Boarding-House stands on debatable ground, between the junction of these extremes, and is a plain brick building, which might be rendered brighter and cleaner-looking by an application of the paint-brush. Mrs. — has occupied it for twenty years—since the death of her second husband.

She is a large woman, with a full face, a hooky nose, and speculative eye, like a Jewish version of Mrs. Trollope's *Widow Barnaby*.[1] Her nose, indeed, is in such undesirable propinquity to her chin as to set one involuntarily cogitating whether her defunct husbands ever kissed her, and if so, how they managed it. She generally appears in a hideous, copperas-colored gown, without any thing white about her neck, and a black wig. In conversation she is chatty and obsequious—especially if you are an eligible young man in search of board. Single lodgers preponderate in her Establishment, of which her daughters constitute the main feature and attraction. These young ladies are three in number, of the respective ages of thirty, twenty-five, and sixteen, the elder being the result of the first marriage. All three appear excessively affable, amiable and approachable, and it is your own fault if they do not speedily become affectionate also. As they have not the *finesse* and dashing assumption of patrician breeding characterizing the ladies of the Aristocratic Boarding-House Where you Don't get enough to Eat, they make bolder advances, and play a coarser game generally. Like them, however, each has her peculiar *rôle*, and though quite a penny *rôle* in comparison with those of the brilliant misses described in Chapter Five, contrives to carry it out with that vigor of which only a woman in quest of a husband is capable.

Admitted into what Mrs. — terms their "pleasant social circle," you are, in the phrase of Inspector Bucket of *Bleak House*,[2] "reckoned up" in a twinkling, and, according to your idiosyncrasy, made over as a lawful waif and stray to one of the three young ladies. They may be thus discriminated. No. 1. Poetic and strong-minded, the last quality subject to modification according to the humor of the destined victim. No. 2. Religious. No. 3. Gushing and exuberant. One would suppose that each of them had studied Phrenology at our friends Fowler and Wells,' and there formed different estimates of the thickness of the masculine skull over various organs; No. 1 determining on reaching the brain through *Firmness* and *Ideality*, No. 2 attacking *Veneration*, and No. 3 *Amativeness*.[3]

Each, then, and in dubious cases, all together, unmask all their batteries of fascination to reduce the Malakoff of your bachelor heart to capitulation.[4] No. 1 listens with grave attention to your remarks, and is surprisingly of your opinion on politics, literature, and fashion—though for the latter she cares but little, despising all "frivolities." She supports you in argument, even to the extent of hinting pretty broadly to your opponents that they are ill-bred, and know nothing of what they're talking about. She thinks women ought to have the privilege of voting, and "knows somebody" (with a corner-of-the-eye glance at you) "who *she'd* send to Congress—if she could, but won't tell *who* for the world." She believes strongly in Alexander Smith's *Life Drama*,[5] and likes to get you to read Byron aloud—but, of course, is entirely unacquainted with *Don Juan*,[6] though, singularly enough, the volume (her property) always opens at that naughty poem. And when, on one occasion, your copy of Walt Whitman's *Leaves of Grass* disappeared for three whole days, she it was who brought it to you, having discovered it behind the sofa, where it had unaccountably slipped.[7]

If you are a mildly-developed young man with religious proclivities, beware of No. 2. She teaches at Sunday-school, and belongs to a society which instigates lady-brigands to wait upon down-town merchants, editors, and business men generally, in their offices, there to solicit subscriptions for an impracticable charity. She is a church member, and will denounce the *Schottische* or *German* on the smallest provocation. It is rumored that she carries in her bosom the miniature daguerreotype of a gentleman studying for the ministry,[8] together with a small theological pamphlet bearing the title of "Milk for Babes." All burlesque phrases applied to aught that may be supposed serious—such as the over-quoted drollery of "Harp of a Thousand Strings"[9]—shock her inexpressibly. And an artist-boarder once incurred her lasting displeasure, when requested to sketch Moses in the bulrushes for her album,[10] by depicting a terrified Jew peddler between two rushing animals of the bovine species.

No. 3 is at once the belle and boast of the Establishment, being both prettier and younger, and therefore more attractive, than her sisters. She is an arch coquette, and, like most coquettes, sometimes ventures very far in flirtation, and is most accessible to the more daring of her admirers. She prefers a game of romps or blind man's buff to books or conversation, and, in the latter sport, it is delightful to see her dart into corners to avoid your outstretched arms, uttering the most musical of little shrieks all the time until caught—when she vows it's "not fair," and that she will retaliate. And be sure, if her endeavors be successful, that she will pull your whiskers and feel your moustache in order to identify you.

Some characteristics the ladies possess in common. They are equally partial to moonlight walks on summer evenings, to sitting at the open windows before the lamp is lit, and to lingering on the doorstep—all in company with the gentlemen, who are kindly permitted to smoke on these occasions. Sometimes No.

3 condescends to ignite a cigar for some favored boarder, and even to apply her own rosy lips to the same, returning it with much coughing and the assertion that she "quite likes it." Upon which, if you remark that it's like getting a kiss by deputy, she slaps you, laughs, and runs away, but unwilling to risk hurting your feelings by the apprehension of her displeasure, comes back again almost immediately. We have known her to be kissed in the passage, and to take it very quietly. But such indulgences, as you will probably find, almost invariably precipitate a matrimonial engagement, which will be broken in a month by the discovery that others have enjoyed, are enjoying, or may enjoy, the same privileges. No. 3 has jilted more swains than you can count upon your ten fingers, and that too entirely in deference to mamma and the almighty dollar.

A thorough-going Old Soldier is Mrs. —. She lets no opportunity of praising "her dear girls" escape her. She wonders how any one can be insensible to their charms of mind and person. They are *so* good, *so* amiable, *so* dutiful, *so* industrious, that she don't know how she shall ever make up her mind to part with them. He who wins either will indeed gain a treasure, and must himself be a paragon—the model and quintessence of every manly virtue ere he obtains *her* consent. Notwithstanding which, we once overheard her tell No. 1 that she was "real sick of her," and wished to—that "some *Fool of a Man*" would take her off *her* hands. It made a great impression upon us at the time.

If you are supposed to entertain a *tendresse* toward No. 1, you learn at the tea-table that "that delicious cake" is of *her* making; an admirer of No. 2 is privately informed that *she* clothes half the poor children in the ward; while No. 3 cuts out her own dresses, and isn't "such a mad-cap as she seems," but will sober down into a "most excellent, affectionate, warm-hearted girl." All of which you may believe or not; but if you incline to the bright side of the picture, we shouldn't advise you to darken it by looking very closely into the landlady's face. For it is ominously suggestive of what "the girls" *may* look like in advanced life. We have known a budding offer for No. 3 blighted by this simple circumstance.

Not content with the matrimonial opportunities afforded to them by their mother's Establishment—which may be looked upon as a hymeneal man-trap—the young ladies occasionally try elsewhere for victims—even at the risk of meeting victimizers. There are stories afloat among the more knowing boarders, of "the girls" having answered matrimonial advertisements, and we can depose to the fact that when the *Phyfe* correspondence got into the papers Nos. 2 and 3 were singularly agitated. All three will admit that they have been to *Madame Morrow's* to have their fortunes told—if not to other "Witches of New York," also.[11] But then ten times the wit and humor of our friend "Doesticks" would hardly suffice to keep "young ladies" away from such places.[12]

Whether they act in concert on a common understanding, or carry on the war, individually, each on her own hook, we never were able to ascertain. Certainly they appear to live in remarkable unanimity, and if squabbles occur, the Napoleonic axiom of washing dirty linen at home is strictly observed.[13] Even on rather provoking occasions—such as the discovery of one sister in the chamber of a boarder presumably devoted to the intruding party—no loss of temper has resulted. They twine arms round one another's waists in the sweetest sisterly fashion, talk awhile with you, and presently skip away, leaving you puzzled, enchanted, or amused, according to your temperament.

We have little to say of the diet of this Establishment, or of individual boarders: the former is but indifferent, the latter (as has already been observed) consisting, generally, of young men—*who do not stop long*. Perhaps the young ladies rather *over-do* the Art of Fascination; perhaps the prospect of such a mother-in-law terrifies the gentlemen. Any way, Nos. 1, 2, and 3, continue unmarried. We shouldn't wonder if the younger sister finally effected it, and take this opportunity to advise her future husband to immediately emigrate with his bride to California, to change his name, and repudiate all connection with his wife's relatives. Following this counsel he may stand a chance of happiness.

CHAPTER XIII

The Cheap Hotel Boarding-House

In one of those business-like thoroughfares which are peculiarly characteristic of the lower part of New York—whose dusky red stores have iron shutters, and the names of their occupants painted up in black letters upon a white ground—whose sidewalks are perpetually blockaded by bales, barrels, and boxes—where the pedestrian's progress is rendered perilous by the transit, on *skids*, of unwieldy merchandise from cart to store, or *vice versa*—where, throughout the week, wholesale traffic reigns, and which, on Sundays, has a very funereal and dead-wall aspect—is a huge, seven-story, corner building, bearing its designation in proportionate letters. It is at once a cheap Hotel and Boarding-House.

A showy bar-room, furnished with the usual amount of plate-glass, many-colored liquors, cigar-boxes, etc., occupies the front of the lower story. Here, when there are but few customers, a portly German, of some eighteen stone weight, may be seen reclining in an arm-chair, half asleep, yet, with the instinctive vigilance of a landlord, keeping one eye open. He is wide awake enough of evenings, and of all evenings in the week, that of Saturday. Drop in then, you will find him the center of a busy scene, and ready to take drinks, successively, with every individual member of a motley and miscellaneous crowd there assembled. Boarders pay up, for the preceding week, at this period, and much mirth, but more noise, is in progress everywhere. Men clustering in front of the bar; men sitting, spitting, drinking and smoking round the stove (if in winter), men bending over the bagatelle-table at one end of the room, men cursing, quarreling, or striking the table at cards,[1] and men engaged in the quieter games of checkers or dominoes. A fog of tobacco-smoke, and a perfect Babel of clamor prevails,[2] the language used being as various as the speakers, but, as may be guessed, the "rich Irish brogue" which General Scott found so charming while on his presidential canvass, is predominant.[3]

Most of the boarders—the house accommodates upward of eighty on the average (sometimes more)—are laboring men, having employment in adjacent wholesale stores, about wharfs, etc. It is, by express rule, a bachelor Establishment. A stair-case, rather dirtier than the middle of a street on a rainy day, gives access to the upper portion of the house, which is divided into innumerable rooms, of different degrees of smallness, some containing three beds, the majority only one. They are plainly furnished, and indifferently supplied with water, but one ewer being allowed to each chamber. The servants, unlike their master and mistress, are Irish, but have dwelt so long in the establishment as to have become comparatively Germanized, and one of them—a character in her way—can talk *Deutsche* like any native-born Teuton.[4] They are mostly ugly girls, of squat figure, very good-humored, slatternly, and industrious.

When the dinner-bell rings—at noon precisely—there's a rush of men from the bar-room to a large apartment immediately over it—(occasionally used for public meetings, clubs, etc.). Every body helps himself at table, and, considering the limited space afforded for elbow-movement, the meal is disposed of in a miraculously short space—about ten minutes sufficing to "get through" with it. Quantity rather than quality is looked for at the hands of the caterers, and they do their best to satisfy this expectation. Colossal joints of coarse meats already cut into slices, pyramids of potatoes, swamps of squash, and acres of collapsed cabbages—all having received extreme unction in liquid grease—disappear as rapidly as if each boarder had made a private arrangement with Nature for a perfectly unlimited supply of gastric juice. A company of ostriches, dining on flat-irons, *à la maître d'hôtel*, horse-shoes, *au gratin*, and ten-penny nails *confiture*,

could not be less apprehensive of indigestion. The acknowledged mode of proceeding appears to be seizing upon the dish placed before you, and "going into" it without wasting time by looking for other condiments than those at hand. Veal preponderates over other meats—why, we don't know. Sundays are celebrated by sumptuous banquets of strongly-scented ham and oyster-soups—which last are provocative of much emulation. For the bivalves, in addition to being of dwarfish and withered aspect, are so few in number that you might fancy them swimming round the tureen in disconsolate search for one another, and happy to be brought into companionship by the first dip of *the* successful boarder's spoon. On Sundays, too, a little more leisure is vouchsafed to the meal—it is not disposed of under fifteen minutes. But if you come in later, only a chaos of fragments, bones, and cold vegetables, awaits you.

The landlady, her daughter, and the servants, wait at table. The first is a spare little woman, very active and alive to the main chance—so much so, indeed, that we have heard it asserted by one of her boarders, that she "would skin a flea for the hide and tallow." But this we incline to regard as a mere poetic figure of speech, as the few fleas in her establishment, so far from being flayed, are generously allowed to puncture the skins of the boarders. One thing is unanimously admitted, that Mrs. — is always very kind when a boarder is sick. On the whole she is popular, and deservedly so. The lodgers are rough, careless, hard-working men, but generally good-humored and kindly, and, like most persons in humble life, always willing to assist one another when occasion calls for it.

Mrs. —'s daughter is a young lady of eighteen, possessing fashionable aspirations, and much admired by the good-looking young men boarders. She appears in great splendor at the *yearly balls*—for balls are got up at our Cheap Hotel Boarding-House—the boarders subscribing for a band, inviting their lady-friends and relations, doing every thing complete and proper, and keeping it up, too, just for all the world as though they lived in the Fifth Avenue, and owned—not worked in—down-town stores. And we don't know but that they enjoy themselves quite as much as richer folks—perhaps more, as such entertainments are of less frequent occurrence with them, and therefore more keenly appreciated. Any way we are sure that the big room over the bar presents a pleasanter appearance when occupied by some two hundred couples, gaily gyrating in the *Schottische* or *Polka*, than when thronged by a mob of heated, brawling, foul-mouthed, rowdy politicians. We have seen it under both aspects, and ought to know. (Our Cheap Hotel Boarding-House is quite the "Headquarters" of the down-town Democracy during popular Elections. We shouldn't advise any body to try and vote any ticket but that favored by the unterrified, in the immediate vicinity.)

For our portly landlord, he is a prosperous man, and apparently gets rich and stout in proportion as he grows older—wherefore we see no reason why he shouldn't rival the wealth of Astor and the bulk of Falstaff.[5] We believe him to be a good fellow—as an act of Samaritanship,[6] performed toward a sick carpenter, may testify. He kept the man at his own cost rather than send him to a hospital, and subsequently advanced the money to bury him. Yet a parting word of censure. Perhaps some of his boarders might hold their hard-earned dollars more closely but for the existence of his *bar*, and its facilities for drinking and card-playing. We have heard of cases in which the latter has only been abandoned in the bar-room to be recommenced in the apartment of one of the gamblers, there to be continued until the rosy smile of a new-born day lit up the opposite house-tops, and reproached the haggard-faced victims for their desecration of the peaceful night. And though our Cheap Hotel Boarding-House be conducted as decently as is possible, we can yet fancy a better home for working-men than we have just described.

CHAPTER XIV

The Boarding-House Where the Landlady Drinks

WE once had had three weeks' experience of an Establishment which can only be rightly discriminated by the above title.

It happened in consequence of a change of dynasty in our, then, Boarding-House. We were made over, in company with a house-full of fellow-victims, to a new landlady; the former—a handsome Kentuckian—relinquishing the business for private life. The tenement was a spacious, old-fashioned one, in a street south of Canal, running west-ward from Broadway. It had been admirably ruled under the former proprietorship. How we fared with the new, we shall proceed to relate.

Mrs. — was a woman of fifty, with a flushed countenance, a nose like a bulbous strawberry which had been left out in the rain so long that the color had got partially washed out of it; and a rheumatic husband, of feeble intellect and demeanor. His occupations seemed confined to befogging himself with yesterday's newspapers, opening the street-door upon unnecessary occasions, getting in the way of the servants when they laid the dinner, and justifying the appearance of that meal when served before or behind the proper hour, by the production of a large silver chronometer, the veracity of which it was impiety to question. His lady's peculiarities, however, can not be dismissed so easily.

The lessee of a Boarding-House succeeding a popular predecessor is likely to be very closely scrutinized by her lodgers. They are apt to be suspicious of deteriorations in diet and other alterations for the worse; and, if any peg to hang complaints upon be discoverable, the new landlady will soon find abundant illustration of the truth of the copy-book proverb, that "Comparisons are Odious."[1] In the present instance, the boarders had good reason for grumbling.

Instead of the palatable soup heretofore initiative of dinner, a liquid abomination apparently derived from boiling dish-clouts in equal proportions of dripping and water, and subsequently flavoring with cayenne pepper and salt, was substituted. In place of goodly joints of boiled, and baked (roast is unknown in ALL Boarding-Houses), we entered upon an interminable prospect of over-cooked pork—that *Monsieur Tonson* of Boarding-House tables.[2] Coffee became cloudier, tea of a more delicately resinous hue, sugar grittier, milk more calcareous. Fish of evil odor appeared. Hashes and stews began to preponderate over substantial dishes. Every thing culinary was subject to the dismalest deterioration. Added to which our landlady's behavior, at table, began to be very extraordinary.

She came to dinner with a very red face, and a curiously hazy appearance about the eyes, accompanied by a sort of spasmodic wink. Her conduct while presiding was singular and disconcerting. She assisted the boarders to food in an arbitrary and inconsistent manner, heaping some plates to an extent sufficient to satisfy the appetite of a hungry giant, while others received no more than could have been easily disposed of by a full-grown canary. When their return hinted dissatisfaction at these proceedings, she *reversed* her blunder, indulging at the same time in a confused and hiccupy monologue about "people not knowing what they wanted." Her carving was odd, and productive of strangely-shaped wedges of meat. She used the big knife and fork in a very startling manner. We have seen her eat her own dinner with these utensils, subsequently wiping them on her sleeve.

Furthermore, she occasionally evinced a preternatural liveliness, and made wild dashes at conversation, addressing remarks about the weather to boarders at the remote end of the table, or violently requesting their approbation of the dinner. Frequently, too, she became impressed with the singular notion that certain individuals were fond of particular dishes, and, especially, that her husband liked *beans*. There was a peculiarly disagreeable kind of them (which tasted like something between bees-wax and bitter aloes, and always got harder by boiling) prevalent at meals, and in spite of Mr. —'s feeble disclamations, his lady *would* favor him with immense quantities, heaping them on his plate with her own fair hand, also sending the servants, with dishes full of the obnoxious vegetables, to him. Once we saw *four* of these in front of the unhappy gentleman.

During these rather eccentric proceedings on the part of our landlady, a corpulent, puffy-faced boarder, who invariably sat on her left hand, gradually emerged into notice as pre-eminently distinguished by her favor. They laughed and talked together a good deal, and at length proceeded to what might be termed ornithological endearments, such as *chirping*, and calling one another "*Dickey*," and even reciprocating chuckings under the chin. This boarder had made his appearance in the house in company with his fair friend and her husband, and was, we presume, an old acquaintance. Whispers circulated that he owned a small groggery, and took the rent out in spirits, which he and the landlady drank together. We incline to credence in that statement.

Of course, these peculiarities of conduct attracted considerable attention on the part of the boarders. Many were amused, some scandalized, and a few disgusted. Our landlady's eccentricities took other out-o'-the-way forms, besides those enumerated. There was a certain Frenchman, who, having only been fifteen years in this country, of course, didn't understand the language, and to him, exclusively, Mrs. — once chose to address her conversation for three successive days, over the dinner-table. She called him *Moo-soo*, talked horribly dislocated English, smiled, and winked, and was, in a word, so distressingly attentive that the poor foreigner presently hit upon the idea that he was being ridiculed, confined himself to his room, had his meals brought up to him, dwelt in an atmosphere of *cigarettes* and unmade beds (he used to shriek at the servant if she opened the window) till his week was up, and then left. Which incident brings us to his successor, who subsequently became a prominent character in the Establishment.

Occupying the adjoining apartment, we were a little surprised on the morning after his arrival by his manner of dressing; which, apparently, consisted in putting on a pair of creaking boots, walking about in them for half an hour, and then going through various gymnastic performances over chairs, accompanied by lively imitations of the cries of an entire menagerie. Subsequently, when we became acquainted with him, he explained these proceedings as being resorted to for the healthful development of lungs and limbs, and told us his history. He was a down-east Yankee, had traveled over three fourths of the globe, and tried an infinite variety of avocations, including practice of the law, driving an omnibus, peddling stoves, editing a newspaper, selling patent medicines, officiating as clerk in a dry-goods store, as Mormon preacher, and Daguerrean artist, with much more than we can remember or chronicle. He had just then returned from California, with some money, and the resolve to get up a big panorama of the whole of the United States,[3] *on the scale of one foot to every mile*. This intention he prepared to "put through" by papering up the lower window of the attic (it had a north light), purchasing an immense roll of canvas, several white-wash brushes, and bucket-fulls of paint, and a barrel of turpentine. Also he cultivated the acquaintance of artists, one of whom ornamented the whole side of the room with a ghastly cartoon personating Cholera as a gigantic, demonized skeleton, flying at the spectator with extended arms, which so appalled the servants (it was during the prevalence of the pestilence in 1849[4]) that complaint was carried to the landlady. She had the room white-washed, but with indifferent effect, for the plaster being laid on but sparingly, the figure still loomed up, awfully, beneath it.

Our neighbor, in pursuance of his panorama project, found it necessary to decorate his room with all sorts of prints from newspapers, books, magazines, etc., in the short space of a week converting the sides of the apartment into an extemporaneous picture-gallery. Moreover he took to fancying animals, and brought home a couple of monkeys and a bull-terrier. These, however, he did not succeed in domesticating. After a combined attack upon a stout Irish chambermaid, in which one of the monkeys sprang upon her shoulders, while the terrier seized her by the ankle—from which he was with difficulty detached—our friend gave up his pets, and, subsequently, the dog bit one of his companions' heads off.

These proceedings, and a habit of sliding down stairs on the hand-rail, brought our neighbor into antagonism with the landlady. He received notice to quit. Considering himself an aggrieved person, his last week's sojourn was especially devoted to the development of Mrs. —'s peculiar weakness. He produced bottles of champagne at dinner, and induced her and the puffy-faced boarder to partake of more than was good for them—a highly unnecessary proceeding. He strove to draw them out in conversation, addressing them in lengthy and flowery speeches; frequently—when they were *very far gone*—of a fearfully incongruous and nonsensical description. As thus: he would ask Mrs. —, in a perfectly grave manner, whether she was aware that All the World was Sad and Dreary everywhere he Roamed, and that O! Darkies, how His Heart grew Weary, now that Forty-Nine Right-Angled Triangles had combined with Phosphate of Pickled Salmon to derange the Equilibrium of the Tropic of Capricorn! at which she would smile and look edified. The effect on the other boarders may be imagined.

Not only that. He was suspected of much more. Of instigating colored females of disreputable appearance to call for the puffy-faced boarder during his absence, and instructing them to leave insultingly familiar messages about wanting him to come round to *Pete's* on the *Points* "as there was gwine to be a *hop*."[5] Of getting a heavy box containing several bricks and a dead cat forwarded, from Boston, to the landlady, per express, carriage unpaid. And, also, of offering, per letter, in Mrs. —'s name, to adopt advertised babies, requesting their owners to bring them to her residence (at dinner time) for the purpose of inspection. We have seen three women sitting together in the front parlor, each with a baby and an epistle purporting to be from our landlady—describing herself as "a childless widow." But, perhaps, a still more unjustifiable trick celebrated this unscrupulous boarder's departure.

Most readers are aware that all vendors of patent medicines, and such articles as appeal to the infirmities of mankind are eager for testimonials of cure—especially when authorized to publish them. This fact our expelled neighbor availed himself of. He wrote—again in Mrs. —'s name—to upward of a score of well-known nostrum-mongers, graciously intimating that they might make what use they pleased with the communications. Next week's Sunday papers contained accounts how our landlady had been afflicted with every conceivable malady that flesh is heir to, even from her earliest years to the time that she obtained convalescence from —'s pills, balsam, bitters, trusses, etc., etc.—as the case might be. There were even testimonials in regard to an admirably serviceable wooden leg, and eulogiums of a Broadway *perruquier* in grateful acknowledgment of his unguent having clothed "a totally denuded scalp" with flowing ringlets.[6] Our landlady's fury that morning was fearful to look upon.

She took to drinking worse than before, and became morbidly suspicious of every body. This, incidentally, induced our departure. We, being at dinner one day, happened to whisper to a fellow-boarder something provocative of a smile, when Mrs. — fancied we were blaspheming the victuals, waylaid us in the passage, and requested us to find another Boarding-House. We did so. There were very few boarders remaining at the time of our departure, and we believe the Establishment resulted in a financial smash shortly afterward.

CHAPTER XV

The Boarding-House Whose Landlady Likes to Be Ill-Used

This is a smallish, four-storied edifice in a wide street, destined ere long to form a thoroughfare only second in business importance to Broadway—we don't care to particularize it more closely. Like its neighbors, it has a plain front of brown cement, and displays modest green blinds at each of its eight windows. A small oval brass plate on the door bears the simple inscription "Mrs. —." She is the landlady.

A small woman with lightish hair and not too much of it, its abnormal color being by no means improved by so indiscriminate an application of dye that the central part of her scalp is palpably purple. An Englishwoman by birth, a widow by condition. Mother, also, of a sturdy, self-willed boy, who gives lively promise of developing into that agreeable style of New York youth prone to loaf round corner groceries nocturnally, there to indulge in the delights of bad cigars and blasphemy.

Mrs. — has kept a Boarding-House for upward of twelve or fifteen years, yet makes comparatively successful attempts at juvenility. She is such a little woman you would, inevitably, under-reckon her age. Were you ungallant enough to ask it, she would simper a good deal and tell you to guess. Probably she is midway between thirty and forty.

Her Establishment is not a large one, and pretty well dieted, its faults lying chiefly on the side of uncleanliness. The little widow bestows so much time on her own personal adornment, that she hasn't any to devote to the nicer details of house-keeping. But we have already described a Dirty Boarding-House *par excellence* and shall say no more on that head. The present Establishment demands our attention in consequence of the peculiar relations which, in our time, existed between the landlady and certain of her boarders—especially one. He was a *Pet Boarder*. We have incidentally alluded to this obnoxious species before. It was here that we first learned the extent of the power sometimes exercised by them.

He—the Pet—was a heavy-looking man of fifty, with a countenance resembling an ugly rhinoceros, black hair, square face, and sullen physiognomy. The boarders said he'd been an overseer—or, as they termed it, *slave-driver*—down South, and there were whispers that he got his living in New York at the gaming table. This might, or might not, have been true, but he certainly appeared to have no ostensible avocation, and came home at all sorts of unexpected hours of the day and night. Ordinarily, when in presence of other boarders, he manifested great taciturnity—being well aware that they hated him—but would relax toward new arrivals, who, however, always went over to the opposition in a week or two—as soon as they found out that he was a *Pet Boarder*.

How it came to pass we never, thoroughly, understood. Certainly not in consequence of his gallantry, prepossessing appearance, or amiability of disposition. He was ill-bred, ill-mannered, and ill-tempered. He never vouchsafed (at least before others) any courtesy—not to say indication of tenderness—toward the landlady. On the contrary, he was generally rude, frequently sulky, sometimes brutal, and often made her cry. And this, we think, gives us the key to unlock the mystery.

There is a species of spaniel-like women who are never so happy as when ill-used. We only state the fact, without endeavoring to explain it. Perhaps they see in the petty despot of every-day life what they themselves *would* be, had they courage—what they *are* to still weaker persons. Apparently extracting a diseased happiness from the consciousness of their own abasement, they seem willing to accept, with slavish gratitude, some churlishly-granted favor as a quittance in full for a month's brutality. Of this order was our little landlady. Other particulars evidenced it as well as her peculiar position toward the Pet Boarder.

To stand high in her good graces it was necessary either to get deeply in her debt, or to treat her, on all occasions, with uniform discourtesy and insult. Pay up regularly, you were but an ordinary, unpleasantly-independent boarder; get in debt, or lead your landlady a dog's life—so to speak—sometimes throwing her a crumb of compliment, and you became, in a manner, privileged. She depreciated you in private, to be sure, and told every body that you owed her money, but she had a secret liking for you, *for having afforded her that pleasure.*

Several eminently gentlemanly boarders, by adopting this principle of action, obtained uniformly more of attention and comfort than ourself, and other punctually-paying blockheads. Some had been her debtors for a couple of years or more. She was accustomed to relate their private histories, telling how, when prosperous, they had deserted hers for more stylish Boarding-Houses—"hers wasn't good enough for 'em *then*, but they were always glad to come back to where they had credit." For a long time it was supposed that one of these—a good-looking young fellow—possessed a place in her affections, as his evenings were generally spent in her company and the front basement, but this was before the advent of the Pet proper. We have also a lively recollection of our landlady's emotion on parting with another amiable defaulter, on the occasion of his going

West. He kissed her, and promised to remit his outstanding account in weekly installments—which, however, abruptly ceased after the initial payment. She, in consequence, took to writing long and diffuse letters—which were passed round and read by the boarders before transmission—to his employers, wherein she requested them to "champion the widow and fatherless," and to "stop it out of his wages." Both of these boarders were favorites in their degree, as were two others who merit particular description. We believe they paid up punctually, yet succeeded in ill-treating little—to that extent necessary to attain her affection.

One, a small, bushy-whiskered Londoner, partial to billiards, and *fast* town-life generally, even maintained a sort of rivalry with the Pet. His low, quaint humor, and great powers of irritation, sometimes enabled him to prove a perfect little fiend to the landlady. He abbreviated her name in an insulting manner, abused her cookery, spoke of her defunct husband—of whom a picture hung in the dining-room—as "that fellow," "that *muff*," etc., and bribed her son to watch, defy, and slander his mother. This course of conduct naturally endeared him to Mrs. —. He was invited to visit her in the front basement, which courtesy he would scornfully reject, preferring unsolicited descents *when he knew the Pet was there*, and his own presence undesirable. Him he would "chaff" in a cool, malignant manner, for hours, attributing the meanest motives to his desire for the landlady's favor, and goading him, by accusations of parsimony, into sending out for oysters and beer, which, when they arrived, he wouldn't partake of. Mrs. — used to fret and fidget on these occasions, and sometimes go out into the passage to cry, but the Londoner always sat his opponent out, if he had to remain till one in the morning.

Speaking of these delicate little attentions, we are reminded of certain traditions relative to a boarder preceding our advent. *His* mode of coercing (and, consequently, winning the regard of) Mrs. —, would appear to have been persistent reproach and crimination of her character. He unceasingly taunted her about her "paramours," and called her "an inefficient man-trap." Once he is said to have greatly distinguished himself by the unprovoked mixing-up, mashing, and general demolition of her gastronomic preparations for New Year's Day. We are credibly informed that she cooked a special supper, that night, for him, in consequence.

But to return to our contemporaries. The other boarder spoken of as holding a place in Mrs. —'s estimation, was also an Englishman, though not a cockney. (The parent country happened to be extensively represented in Mrs. —'s establishment.) He was the greatest "swell" we have ever encountered. He had his hair curled and scented, sported elaborately-embossed shirt-fronts, frills and ruffles, wore studs, pins, brooches, rings, and knick-knacks innumerable, and generally appeared with a rivulet of watch-chain gushing from a horticulturally-embellished vest. In pronunciation he eschewed the letter R, instating W in its place, which, in conjunction with a hoarse voice, and a loud, gasping laugh, had a singular effect. He used to swear at the landlady. You'd find her in tears in the parlor, and be informed how "— had abused her." Be but rash enough to sympathize, she'd threaten him with your championship, and get you into a row. This occurred once, in connection with an artist-friend of ours. He, by-the-by, painted a portrait of the landlady (in payment for outstanding board) and could never make it handsome enough to please her. The sittings were great occasions. Little Mrs. — would attire herself, like Viliken's Dinah,[1] "in gorgeous array" (which was particularly necessary, only her face being required), and thus sit in state, languishing, smirking, smiling, and generally conducting herself as a sick kitten under the influence of laughing gas might be supposed to do—in the front parlor, for whole summer mornings, the artist and a looker-on or two alternately complimenting her, and cutting jokes at her expense. She subsequently drove the

former from the house by persistent requests that he would "touch up" the portrait a little, and make it look lovelier.

We suppose no little woman in the world ever had a larger share of approbativeness. She expected all the male boarders to admire her, and disliked them if they didn't. She was full of little jealousies and petulancies, spitefully resentful of attentions shown to lady-boarders, and addicted to slandering them in a weak manner. She was intolerant of jocular conversation at table, and would snappishly request her boarders "not to talk nonsense." She had a more than feminine curiosity about every thing and every body. We shall not easily forget her indignation on one of the lady-boarder's leaving and getting married, without previously informing her. She assumed a weak-tea sort of religion, which didn't prevent her from being inordinately *sly*, on her own account, and generally uncharitable in her judgment of others. And this, too, in spite of her own equivocal position with regard to the Pet Boarder—who was a married man.

After some month's residence on his own part, he brought his wife to the house. She, a tall, pale, cold-fillet-of-veal-looking woman (we snatch the simile from Dickens, for nothing else will convey our exact meaning), never looked happy, and was very much pitied by other boarders. Our landlady used to simper in an inane, compassionate manner about her, and call her *poor* Mrs. —. She thought her an invalid, and likely to *die* soon. Only on one occasion do we remember the Pet Boarder's wife smiling, and how this came about shall be narrated.

Her husband, as has been stated, was detested by other boarders. Readers who have had practical experience of the quiet, omnipresent despotism established by Pet Boarders—how they influence every thing, from the choice of a dinner to the landlady's courtesy (or want of it)—how they directly, or indirectly, contrive to "serve out" those who refuse to bow to their authority—will readily understand this. There were plenty of minor feuds in this Boarding-House—as there are in all such—but war to the knife (and fork) was the unanimous sentiment against the Pet. The smaller manifestations of this generally consisted in rapidly disposing of the contents of dishes to which he was known to be partial, or passing them to remote ends of the table; admiring "Uncle Tom's Cabin";[2] turning the conversation on the immorality of gambling; doubting the accuracy of his watch, and *pooh-poohing* his opinions on every possible subject.

When, therefore, he brought home a small dog, its owner's name was at once bestowed upon the animal, and a jocular fiction established as to its paternity. But the proverb about presenting a dog with a bad name was not carried out—the animal being rather a favorite than otherwise. And one evening, at the supper-table, the artist (who sat precisely opposite the Pet) took this dog on his lap, permitting him to dispose of a half-saucer full of milk full in the truculent face of his enraged owner. It was simply an absurd incident, but comprised as complete a defiance of the Pet's authority as Tell's knocking the hat of Gesler off the pole.[3] The boarders saw it in that light. The Londoner laughed sharp and cynically, his friend of the frills and the rings burst out into a great haw-haw, an ordinarily stolid printer, after inflaming his face until it assumed the color of a newly-cut slice of beet, exploded in a roar, his good-humored little wife tittered, and even the wan countenance of the Pet's better half lighted up with the semblance of a smile. Finally, a universal grin flashed round the table. This produced a climax. The Pet leaped to his feet and darted, scowling, from the room. And the landlady, gliding behind the offender's chair with an aspect of concentrated fury, *necked* the dog and bore him vengefully into the passage. By the shrill yelps he uttered during the brief transit, we should judge that she pinched him considerably.

The Pet Boarder kept his room for full three weeks in consequence of this. Our landlady took meals to him in advance of the regular ones, and we sometimes heard him growling at her for not having selected precisely what he wanted. The boarders felt intense, though silent satisfaction—but their triumph was short-lived. One by one they began to disappear, some quitting in accordance with their own inclinations (accelerated by Mrs. —'s temper), others receiving intimations that their rooms were "wanted." It became evident that the Pet had resolved upon weeding the house of all who were obnoxious to his power. We were among the earliest to quit.

Since that time we have learned that the Pet has left. Occasionally we meet our former landlady on Broadway. She has a high color and dresses very gaily. We suspect that she rouges with less discretion than of old. But whether other Pets have succeeded the former one—whether her Establishment is conducted on the same principles now as then—or, indeed, whether it is in existence, we are at present ignorant.

CHAPTER XVI

Of a Tip-Top Boarding-House

If at any time during the perusal of the foregoing Chapters we have sunk in our reader's estimation, as manifesting a suspicious familiarity with the dirty side of human nature, we confidently expect that the present one will redeem our character. There can be nothing vulgar to chronicle of the Establishment now claiming attention. We especially plume ourself on having lived in it. Whenever inclined to depreciate, and to think small-beer of ourself, we turn to that page of memory's volume upon which the details are recorded, glance admiringly over them, and hold up our head elate with the consciousness that we had Two Months' Experience of a Tip-top Up-town Boarding-House.

It is situate in a due north-easterly direction from Madison Square,[1] being one of a row of sober-brown houses forming the side of the street which connects two avenues. They are large, stylish, pretentious mansions (at the time of our sojourn yet damp from recent erection), with much ornamental iron work on either side of their heavy flights of stone steps, balconies running the length of the entire row, and windows, cornices, and lintels, of a highly ornate description. Each individual tenement so strongly resembles its neighbors that you can't help fancying that similar locks must have been fitted to the doors, and on coming home at nights, are distrustful of unintentionally effecting an entrance into the wrong domicile.

The lady proprietresses—for there are two, to whom you obtain an introduction through the medium of a mutual acquaintance—only admit a new boarder after the severest scrutiny as to references and respectability. Their Establishment is eminently aristocratic, so much so, indeed, that its gentility verges on the awful, from very intensity. You are supposed to imagine any amount of applicants lingering Peri-like at the portal,[2] to be deeply conscious of your own superior happiness in obtaining ingress, and to deport yourself with equal reverence and humility both toward the house and its mistresses. Which ladies deserve, here, further description.

They are sisters, the elder a widow of five-and-forty, the younger her junior by a few years, and unmarried. Both may be considered good-looking, though their physiognomy is of that sharp-black-eyed, aquiline-nosed, thin-lipped order one prefers to think of in connection with Lady Macbeth and other unpleasantly-dramatic females, rather than to desire its presence as a household companion. Perhaps Mrs. — is the handsomer, matrimony having operated to mollify and tone down the severity of her aspect and temper. Her defunct husband—there is a portrait of him hanging in the sitting-room, representing a square-faced man of bilious complexion, and generally over-shaved appearance—is understood to have officiated as United States Consul to the court of Jonker Afrikaner,[3] or some equally important potentate, and his relict assumes immense dignity in consequence. (She tells you how he endeavored to import a couple of hippopotami who died on the passage.) She is a tall, upright figure, and generally dresses in black velvet, which doesn't tend to relieve the depressing effect of her *tournure*.[4]

Her sister has, apparently, settled down to the grimmest and most uncompromising spinsterhood. She wears her hair pulled violently back after that peculiar French-Chinese fashion, which seems to possess such great attractions to all women whose faces it *doesn't* suit, is partial to exuberant *crinoline*, to botany, and to her nephew. He is a small, but lofty-souled young gentleman of three-and-twenty, afflicted with a weakness of the eyes and knees, a desire to become a great public character, and an overpowering sense of his own importance, and that of the family.

The house is handsomely furnished throughout, exceeding in display the Establishment described in Chapter Five. Combining the probable expense of this with a presumably high rent, we were, at first, somewhat at a loss to conceive how Mrs. — and her sister (who were spoken of as being comparatively unprovided for at the demise of the African Consul), had contrived to commence business in so dashing a way; but the mystery was subsequently explained to us. Among the boarders, we remarked, as especially intimate with the lady proprietresses, a short, black-whiskered, high-complexioned, crisp-looking man of fifty, who owned houses and lots on more than one of the avenues, dealt in land and building speculations, and was generally reputed to be very wealthy. He, so we were privately informed, had advanced the necessary funds. Perhaps, indeed, the entire Establishment was a "speculation" of his.

If so, to all appearance it was a successful one. The majority of the boarders were affluent, or desirous of seeming so, and willing to pay for that privilege. Mrs. — (who, in virtue of her widowhood, assumed the part of landlady *par excellence*) professed a more than *Mrs. General*-like contempt for money, making her sister collect the bills, and occasionally using her as a pecuniary *Jorkins*;[5] yet it was advisable to have a very definite understanding as to terms, or you would, invariably, find little "extras" crowding into your weekly accounts—to dispute which, with a lady of Miss —'s dignity and antecedents, was really a formidable undertaking. You might, with as much consistency, have submitted a question of absent shirt-buttons to Mrs. Siddons,[6] or suggested to Zenobia,[7] when in reduced circumstances, the propriety of taking in washing.

There were upward of five-and-thirty boarders, over half of which number appertained to families who preferred this mode of residence on the score of fashion or—convenience. The wives had mostly made feeble attempts at house-keeping subsequent to marriage, and finding themselves as much at home in it as a kangaroo in a diving-bell, had "given up" in despair, declaring that domestic duties were "a real plague," and "those Irish enough to worry any body's life out." The husbands—devoted to business and money-getting—could scarcely miss what few of them had experienced—a home—and perhaps preferred confining their domestic expenses to definite weekly or monthly payments. So the gentlemen were satisfied, the ladies relieved of the trouble of house-keeping, and the children sent to school at an early age, where they took the initiatory steps toward becoming as happy and as useful members of society as their parents. We only remember one in connection with the Tip-Top Boarding-House—a pretty but horribly-spoiled little girl, the daughter of a good-looking widow, who was, herself, somewhat of a character.

She possessed an estate on Staten Island, but preferred New York during the winter from mingled motives—economy and love of flirtation. She lived—with her child and servant—in an attic, had a remarkably sweet voice, a $700 diamond necklace, and a mild *penchant* for herrings, cheese, and brandy and water—as we judged from olfactory testimony on going up-stairs nocturnally. She was of plump, buxom figure, yet so much disposed to deprecate her general tendency to jollity of appearance that upon our alluding to the *double-chinnyness* probably awaiting her, she actually tied her head up in a handkerchief for a day or two to repress it! She precipitated herself from violent friendships with lady-boarders to the very opposite extreme of the social compass. Her vivacious temperament impelled her to the utterance of loosely-generous promises—which she was very chary of redeeming. (We remember her rashly volunteering a $100 wedding-dress to a lady-boarder, in order to get off from paying a forfeit *philopoena*,[8] and being in a state of great apprehension subsequently in case it might be looked for.) She—in common with most widows—professed an indifference toward further experience of matrimony, but cavaliers of about the age of her eldest son used to call upon her. Sometimes she had rows with the servants on their objecting to tell gratuitous fibs about her not being "at home" to these gentlemen. Indeed, she was continually in hot water, having contracted an unlucky habit of tattling herself into scrapes. We were present during an altercation between her and a longitudinal Scotchman (engaged in the wholesale liquor business) in which she expressed a desire to bite off his nose; and afterward offered, over the supper-table, a reward of $100 to any body who'd cow-hide him. In the language of "sporting" men, there were no takers. Withal, Mrs. — could be very agreeable when she pleased—as the landlady remarked, privately. And then she was *very* good-looking.

The remaining boarders comprised an equal number of single young ladies and gentlemen, many of the former having quitted their parents' homes "because it was dull," or for some equally excellent reason. Had you hinted to them the possibility of danger from being brought into contact with men of unknown, and perhaps not irreproachable characters, though of stylish exterior, they would have laughed, and Mrs. — grown indignant. As well fancy a Tombs lawyer obtaining admission into heaven as such an individual into *her* establishment. It was an up-town, patent-polished, carved and gilt edition of Eden, only people dressed in better taste, got up balls, and had a greater variety of dishes for dinner. Yet we have heard some of the gentlemen boarders converse among themselves—and about the young ladies, too—in a manner not compatible with the strictest propriety. But, to do the ladies justice, they appeared able to take care of themselves.

Prominent among bachelor-boarders was a bushy-whiskered man of forty—young, therefore, only by courtesy—for, in addition to his age, he was prematurely bald. Yet he achieved prodigious popularity among the ladies, whether married or single, especially the former. He had an elaborate foppishness of manner, an air of grave, confiding gallantry; and would utter solemn platitudes with an accent of such impressive sincerity as to convince any feminine listener that he was the most tender, most susceptible, most excellent, most gentlemanly of mortals. Privately, he was the *loosest* talker in the community.

This gentleman, if we recollect aright, in company with a couple of lady-boarders, originated what might be termed a Mutual-Admiration-and-Matrimony-Promoting Society, to which one especial evening in each week was devoted. The club—for so it was called—also met at the residences of outside members—chiefly Boarding-Houses. We were not honored by a fellowship, though present on several of these interesting *reunions*. The company assembled at about an hour and a half after dinner—say eight o'clock—and having transacted the more important business (such as going over the minutes of the preceding meeting, balloting for new members, etc.) within closed doors, admitted the uninitiated to the succeeding festivities. These generally commenced by the ladies and gentlemen reading passages from the poets, or essays of their own composition, on subjects previously dictated to them by the chairman—our bushy-whiskered friend before spoken of. He had but a feeble imagination, and would set ladies to writing scathing denunciations of the use of tobacco (*he* couldn't smoke, and was consequently "down on" the weed), and gentlemen to disquisitions on the relative tendencies of the works of Tennyson and Tupper.[9] Sometimes we had recitations and once a male boarder favored us with a dismal "Ode to the Memory of the Pilgrim Fathers," five newspaper columns in length (he got it inserted, subsequently, in a country journal, and was so complimented by the chairman—who manifested anger at seeing members whispering with the girls instead of listening—that he promised to write another, and might have done so had not some judicious friend stolen his rhyming dictionary. Our chief made but one attempt at distinguishing himself, when he essayed to read *Hiawatha*,[10] broke down most signally over the hard Indian names, and sulked for the remainder of the evening, all the coaxing of the ladies proving insufficient to restore his good-humor.

The Society was more successful in the musical portion of its entertainments, for many of the ladies played brilliantly and sang vociferously. And a gentleman of poetic aspect—which is to say, having long, dark hair, and reversed shirt-collars (he was in the express business down town)—accompanied himself upon the guitar. He had a good deal of fun in him in spite of his exterior, and used to sing a *Hood-like* Serenade of his own composition,[11] in a manner that brought tears into the eyes of the fair auditors, who declared it "beautiful," and demanded copies for their albums.*

But such diversions, though presumably the ones for which the Club was established, proved infinitely less attractive than the dance and game of romps or forfeits—instituted after a general failure in an attempt at acting charades—which always terminated the evening's entertainments. We must say we enjoyed Blindman's Buff immensely in the Tip-Top Boarding-House, not to speak of Hunt-the-Slipper and Fox-and-Geese—the title of which last, by-the-by, might have suggested, to a cynic, an ominous moral. Both ladies and gentlemen, single and married, "went in" for these sports with such ardor as to provoke an occasional remonstrance on the part of the spinster proprietress. (There was, in truth, a mild conspiracy to keep *her* at piano-duty.) A sense of delicacy so nice as to constrain its possessor to the substitution of the words "*stepper*" or "*walker*" for a turkey's *leg*, at dinner (it is our belief that Miss — would have suffered martyrdom rather than have used that vulgar substantive) could scarcely fail to receive

* In case lady-readers may be desirous of following their example, the poem is here subjoined, by special permission of the author. Music publishers are herewith presented with a gratis copyright.

Tune—the Dead March in *La Gazza Ladra*,[12] played rapidly.

O Lady, wake! the tuneful fox
  Is twittering in the emerald sky—
The star-fish 'gainst thy casement knocks;
  And in thy chamber, fluttering nigh
The taper's flame, with silken wing,
  The fragile penguin circles round,
While, luridly, night's shadows fling
  A ruddy darkness on the ground.
O'er the Campagna's bursting waves
  The giraffe whistles wild and shrill,[13]
While her small beak the simoom laves
  Within the azure daffodil.
Sweet influences below, above,
  An Iris-tinted clamor make—
All wooing forth my lady-love
  To walk abroad. O Lady, wake!

an incidental shock or so. And the ladies and gentlemen *did* romp considerably. So much so that sometimes a husband exhibited symptoms of jealousy—which was, surely, very unreasonable, as he had an opportunity of paying attention to other ladies, and could any thing be fairer?

At all events, Mrs. — couldn't help it if ladies *would* flirt. She thought prudery uncalled-for in *her* Establishment. No ill thing was there to be guarded against. As for such little incidents as a male boarder making love to a married lady who had recently quitted, and was then engaged in getting a divorce from her husband, why, they were, of course, perfectly proper.*

Yet a circumstance *did* occur which proves that scarcely any amount of precaution can preserve the very cream of society from being ruffled by extraneous flies. We do not allude to the atrocious case of the miscreant of gentlemanly exterior, who boarded for five weeks—and indeed comported himself every way in an unobjectionable manner, but subsequently proved to be an *actor*—to the immense disgust and indignation of the lady proprietresses. (Their son and nephew, by-the-by—the weak-eyed young gentleman before alluded to—threatened to kick the offender wherever he met him, but we haven't heard of the *rencontre* coming off yet.)[14] The incident, as narrated to us (it chanced a little before our time), happened as follows:

There came, ostensibly from New Orleans, a handsome dashing lady, with a French title, who, taking up her residence at our Establishment—we presume she had a letter of introduction, or Mrs. — wouldn't have admitted her—speedily excited quite a *fureur* of admiration among the male boarders. She smiled so sweetly, talked so affably, had such a *piquant* foreign accent, such delicious *naïve* ways, that all the gentlemen adored her, and brought home *bouquets* and opera tickets innumerable. The ladies, too, though naturally disposed to contemn a pretty woman, could not resist her stories of the Empress Eugenie,[15] and the Parisian court. They consulted her about the fashions, and were emulous of her company on Broadway. The bushy-whiskered boarder presented her with a lap-dog, and wanted her to read Racine to the Society.[16] The weak-eyed young gentleman put himself through a severe course of French in order to pay her compliments in her native language. Even Mrs. — relaxed her dignity toward her pretty boarder—and told her in confidence diverse particulars as to the habits and dispositions of the gentlemen. Which, as subsequently appeared, she turned to advantage.

Presently, however, awful rumors came to ear, of her being seen with gentlemen on the avenues, in fast-going buggies, and at theatres. It was remarked that

* Apropos of this, we have met so many divorced ladies in Boarding-Houses as to be almost inclined to infer a mysterious connection and sympathy between them. Let no reader rashly venture to contradict us on the strength of his individual experience. He mayn't have known the true position of his fair co-boarders. Half the ladies who are compelled (of course by the villainy of their husbands) to effect a divorce, immediately sink antecedents and start as *Misses.*

though she had a large circle of male acquaintances, no lady visitors ever called upon her. Certain milliners and dress-makers, to whom she had become known through the medium of the boarders, began to complain of large outstanding debts. She occasionally disappeared for a week or so, avowedly on journeys to Washington, where, she said, she had friends. Finally Mrs. — met her, one evening, in Broadway, in company with one of the married gentlemen boarders, *disguised in male costume.*

A furious row took place in consequence, in which the Frenchwoman made use of language—as Mrs. — declared—absolutely unmentionable. The crisp-looking capitalist had to be called in to effect her removal. Two days afterward another gentleman (not the one who had assisted at the *promenade à la Amazon*,[17] but also a married man), deserted his wife to join her. They sailed for Havana by that week's steamer. And, from some remarks dropped on our arrival, we fancy that *nearly all the male boarders* had been privately and extensively victimized in the way of loans to the lady.

CHAPTER XVII

The Boarding-House Where You're Expected to Make Love to the Landlady

WE had known more than one Establishment which possessed this characteristic in an imperfectly developed degree, but until Destiny, foreseeing our present task, guided us to the abode we are about to describe, never had we beheld it in full completeness. As it was the dominant peculiarity, we so entitle the Chapter.

The landlady in question was a large widow, her house a moderately-sized, timber-framed one, some distance up-town, in a side street, leading off from one of the avenues. Close by were handsome mansions of free-stone and granite, presenting a genuine New York contrast to the unpretending tenement, which, with a couple of neighboring houses, stood modestly back some dozen yards or so from the line of the newly built street, the space thus gained being laid out as gardens. Altogether the spot was unique in its way, and but for the clatter of the passing cars you might have fancied it rather out-of-town-ish. The widow had lived there some years before commencing keeping a Boarding-House. We should scarcely have fancied it a favorable locality for one, but Boarding-Houses in New York are like dust in summer and mud in winter—everywhere.

The place was recommended to us by a recent inmate, notwithstanding the circumstance of his having quitted it in disgrace, in consequence of the perpetration of a wretched pun over the breakfast table. (He had alluded to the "Tragic *Mews*" in connection with sausages.[1]) The landlady was very sensitive and wouldn't overlook the offense. He also thought of getting married, which act of presumption she highly resented, considering her boarders' allegiance as due to herself alone. Thus forewarned, we became an inmate of the widow's domicile. Just then we were desirous of a quiet abode, having considerable literary labor on hand. We did the Parisian correspondence for two Sunday papers, supplied a third with a "thrilling local romance" (entitled the Ghouls of Gotham, or the Magnanimous Manglewoman and the Blood-Stained Shirt), wrote testimonials for five patent medicines, rhyming advertisements for a puffing tailor, and also composed tracts for a religious Society.*

We found things pretty satisfactory. The house was neatly furnished and very cleanly, the diet of endurable quality, and not worse cooked than we naturally expected in a Boarding-House, the landlady good-humored (especially toward a new boarder), and there were no children, the youngest resident being a lad of thirteen. Mrs. — had a family of five, three of whom were yet inmates of their mother's dwelling. We shall speak of them presently, our immediate attentions being due to the lady.

She was a fat, jolly-looking, sun-flower of a woman, a little over forty, and had doubtless been a showy beauty in her day, which the fact of her having contracted a very early marriage also corroborated. Of course, being the mistress of a Boarding-House, she had seen better days. Her husband, according to his widow's account, was a speculative builder, whose various enterprises had terminated in bankruptcy, before the word had become synonymous with assigning a few cool thousands over to a relative, ignoring one's debts, and making a fresh start in life. He, she said, had *adored* her, and would relate plenty of instances of his affection; giving you to understand that when he died her heart was broken into so many bits that she didn't care about trying to rivet them together; and the "fount of her tears sealed up." Which probably explained her present lively and somewhat selfish zest for existence.

There are women on whom it's unsafe to bestow too much affection; who may be petted like lap-dogs, into becoming nuisances to themselves and the community. Our landlady was of this kind, and we're inclined to think her husband had helped to spoil her. All her characteristics—ostensibly genial and jolly enough—radiated from one center of unconscious egotism. She believed herself to be a very phoenix of widows—the most unselfish, warm-hearted, and undeservedly persecuted of mortals. (The latter in consequence of the reverse of fortune following her husband's bankruptcy.) What she had gone through "nobody could have any idea of." All the world had behaved shamefully to her, and if she forgave it, 'twas only in virtue of her angelic nature. As with the past, so with the present. A long arrear of comfort being due, it was her duty to take it out as energetically as possible. She had a right to expect things to be "made

* Those entertaining little books, so well calculated to diffuse spiritual instruction among the humbler classes of our city population, and known as "a New Birth for Newsboys," "Pea-Nuts and Perdition," "The Hydrant of Grace," etc., are from our pen. We mention the fact in order to damage their sale, as we didn't get paid for writing them.

easy" *now*, and that every body, especially her children, should immolate themselves to her.

Her remaining characteristics were congenial. She had a good appetite, and went to church twice every Sunday, on the principle of securing snug quarters in the next world as well as the present. She was vehement in her likes and dislikes, generally expressing herself in a violent and explosive manner. She got unnecessarily enthusiastic or denunciatory on the smallest provocation, and if you didn't tune your humor by hers, was offended. When pleased, she laughed inordinately; when angry, became red in the face and assumed an inflated appearance, which, in a lady of her size, was undesirable. Only by making love to her—hot, strong, and frequent—could you secure and retain her good graces.

We were rather amazed, at first (despite our friend's information), at the extent to which this rule appeared to be practiced. Mrs. — presiding at the head of the table in a rich plum-colored dress—she specially affected such tints as made her look larger and hotter—sat blushing and blooming like a big cabbage-rose, or over-blown peony, while half a dozen men vied with each other during the intervals of mastication, in affected rivalries and rhapsodies on the subject of her charms. The enthusiastic, the jocular, the hopeless, the matter-of-fact, the jealous lover each found a representative; each part being caricatured to the utmost capacity of the actor. We soon found it was a recognized institution, and as much looked-for on the part of Mrs. — as one's weekly payments. She would as willingly have pretermitted the one as the other. Unless you had a morbid inclination for indifferent commons, short answers, and sulky glances, you straightway followed suit and played your best trump cards of compliment.

You couldn't blaze away too hot or heavily; nor need you be over choice as to the quality of your ammunition. Be sentimental, comic, serious, what you would—suit yourself—only recollect you were expected to be in love with Mrs. —, and to talk accordingly. (We went in for the gloomy and sardonic, and were considered eminently successful in that line.) Every body had his *rôle*. You couldn't get along at all, without complying. And, as "in a multitude of counselors there is safety," so, among a host of burlesque admirers each one may comfort himself with the thought that there's little danger of his individual victimization. Had not this impression been universal we might have been staggered at the daring of gentlemen boarders.

In truth, it was all very innocent, though supremely ridiculous. We don't think our landlady had any intention of getting married, unnatural as the assertion—in connection with a widow—may sound. Very probably she would have demurred against any formal renunciation to that effect, preferring to retain, though in a hazy, indefinite shape, the pleasurable self-elation instinctively awakened in the feminine mind in conjunction with the subject. But we are convinced such speculations would remain such. Not that she entertained a moment's doubt of the *possibility* of their realization, for she certainly lay down each night with the conviction that not a male boarder but would have been happy to have succeeded the departed builder. We suppose her immense appreciation of general incense operated as a check to prevent her narrowing her (presumed) sway to a single worshiper. It was a species of innocent feminine Mormonism. And without asserting that she received such indiscriminate homage as perfectly genuine, we yet maintain that she had no doubt of its being based on fact.

As intimated, the number of boarders was limited, consisting of five bachelors, one married man, and a solitary spinster. The men had employment down town, where they remained till evening, at which time (our sojourn occurred in winter) there was a general *re-union*. A small annuity afforded our only lady boarder the means of subsistence. She was a little squeezed-up-looking old maid, addicted to snuff and India-rubber overshoes (which she wore in-doors), subject to colds in the head, and generally antagonistic to the landlady and to street organs. The "goings on" of the one and the performances of the other always excited her lively indignation. Hence the boarders were prodigal of gallantries and cents in developing both peculiarities. We have known Italian minstrelsy to be in operation in front of the house from 8 to 12 P.M. Upon which occasion Miss —, after an abortive attempt to salute the offending musician with the contents of her ewer, denounced every body, and went to bed with cotton in her ears. She was also extremely fastidious as to questions of propriety. Our apartment adjoined hers, and we believe she spent the night of our arrival in cramming curl-papers into every conceivable chink and cranny intervening; besides telling the landlady with a shudder of horror, on the following morning, that she actually heard "the feller" pull his boots off. We believe she would have quitted the Establishment but for some feeble designs on the celibacy of the landlady's elder born.

This was a tall, round-faced, light-haired, and whisker-less young man of three-and-twenty, who might, intellectually, have been described by a homely metaphor in use among housewives, as "rather slack-baked." He didn't approve of theaters, couldn't endure tobacco, liked Miss Warner's novels and Tupper's poems,[2] attended a Bible-class on Sunday afternoons, and was publicly snubbed and depreciated by his mother—it being, indeed, that excellent matron's custom to treat him as though he were a natural fool upon all occasions. She'd tell him, when in conversation with others, to hold his tongue, and not to expose himself. She would narrate particulars of his entertaining hopeless passions for a series of young ladies, and generally indulge in confidences calculated to make a listener get hot and uncomfortable—when in presence of their hero. Her second-born was in California. No. 3 came home but seldom, being employed as a governess in an Up-town family. No. 4 was a very pretty girl of fifteen, with soft, bright eyes, and curling hair, and of a most lively but variable temperament. Her mother had a trick of discovering entirely imaginary attachments on the part of young gentlemen for this daughter, and warmly abetting or indignantly repelling them. No. 5 (the youngest of the family) was a singular youth, who nourished wild ideas about constructing an omnibus, using cats or goats as a propulsive power, and making a large fortune on Broadway by devoting his vehicle to the accommodation of fashionable youth. With which view he haunted lumber-yards, soliciting contributory bits of wood from the proprietors, and, also, set traps of clothes' lines and balls of twine in the back-yard, to secure the necessary quadrupeds. When the family met together, a great deal of kissing always took place. They were very affectionate. You couldn't spend an evening in their company without witnessing at least two or three osculatory performances. Mrs. — would set them at it on the smallest provocation or none at all.

But our reminiscences of her Establishment are not entirely of a whimsical character. We have alluded to the existence of a married boarder, who, in spite of that qualification, was rather a favorite of the landlady's, and, indeed, of the lodgers generally. A lively little Italian, with jet black eyes and curly beard, he worked hard at his trade of jeweler all day, and played the fiddle of evenings. He had a laugh and friendly word for everybody, and a perfect dictionary of compliments in broken English for Mrs. —, to whom he confided all his hopes and expectations. His wife and family were in Italy. Six months back he had sent money for their transmigration through the medium of a fellow-countryman, who had proved dishonest. In due time he was again enabled to forward the necessary sum, and, presently, to announce with infinite glee and excitement, their embarkation. Day by day he counted the time which must elapse between it and the probable date of their arrival. When the ship became due he could scarcely contain himself, and his interest communicated itself in a minor degree to the boarders, who always looked in the morning's papers for the desired intelligence. It never appeared.

It was savage winter weather, and men talked of terrible storms at sea. There were vague guesses and conjectures as to the cause of the detention of a missing vessel, hopes growing fainter, week after week, and, at last, a shuddering conviction that far down in the solemn depths of the Atlantic the luckless ship lay, and that the poor Italian would see his wife and children Nevermore—.

His grief was piteous to look upon. And one unquiet night, when the wind blew with a dull, hollow clamor awesome to listen to, when the casements rattled as though shaken by wrathful hands, when the snow-flakes fell fast and blindingly in the face of the pedestrian, and newly coated the dirt piles in our never-cleaned streets—the poor Italian crept home—to die. He was found, on the following morning, stark and cold in bed, but with a quiet smile on his face. He had taken poison.

CHAPTER XVIII

Of Another Mean Boarding-House

This Establishment—which, in point of pretensions, might rank between those described in Chapters the Fifth and Eleventh—is now happily extinct; we therefore, as usual, speak of it in the past tense.

It was located in a dozy, shady street, particularly affected by hand-organs and children, and not far from St. John's Square.[1] Exteriorly, a plain, substantial, red-brick edifice—interiorly, a decent, though meagerly-furnished one—gastronomically, a *mean* one. And as its meanness developed itself after a peculiar fashion and led to singular results, we devote this chapter to particulars.

The landlady—familiarly known as "the Ogress," or "Meat-ax," from a presumed resemblance of her countenance to that instrument—was a thin, spare, hollow-eyed woman of fifty, with a curiously-cracked voice, an over-allowance of nerves, a daughter of similar construction, and an elderly husband—originally, we believe, a bellows-maker. He had, however, long abandoned business, being afflicted with rheumatism, and now devoted himself to chewing tobacco, and the marketing of the Establishment. Miss —, though a virgin of six-and-twenty, might have been mistaken for her own mother, but for one happy peculiarity of feature. She had a particularly large nose, and although the Slawkenbergian promontory was forcibly defined throughout the family,[2] *hers* rendered the others decidedly insignificant. She always rose at an unnaturally early hour on winter mornings (and, like most persons guilty of that unpleasant virtue, "took it out" of mankind in talking of it), thought she looked "cunning" in a leathern belt, and hated the boarders. We shall have more to say hereafter of her remaining characteristics.

The inmates of the Establishment were mostly of the male sex, and fluctuated from ten to twenty, generally inclining toward the lesser number, half of whom were our personal acquaintances. But for this, our stay would have been very brief. Companionship makes almost any thing endurable. No doubt one's objections toward being hanged would be considerably lightened were a dozen friends to share the same fate. At least, the principle proved correct with regard to the comparatively minor miseries of the Mean Boarding-House.

If our landlady and daughter had been brought up in entire ignorance of the primitive arts of eating and drinking—never discovering that people did such things until the respective ages of five-and-forty and twenty-one—they couldn't have regarded all gastronomic indulgences with greater severity. *Appetite*, in their eyes, was not only the Seven Deadly Sins combined,[3] but the Unpardonable One into the bargain. The very genius of Famine might have been the familiar *Lar* (or household deity) of the Establishment.[4] We will endeavor to describe its domestic—not economy—but parsimony.

You took your place at the dinner-table, observing that the bread was cut very thin, and the butter contained in *one* of the smallest plates you had ever seen out of a doll's house. When the dish covers were removed—by the daughter (for Mrs. — kept no "wasteful slut of a servant"), you found cause for astonishment at the small quantity and meager quality of the food provided. Be assured that you would be helped in proportion. You got a minute fragment of meat which could easily be disposed of in three mouthfuls. Influenced by modesty, you made *five* of it. After a hungry pause, you sent your plate up again (waiting, under the wild expectation of being asked, always proved ineffective), and obtained a still smaller moiety of meat, but a liberal allowance of bones. When, being a new boarder, you despairingly fell back upon the potatoes (there were plenty of *them*), drank large quantities of water, and allowed your plate to be removed, with the secret resolution of "making up" at the expense of the pastry—in which you were again baffled—unless you liked pies made of tomatoes with the skins on, and sweetened with watered molasses.

Such, in general, was a new boarder's initiatory experience, which he might be expected to endure for from one day to six, according to his temperament. Hunger, however, invariably stimulated him into energy. He sent his plate up repeatedly, three—*four*—FIVE times. He made dashes at the bread with his fork, indecently impaling and securing half-a-dozen pieces. He arrogantly demanded that remote dishes of vegetables should be passed to him. He ignored the necessities of his neighbors, yet felt a savage pleasure in handing the pickles that they might still further provoke already exasperated appetites. He gnawed bones, and sopped up gravy with his bread. He began to look upon the landlady and her daughter as his natural enemies, and to wonder whether a chameleon didn't suffer a good deal in getting used to its mode of life. He remembered the lady-*ghoule* in the Arabian Nights,[5] who fed herself by picking up grains of rice with a pin, and shuddered at the possibility of Mrs. and Miss — resorting in private to the other diet attributed to that person. He speculated as to whether they might not have some relative engaged in the undertaking business. He became suspicious of their retiring to snug after-dinners in the basement, and vented such opinions to fellow boarders. He felt himself capable of appreciating that hungriest of books, the *Adventures of Lazarillo de Tormes* (in case he had read it),[6] and thought Cannibalism, in cases of disasters at sea, perfectly justifiable. Finally he grew very thin, and went away, took extraneous meals at restaurants, or resorted to such surreptitious proceedings as we shall have occasion to relate of ourselves.

It has been stated that the landlady was *nervous*, and that her daughter shared that characteristic. Now this rendered both especially impressible to unpleasant incidents, such as fires, murders, and other social calamities, and it was easy to adapt the feeling to the production of desirable results. As thus. Each boarder (sharing the secret) would, on making his appearance at the dinner-table, relate some harrowing circumstance as having occurred under his individual notice, or reported in the newspapers. (None were taken at the Mean Boarding-House, from motives of economy.) Now it was told how an Irishwoman had scraped her twin children to death with oyster shells, or severed their heads from their bodies with a fragment of looking-glass; now, how a member of Congress had scalped a political opponent, on the floor of the House, after gouging out one of his eyes, or biting off one of his ears; now, particulars would be vouchsafed of an awful conflagration, in which the entire inhabitants of a Lunatic Asylum had been roasted alive in their cells; now, how a band of emigrants on the overland journey to California had been impelled by starvation to become Anthropophagi,[7] commencing by eating up all the old women. Upon which Mrs. — and her daughter would start and shudder, beg the gentlemen to desist, resort to smelling salts, and finally retire precipitately from the room—when the triumphant boarders (who didn't at all mind Mr. —) *were able to help themselves.* And though our landlady must, in time, have had suspicions of the apocryphal nature of these narratives, it was but seldom that she could resist their influence. Miss — did, some times. Occasionally the boarders varied the dodge by the narration of hideous dreams.

Nor was this all. Hunger, says the proverb, will break through stone walls—how much more, then, the silent watches of the night? A nocturnal foray having discovered the existence of a huge padlock, on the kitchen-door (the key of which Mrs. — deposited, every night, beneath her pillow), some brilliant spirit—anticipating the expedient of Mr. Sparrowgrass[8]—suggested whether it might not be practicable to descend into that culinary locality by means of the dumb-waiter, by which dishes were hoisted up to the dining parlor. One trial—as advertisements say—proved the fact. The shelves being removed, the lightest weight of the party could, with comparative ease, deposit himself therein, and in that position was carefully lowered below, from whence he sent up the entire contents of the larder. We shall never forget the mute astonishment which greeted the appearance of a *turkey*—of whose plump carcass comparatively little had vanished! That turkey was an entire stranger to *us!*

Our darkest suspicions were confirmed. It *was* true, then! The family catered for themselves on a different scale than for their famished boarders.

Could Mrs. — have descended from her third-floor-front into that back-parlor, at the ghostly hour of midnight, she would have beheld a spectacle which might have irrecoverably damaged her nerves for the remainder of her existence. Six hungry individuals, in shirt sleeves, and similar free and easy *deshabille*, with a goodly array of viands before them—for our discoveries did not end with the

turkey—were seated at the table, by the light of the half-turned gas-jet, in subdued revelry—even as though spectres, or *double-gangers*,[9] as the Scotch term the apparitions of living persons, were mimicking our mid-day proceedings. No shadowy repast, however, was it, but the most satisfactory one we had eaten within those walls. A second descent with empty dishes and the skeleton fowl, concluded our proceedings, and then, with a full stomach and tranquil conscience, each individual sought his pillow.

Our landlady's countenance wore a troubled look on the following morning. She said not a word, but appeared horribly suspicious. We turned the conversation on Spiritualism, and instances were related of singular freaks on the part of supernatural visitors, such as committing robberies, *setting fire to houses*, etc. We also talked of mortal burglars. Mrs. — preserved a grim silence. It was plain that she distrusted her boarders' agency in over-night's proceedings.

Her husband had a conference with the policeman of the vicinity and induced him by a promise of prospective dollars (to be paid on the capture of imaginary delinquents), to watch the area of the house during the hours of night and early morning. But, as may be imagined, no discovery ensued from *that* quarter. And the policeman—not getting the reward—subsequently revenged himself by violently ringing the street-door-bell between the hours of 3 and 4 on several consecutive mornings, as also by throwing ash-barrels into the area. "Stolen waters are sweet," and we have Solomon's testimony as to the attractions of "bread eaten in secret."[10] Our midnight revels were continued, at such intervals as prudence dictated, until an unlucky *contretemps* marred all. Our light-weight voyager chancing to be sick one night—we believe alternate hunger and plenty disagreed with him—a heavier friend volunteered to descend in his place. It was with much difficulty that he contrived to squeeze himself into the recess, and, as he descended, the rope—alas!—broke—! A swift, sharp, rattling sound, followed by a heavy concussion—and, we shame to say it, his companions fled, leaving him to his fate. He spent the night on the kitchen dresser, among innumerable cockroaches, and nearly frightened Miss — into a fit when she unlocked the door on the following morning. Nor did he wait the advent of the landlady to decide on his certain expulsion, but hurrying his personal property into a valise, incontinently decamped, with no other words than sufficed to convey a strong sense of indignation at the conduct of his fellow-boarders. And—we blush to record it—the entire blame of our midnight ravages was permitted to rest on his memory. His behavior *and appetite* were voted atrocious.

But all of us had to follow very speedily. After this untoward discovery our landlady locked the doors of both parlors, regularly, at ten o'clock, and for a time insisted on her husband sleeping on the dining-table, as an additional security. We could hear him snoring, even on the second floor, where we were domiciled in a small apartment in which the proverbial feat of "swinging a cat," could not certainly have been accomplished without damage to the head or tail of the animal. Mr. — was a terrific snorer. The boarders asserted that his wife had to plug her ears with cotton in order to avoid being kept awake by his incessant performance on the *nasocleide*. But to the cause of our removal.

The increased strictness of discipline, then, reduced us to the most painful privations, which came to a crisis on the landlady's going out of town, and leaving her daughter to assume official responsibilities. That well-nosed virgin, whether influenced by a deep sense of the trust reposed in her, a desire to merit it, or natural parsimony, exerted herself so as to bring matters almost to the famine pitch. She laid in a large quantity of salt mackerel—such as one sees barreled and steeping in strong-smelling, mustard-colored liquor about the streets abutting on the North River[11]—and intensely pickled pork, upon which dainties we were dieted, without the slightest variety, for a whole week. It is true, however, that different modes of cooking these delicacies were resorted to—the prevailing one being interring and then baking them in batter—thus producing a sort of pudding. More detestable culinary compositions it might be impossible to imagine. The seventh appearance of these at the dinner-table produced an open rebellion. In ominous silence each boarder received his moiety of the obnoxious food, allowing it to remain, untasted, before him, until all were served. And then, at a given signal (the ring-leader's blowing his nose violently), each conspirator suddenly reversed his plate and its contents on the table-cloth, rose, wheeled about, and gravely stalked from the room. Miss — uttered a sharp little scream, her father an incoherent exclamation, the boarders uncognizant of the secret stared in blank amazement, as the defiant ones, closing the door with a bang, sought an adjacent restaurant, there to dine in plenty and triumph—only returning at a late hour for their baggage.

We have already mentioned that the Mean Boarding-House has ceased to exist. Some unhappy man—Heaven knows why—married the daughter, and Mrs. —(now a widow—for her husband has gone to that bourne,[12] where, it is to be presumed, tobacco and rheumatism are not)—resides with her son-in-law. May he possess the endurance necessary to sustain the combined afflictions!

CHAPTER XIX

The Family Hotel on Broadway

A WHITE marble or free-stone front, one to two hundred feet on the fashionable side of our principal thoroughfare, and six or seven stories high—a main entrance over twenty feet wide, and a hundred deep, with private ones in proportion—offices, saloons, parlors, ladies' and gentlemen's reception-rooms, dining-rooms, reading-rooms, bath-rooms, bar-rooms, ordinaries and tea-rooms—apartments of all sizes and degrees of luxury; rosewood furniture, velvet tapestry, gorgeous chandeliers, huge mirrors, fresco paintings, high ceilings, a stair-case twelve feet wide, with landing-places over twenty, on each floor—accommodations for four or five hundred guests, armies of waiters, a heating apparatus located in a rear street, a throng of idlers at the door, arriving and departing vehicles, people up-stairs, down-stairs, and in my lady's chamber—all this, and how much more, is suggested by the words "a Broadway Hotel"?

In a preliminary chapter we have intimated that this class of Establishment scarcely comes under our province. Though possessing their characteristic, and indeed individual features, they are conducted upon so vast a scale as to afford but little scope for the portrayal of those personal traits which form so large an aggregate in less comprehensive structures. Boarders in a hotel may know much or little of each other, according to mutual inclination, but, necessarily, only the outside and general aspects of character will be visible. You can't sketch very minutely in the midst of a crowd, and might as well attempt to describe the doings and peculiarities of the inhabitants of an entire street as to take pen-photographs of the various and ever-changing guests of the Cosmopolitan,

St. Nicodemus, or other "traveler's houses."[1] The man who sits beside you at dinner is as much a stranger as he who jostles past you in Broadway. He may be either a senator or swindler, and you are as little surprised, three days hence, to learn that he is a millionaire, as that he's going to be hanged.

In truth these lordly caravansaries are no bad types of our civilization—being very splendid, very showy, very pretentious, very expensive, very uncomfortable, and containing all sorts of incongruous elements. Whether both be not susceptible of considerable improvement, might be a question of some delicacy. We (of course) have unbounded faith in social democracy, and are not prepared to deny that living in a big Broadway Hotel is the *ne plus ultra* of existence.

The one we purpose to speak of claims a place in our volume over grander competitors, in consequence of its possessing (in common with a few others) something akin to a private character. Families affect it rather than transitory boarders, though there are, occasionally, plentiful sprinklings of the latter. But the population is neither so migratory nor so large—and therefore the better fitted for our portrayal.

We shall not describe its location, general appearance, or detail management. We don't know its landlord. He may have commenced life as a waiter, bar-tender, hotel-clerk, or steamboat-steward—from each of which avocations (we are told) landlords of big New York Hotels have risen. He may be a gentleman of education and refinement, or as ignorant as a newly-imported Irishman or a poor Southerner, for aught we know to the contrary. Certainly his Establishment is an ably-ruled one, and his guests' senses as luxuriously catered for as in more pretentious rivals. Upward of two hundred persons find temporary or permanent accommodations within its walls.

The latter belong to a class we have already had occasion to speak of as constituting the majority of the inmates of the Tip-Top Boarding-House. Perhaps they're a trifle wealthier, but this is by no means certain. Young lawyers and lawyer-politicians, editors, publishers, opera singers, and professional men generally; a few Broadway store-keepers, brokers from Wall-street, and down town merchants—these, single and married, with many others of less definable position and vocations, live in our Family Hotel. Men of independent incomes, fast youths who are not only aware that their "old man was born before them," but have also arrived at the pleasing conviction that his industry, or acquisitiveness, has anticipated any necessity for labor on their part (except it be in the way of getting rid of the parental dollars); families from the country (during the winter months); wives who like "society"; widows who wish to change that title, or who have grown-up daughters; and egotistic old bachelors—all who, influenced by fashion, inclination, dislike to the responsibilities, or indifference to the pleasures and sanctity of *home*, may be supposed to *prefer* the mode of life—are here, New Yorkers preponderating. Some have boarded from year to year, being quite *habitués* of the place, and entertaining no intention of quitting it. Others accept it as a period of transitory splendor, to be merged into the obscurity of private boarding, or housekeeping, when increase of family or shortness of means compels.

Perhaps, in the latter case, antecedent hotel experiences hardly conduce to future happiness, or to fit either wife or husband for the cheerful performance of their respective duties. Let us glance, though cursorily, at the inevitable routine of life in our fashionable caravansary.

Being emancipated from all those household ministerings, and little domestic cares which are so truly degrading to the feminine character, lady-boarders have leisure to devote themselves to the more intellectual arts of dress, and general fascination. In a fashionable hotel you *must* dress fashionably—of course. Who could think of sitting down to a dinner at which two hundred guests assemble—where, at a given signal, an equal number of carefully-drilled waiters remove the dish-covers with a dexterous flourish of their white-gloved hands—where a band of music, in full blast, accompanies general mastication—in other than ball costume, or something very near it. Indeed, even in the forenoon, what lady, with *any* respect for herself, would risk the chance of being *seen* in a plain morning-frock? Though, to be sure, we have heard of high-born dames in England and France (whom, as simple republicans, we are naturally anxious to resemble) *do* dress at such times with exceeding simplicity. But perhaps they can't afford to do better. Any way the wives and daughters of free-born Americans have a right to sport their silks and satins at what hour of the day they please, whether in the *boudoir*, public sitting-room, or on Broadway. What's the use of dressing like a rainbow gone mad, if people are not to look at you?

At our Family Hotel, during the winter season, weekly balls are a regular institution; and these, it is said, form no small attraction to boarders, some abandoning private residences in order to secure admission to them. They are got up on a scale of unexampled splendor. Now, perhaps, there can be no pleasanter social spectacle than upward of a thousand handsomely-dressed ladies and gentlemen in a brilliantly-lighted ball-room, intent on mutual enjoyment; yet, it may be questioned whether such periodical indulgences are conducive to the production of domestic tastes in man or woman. A young wife is not in the best of health or temper on the morning subsequent to six hours' active performance of polkas, cotillions, quadrilles, schottisches, etc. Nor is her husband in the best order for going down town, subsequent to those dozen bottles of champagne disposed of in company with a few jolly fellows in the supper-room, after the ladies had "got through."

But, says the lady reader, you wouldn't have people always mewed up in their own apartments? There's little cause for apprehension on that score in our Hotel. Stroll into the drawing-room of an evening, you will see they know how to amuse themselves. If Mrs. A is coquetting with B, who can blame her? She is young, and pretty, and rather neglected by A, who has contracted a taste for billiards and dissipation generally, and is probably rather drunk in some adjacent bar-room at the present moment. In fact, his lady has nothing to do but flirt—and does it accordingly. And if C (who is a married man, and ought to know better), is talking eloquently to Miss D on some subject which brings the blood to her cheeks (rendering her *rouge* unnecessary for the moment)—people *must* be sociable when they meet in the same saloon, evening after evening. 'Tis their own fault if worse occur. Yet perhaps it's not always advisable to run such risks, as a big hotel must inevitably present. Among two hundred persons some few *may* be characters one wouldn't wish to see one's wife waltzing with. It is however, but justice to say that there are boarders as exclusive in their habits as is possible.

Both ladies and gentlemen finding so many attractions soliciting their attention, it is but little wonder that the claims of the rising generation are overlooked, or, at least injudiciously provided for. Sanitary people assert that children's appetites demand little beyond bread, milk, water, sugar, light broths, and such simple diet; but juvenile American stomachs are not to be dictated to after that fashion. The boys and girls at our Family Hotel have an especial table set for them, about an hour earlier than their seniors' dinner, where they indulge in hot, unctuous soups, highly-spiced French cookery, stale pastry re-warmed, dishes made indigestible with melted butter, cakes, tarts, comfits, pickles, and sweetmeats. Their breakfast comprises strong coffee, hot rolls, and molasses. As for exercise, their mothers can't be troubled with them while going out shopping, so they're confined to a room devoted to that purpose, or allowed the opportunity of running about the house, being chidden for entering saloons, and listening to the oaths and improving conversation of the waiters, or hearing them make love to the chamber-maids. If they don't thrive under this treatment, but become excitable, nervous, and sick, the doctor is called in to remedy matters.

—But then the children are always very prettily dressed. If five hundred dollars can be used up in the way of lace, embroidery, frills, rosettes, and ruffles on the person of a "blessed baby," so much the better.

It scarcely comes within our province to do more than just hint at certain other peculiarities incidental to life in a New York Hotel. Our instance of the lady-sharper in the Tip-Top Boarding-House has often been dwarfed by the ingenuity and audacity of *chevaliers d'industrie*, as exercised at the expense of both landlords and lodgers in these giant Establishments, nor are swindlers of the softer sex uncommon. We have heard of gentlemen of *distingué* appearance being discovered with spoons in their pockets; of ladies of equivocal character obtaining admission for equivocal purposes; even of mothers trusting to their own charms, or those of their daughters, to discharge pecuniary obligations. But the last sounds like a slander, and we don't believe it.

CHAPTER XX

The Artists' Boarding-House

Artists do not, in general, affect Boarding-Houses. Whether their profession—which in some cases appears to have a tendency to the development of eccentricities of costume and character—renders them averse to any routine existence, or whether an untrammeled life better accords with the necessities of their position, we do not venture to decide, simply stating the fact. Some prefer taking their meals at restaurants, bivouacking at night in their studios or offices amid the heterogeneous medley of articles only to be seen in such places—as plaster-casts, boxing-gloves, easels, squares of canvas, skulls, fencing-foils, portfolios, pipes, armor, weapons, and sketches. This, though endurable enough in summer (when a bachelor on the right side of thirty feels three fourths independent of the necessity of a home, and can stick upon his office-door the inscription "Gone to Nootka Sound[1]—Back some time in the Fall," without consulting any body), isn't agreeable in winter. Camping on the floor with a buffalo-skin for mattress and counterpane, a pair of boots and an old coat a pillow, proves monotonous, not to say dreary when the snow lies nine inches deep on the window sill; even if you haven't to journey to the next grocery-store in the morning, for water to wash with, as the Croton is frozen in your building. Therefore artists who like Robinson-Crusoe-ing in the summer, frequently board during winter. It was under the latter aspect we had an opportunity of observing them.

Bleecker-street is, *par excellence*, the street of Boarding-Houses. What tenement is not a shop may be safely assumed as devoted to the accommodation of the boarding public. On summer evenings not a stoop but has its knot of male boarders "cooling off" after the heat of the day; not an open parlor-window but frames loveliness enough to knock any "Book of Beauty" into a cocked hat; the whole thoroughfare, indeed, presenting a continuous gallery of metropolitan manhood and femininity. Our Artists' Boarding-House was in Bleecker-street.

We remember its proprietress as the most deservedly popular of landladies. She shone equally in her social and professional capacities. Her temper and beef were beyond all praise, her morality and mutton of the best quality. In spite of fourteen years of Boarding-House life, she had retained such refreshing simplicity of character as to be totally ignorant of the meaning of the words "brandy toddy" (upon their utterance by one of the inmates of her Establishment); to merely associate the idea of some flexible substance with "bender," and to consider a work of art alone suggested by "bust." She held very strict notions of propriety, thinking that a husband ought not to appear with his coat off, in his wife's presence, under any circumstances. She had a natural turn for match-making, and believed that at least *one* marriage ought to come off every year within her Establishment. And, finally, she used to immolate herself on the altar of an old lady-boarder who had her meals served in her own room, and was a mysterious personage, generally.

There might have been from fifteen to twenty persons resident at Mrs. —'s, of whom half-a-dozen were artists. Numerically, therefore, they were in the minority, socially they assumed prominence enough to justify our selection of the present Chapter's title.

We shall only speak of the professional boarders. None of the artists dined at Mrs. —'s, save on Sundays; being engaged at their several studios, offices, *burins*,[2] etc., during the day, to reunite at evening. This generally took place in the front basement, a largish room on a little lower level than the side-walk—just the sort of apartment ordinarily occupied by Doctors.

Nominally this chamber belonged to the two who slept in it, practically to the artist fraternity. We shall take what the poet of *Idlewild* denominates "Hurry-graphs" of some of them.[3] Our first selection is the Comic Artist.

If there be a popular superstition to the effect that "funny men," whether wielders of pen or pencil, are an obstreperously hilarious generation, he was a signal contradiction to it. You wouldn't have noticed any thing especially comic about him. He was an individual of quiet exterior and observant eye. He had the air of a gentlemanly fellow, with not too much to do on his hands, and a steady conviction in his mind that he ought to be deliberately miserable. We once knew a Methodist minister who, simultaneously with a bad attack of tooth-ache, lost his situation in consequence of the generally terrific nature of his discourses, which had driven several old women (of both sexes) crazy. Well, our Comic Artist resembled him—only he had a moustache, and seemed a little more despondent, as being less assured of the safety of his soul.

The amount of work he "got through" with might have amazed any body—but a Comic Artist. There seemed no end to his labors. Ixion's wheel, or Sisyphus's stone-rolling were nothing to them.[4] Contemplating the piles of "big cuts," "little cuts," "cuts" of all shapes and sizes, "cuts" for comic weeklies, "cuts" for comic monthlies, book illustrations, magazine illustrations, designs for posters-drawings in short of every conceivable and inconceivable character—contemplating these, we say, to the unceasing production of which our artist's time was devoted, it is probable that the Tartarean gentlemen recently mentioned had an easy time of it compared with him.[5] He must have used up whole forests of box-wood, ship-loads of pencils, barrels of flake white, and quarries of pumice-stone in the exercise of his profession!

In blazing away at the peccadilloes and follies of human nature, he sometimes manifested a sublime independence of the canons of art. His notions of proportion were generally regulated by the size and quality of the box-wood blocks he worked upon. The dislocation of a limb in order to bring it into a certain part of the picture, or to avoid a knot, was a little artistic license of which he frequently availed himself. He would draw a disjointed young man of the first fashion, eight feet high, conversing with a fractured belle whose arms terminated at her waist; in the back ground a number of dancers tripping it on the light fantastic flat-iron—such being his notion of feet; while a baboon—his conception of an Irishman—handed round refreshments. But what were these little defects in comparison with his merits, his exquisite perception of the ludicrous, his instinctive love of the beautiful, his pictorial philo-progenitiveness,[6] his extraordinary powers of burlesque.

A greater contrast could hardly have been conceived than was afforded by another boarder. Like the hero of Tennyson's ballad,[7] he was a "landscape-painter," and quite a young lady's *beau ideal* of an artist. He had long, dark hair, semi-melancholic eyes, a Vandykish beard.[8] He wore a wide-sleeved-and-slashed-black-velvet coat, a broad *sombrero* hat, was over six feet high, and generally resembled a consumptive younger brother of Charles the First of England run to seed. (He didn't look so poetic in his *atelier* costume, a ragged jacket, pants on which he used to try his brushes; and his hair tied behind with a bit of string.) We called him the "Picturesque Anachronism."

He painted big pictures of mountain scenery with brilliant molasses fore-grounds, cylindrical water, and impossible Indians. (He spent half the year among the Catskills,[9] his rural attire comprising a few bowie-knives, sundry hatchets, an alpenstock or mountain-pole shod with a spike, and huge jack-boots.) His friends and companions were at the pains—in consideration of his appearance—to invent all sorts of startling and ingeniously-elaborated narratives, wherein he figured as a heroic miscreant of Southern birth, guilty of romantic villainies enough to set him up as hero for a hecatomb of yellow-covered novels.[10] In point of fact, he hailed from down East,[11] and hadn't been further south than Philadelphia in his life. But to this hour we suspect him of a latent admiration for the character ascribed to him.

The others we shall dismiss more briefly. One was a young Englishman of unpleasantly rampant animal spirits, addicted to practical jokes, to saying the most insulting things with the most good-humored air in the world, and to burlesque opera vocalization—in which he and another of the party greatly excelled. We believe he had commenced art-life on a Panorama which didn't pay—probably in consequence of his being engaged on it. He now drew for books and newspapers. A fourth had an intellectual-Jack-Sheppardish physiognomy,[12] and a queer, semi-Manichean system of philosophy which inculcated that nobody could be happy without somebody else being simultaneously miserable.[13] He painted in oil, and was suspected of writing pretty songs and lively stories—with artists for their heroes—for a Sunday newspaper. A fifth played on the guitar; a sixth had a red beard, and was very near-sighted—which is all we can recollect about them.

These, then, constituted the Artist Community. The basement in which they—to use a Scotticism—foregathered, was characteristic of its frequenters. No amount of attention on the part of the chamber-maids could make it look tidy. All freshness and elasticity was squeezed out of the beds by four or five gentlemen sitting or reclining on them at the same time, amid tobacco ash and cigar stumps. The chairs contained wash-basins full of indefinite-colored water, which looked as if it had got black in the face in trying to look like champagne. Plaster casts blockaded the windows. Boxing-gloves resembling Scotch *Haggises* (if that be the correct plural),[14] or apple-puddings suffering from the combined attacks of mumps, yellow-jaundice, dropsy, and cramp, littered the floor. Portfolios, yawning like sick oysters disgorging ill-digested sketches, lay around. An easel and lay-figure stood in a corner. Weapons, every one of which had been used for some domestic purpose, from sharpening pencils, toasting bread, opening oysters, cleaning pipes, to poking the fire, covered the table, heterogeneously jumbled together with pumice-stone, crayons, crumbs, charred wood, empty bottles, box-wool blocks, cards for whitening them, files begrimed with black-lead, Indian ink, cigar-cases, sketches, cents, and illustrated newspapers. Here our Artists sometimes worked nocturnally.

Not always, though. They sometimes played. Dropping in of an evening, you might find yourself the amazed center of a half a dozen temporary lunatics indulging in the wildest of gymnastics over chairs, beds, and tables. Or a quiet conversation would be interrupted by the English artist (who, by-the-way, had contracted a playful habit of hurling clubs at the head of any in-comer) commencing a vocal imitation of the newest opera *basso* or *tenor*, when the others joining in, you were incontinently hurried into a Mahlström of melody.[15] Or a boxing match would be in progress. We remember how a gentleman got knocked *through* his recently-completed picture—a ten-feet-by-six one designed for academic exhibition.

During the opera season, however, the basement was often untenanted of evenings, and always on Saturdays, when the party attended a literary and artistic club held at a German tavern, where they sang songs, told stories, made puns, and drank lager-bier. If any of them returned home keyless, between the hours of 1 and 2, they beat devil's-tattoos on the window-panes till admitted. They lay very late in bed on the following mornings, but didn't lose their breakfasts—as

the landlady was very good-natured. Some manifested an indifference to the meal, preferring a short pipe in bed.

Mrs. — was, indeed, the most good-humored of land-ladies, and her house the pleasantest of which we have experience. She overlooked the rough usage of her basement chairs. (The backs generally came out when one sat upon them.) We don't attribute the turning the *statuette* of the Fighting Gladiator with his face to the wall to her,[16] but rather to the unnecessarily rampant modesty of an Irish chamber-maid. We never saw her out of temper but once—when certain of the boarders (not artists) purloined a ham-bone from the pantry at midnight, picked it, and deposited the osteological fragment on the window-sill of the mysterious old lady; getting out of a window on the roof of an out-house to effect the injurious implication.

We don't know if our artist friends are still resident in her Establishment. The advent of summer attracts the fraternity irresistibly from baked side-walks, pitiless sun-glare, and simooms of city dust, to the blue cones of the Catskills, the breezy heights of the White Mountains,[17] the giant lakes of the North, and other portions of American Fairy Land. We may meet them again in winter.

CHAPTER XXI

The Vegetarian Boarding-House (As It Was)

IN commencing the present Chapter we would especially disclaim any intention of describing a certain Establishment yet extant among us. Of that we know no more than that it is said to be conducted on an approach to—though not strictly—Vegetarian principles; and that its proprietor has the reputation of a gentleman and a man of science. Our Vegetarian Boarding-House is an entirely different affair; and, to the best of our knowledge, ceased to exist upwards of four years ago. Yet its peculiarities are worthy of preservation. The tenement was one of those old-fashioned, comfortable-looking, red-brick ones margining the Battery.[1] We became a boarder partly in consequence of this location, though we acknowledge curiosity as our principal inducement. It was sultry July weather, and we hadn't dollars enough to compass rustication. We always loved the Battery before the city authorities made a big dirt-pie of it. The sparkling waters of the bay rippling in golden sunlight, the pleasant rustle of leaves overhead, and the shadow-checkered grass under foot were suggestive of other than city life—and as for abstinence from flesh diet, one doesn't feel very carnivorous in summer, and could give one's self a dispensation at a restaurant, if desirable. So, obtaining an introduction to the proprietor, we became an inmate of the Vegetarian Boarding-House.

He was a tall, spare man, with a large nose, light watery eyes and but little hair, though he wore a straggling hay-colored beard. Like the wise men of old he hailed from the East. His life seemed to have been spent similarly to those of the

Athenians in Scripture in inquiring for *new things*.[2] Not an *ism* whether philosophic, philanthropic or theologic, but had, in its turn, subjugated him. He had shower-bathed his soul with Unitarianism, frozen it up tight in Transcendentalism, thawed it out with Universalism, besmoked it in Swedenborgianism, knocked it higher than a kite with Millerism, let it putrefy in Mormonism, flayed it with Shaking-Quakerism, buried it under General Negation, and dug it up with Spiritualism.[3] He had kept a Water-cure Establishment,[4] visited Icaria,[5] lived in a Phalanstery,[6] and officiated as "Elder" at Salt Lake.[7] He had been ridden on a rail and tarred and feathered, as an Abolitionist-lecturer, down South. He had anticipated Neal Dow in the advocation of the Maine Law.[8] At the time of our sojourn in his Boarding-House he devoted himself, almost exclusively, to Vegetarianism and the Woman's Rights movement.

His wife—taken *after* the Mormon episode—was a little rigid woman, without eye-brows. If the reader can imagine an elderly frog laboring under the combined miseries of a severe stomach-ache and the conviction that he was going insane and had better commit suicide, that will convey some idea of the expression of her countenance. She always dressed in black, wore very scanty frocks, black cotton stockings, and thick shoes. She had accompanied her husband in what may be designated his theologic and social *benders*, in some cases preceding him. She was a keen politician (Whole-Ticket-Died-in-the-Wool-Anti-Union-Pro-Amalgamation-Anti-States-Rights-and-No-Backing-Out Stripe), and studied anatomy with the view of practicing as Doctress. Happily for society in general, she had no children.

There were but few boarders, our arrival completing the half dozen—a select circle of originals as we ever encountered. Before discriminating them into individuals we will speak of the Establishment generally.

Our landlady had as much faith in cold water as Preissnitz or a mermaid.[9] Her house, her person, her very cat was over-washed. If it had rained in-doors all day long the house couldn't have been wetter. From garret to basement, both chambers and stair-case were always in a more or less hydropathic condition. You turned out for an unsuspecting walk of half an hour's duration, to find, on regaining your apartment, the chairs blockading the passage, the *disjecta membra* of your bedstead reclining against the wall, and a stout negress on her hands and knees, scrubbing away with perseverance and energy worthy of a better cause. Perhaps Mrs. — would be superintending—and quite ready to crush you with sanatory authorities in case of objection. Our floor was rendered so damp by these proceedings that we shouldn't have been surprised at seeing a plentiful crop of mushrooms or toad-stools spring up under the washing stand, or to have found an eel in the pockets of the old coat which served us for a dressing-gown.

Ventilation and sunlight were also hobbies of our land-lady. Now, in July, few persons object to the former, but it's not altogether agreeable to sit at dinner in the full blaze of the sun, his rays concentrating with a more than burning-glass power upon your physiognomy—albeit the meal is of a cooling nature. We have seen a gentleman's nose begin to blister, and the cuticle peeling from a lady's countenance. If you remonstrated at such Salamanderish treatment,[10] Mr. — talked about the Arabs of the great Sahara, proved that hats were an effeminacy, and attributed ophthalmia to the use of protectives from the sun's rays.[11] It was one of his peculiarities never to look hot. He might have taken the arm of Shadrach, Meshach and Abednego, in their little promenade, with perfect impunity.[12] Whether addressing a room full of people, digging in the back garden, or presiding at table (we have seen him under each aspect), he was equally frigid and imperturbable.

Our meals—at which we formed a snug family party—were served with uniform cleanliness, and excellently prepared. Every thing was of the herbaceous or farinaceous description, of course. We had no meats, no fish, no gravy-soups. Tea and coffee were also rejected, as stimulants. But every variety of vegetable appeared at our table, as also fruit and pastry. (No butter entered into the composition of the latter, that being a tabooed article.) Bananas, melons, peaches, grapes, oranges, cherries, pine-apples; all the daintier forms of Vegetarian fare were provided with a liberal hand. The display, indeed, exceeded our expectations. We saw Vegetarian diet under its most attractive (summer) aspect. Whether the fraternity were confined to turnips, etc., during the winter season, we can not determine. In spring they generally went out to graze at a country Establishment, located somewhere in Connecticut, and owned by a relative of the landlord's.

Descending from our neatly-ordered though damp apartment, to a breakfast of the material recently described, was agreeable enough. We began to think our Vegetarian friends might possibly be right, and that we, hitherto, had been living in a state akin to cannibalism. We thought of Adam and Eve, in *Paradise Lost*, and of the Angel taking dinner with them. We remembered to have read that Brahmins generally reached a good old age (in the event of their not shortening their days by making fires on the tops of their heads,[13] inserting knives into their abdomens, undertaking to stare the sun out of countenance, or similar devotional proceedings). We looked at the anti-carnivorous passages in *Queen Mab*,[14] and thought of the Golden Age.[15] What if we went in for innocence and vegetables in good earnest? But before doing so we resolved to observe their effects as evidenced by our fellow-boarders.

They appeared generally healthy, but unusually quiescent individuals. First, and most prominent among them was a middle-aged man of loose figure, large, colorless countenance, and little eyes—something like a dropsical turnip, with two raisins stuck in it. In-doors he wore a long, green-baize coat, a straw hat bordered with bright listing, and slippers. He also carried a large, tarnished silver watch, to which, in lieu of chain or guard, was attached a tarry string. The expectation naturally excited by his appearance was more than justified by his opinions and characteristics, in describing which we shall risk the charge of exaggeration, if not of pure invention. He prided himself on being a man of *sys-*

tem. Considering bed an effeminacy, and hurtful to the development of the human body (as affording facilities for laying on one side, and so contracting the chest), he preferred reposing on a narrow plank, placed upon two chairs—being covered only by a sheet. This was his *system* of sleeping. In diet he confined himself to particular dishes, always eating the peel with the fruit or vegetables, whether oranges, peaches, or potatoes, in the belief that removing it deprived them of remarkable stomachic virtues. (He even attempted to devour the rinds of water-melons, cocoa-nuts, and pine-apples, correcting the internal discomposure thereby provoked by taking ginger.) This constituted his system of eating. In drinking he confined himself to water, occasionally flavoring it with boiled onions, a weak infusion of sassafras or lemon-peel, in the beneficial qualities of which he had strong faith.

He was the strictest Vegetarian of the community, and the most intolerant of the flesh-eating barbarians of the outer world. He never used the words *meat*, *beef*, *pork*, or *mutton*; employing in lieu of them such denunciatory terms as *dead flesh*, *cow's corpse*, *butchered hog*, and the like. Wine, beer, and spirits he considered direct inventions of the Arch Enemy. Yet he smoked—not tobacco, but dried sun-flower leaves, thereby producing such offensive odors that he was requested to confine himself to his own room during such indulgences. He had also—so he informed us—once tried a mixture of opium, tea-leaves, and red pepper, but couldn't stand it.

This bit of confidence was vouchsafed in his chamber, whither we were, one day, invited. The room was as odd-looking as its occupant. He had made it an especial condition with the landlord that he should be permitted to furnish it according to his own inclinations—in pursuance of which the ceiling had been painted of a lively blue, the floor of an equally bright green. This, he said, was in accordance with nature. He had even caused the artist to attempt certain extraordinary delineations of birds and butterflies upon the walls (the latter as large as cocked hats), and at about three feet above the wainscot, to depict a row of gigantic sunflowers—the yellow put in without regard to expense. Sunflowers, we imagine, were a weakness of our fellow boarder's. He often wore one in his button-hole in his morning walks on the Battery, and once took to eating their seeds—carrying them about in a large *papier-mâché* snuff-box, and pressing them upon others. Of his origin and past avocations we were unable to learn any thing, he himself maintaining, a resolute silence on these heads. He had arrived one evening with his effects—consisting of a large trunk, a bird-cage, a valise, and a dog-kennel—in a wheelbarrow. The two latter articles were yet extant in the back-yard. Their owner kept a rat in the bird-cage, which subsequently died on his attempting to feed it exclusively on cabbage-stalks.

Some of these peculiarities were communicated to us by a fellow-boarder who occupied an adjoining apartment, and was himself only second in eccentricity to their originator. A thin, eager-looking man, his light reddish-colored hair curled crisply all over his head, like fine mahogany shavings. He stooped in walking, was very near-sighted, and carried an eye-glass. He had adopted Vegetarianism not so much on account of principle as for the better and more unclouded development of his intellect—which he devoted, solely and entirely, to attempts at discovering how the art of *flying* might be rendered practicable. We are inclined to think the celebrated "Moon Hoax" of Richard Adams Locke,[16] with its plagiarized details of winged Lunarians, had first turned his thought in this direction. His room was littered with the *debris* of abandoned aerial machinery. Wings of whalebone-ribbed-india-rubber, to be worked by an abortive contrivance, which seemed a compromise between a coffee-mill and pair of bellows; an artificial eagle's tail, of immense size, with breast to match, and apparatus for inflating it when fastened on the wearer; queerly-shaped balloons like circular sausages, to sustain the imaginary aeronaut, while he won his way through fields of air, by turning a crank which put in motion four large pieces of framed canvas resembling the sails of a mill—these and more ingenious inventions were here. He put them on in our presence, explaining their proposed action, and descanting with enthusiasm on the glory which must accrue to the conqueror of the only element as yet unsubdued by man. Just then he had temporarily abandoned the endeavor to achieve the means of solitary flight, and in conjunction with another enthusiast—we believe a Bowery watch-maker—aspired to construct a machine calculated to accommodate some half-dozen aerial excursionists. One summer's afternoon we crossed to Hoboken, where it lay enclosed within a square of palisading, awaiting the raising of funds necessary to its completion. To the best of our recollection it resembled a sharp-nosed, sharp-sterned canvas boat, containing a little steam-engine wherewith to work two great screw-like fans, a balloon attached to it forming the sustaining power. Our fellow-boarder considered that the means couldn't be too simple. If that qualification were especially demanded we should have thought *him* particularly adapted to the discovery. He had been a clerk in a telegraph office, but relinquished business for his project, and now relied on relatives both for the funds to carry it on, and to pay his board. They sent him letters containing money and denouncing aerial contrivances.

We had two lady-boarders, a mother and daughter, the latter a pink eyed, scared-looking girl of sixteen, who smelt like mice; the former a fat, pale-faced woman of fifty, whose round, protruding eyes, and small, beak-like nose, gave her a strong resemblance to a large white owl. She, with the assistance of the landlady, was engaged in perverting her daughter's intellect to the degree necessary to produce *clairvoyancy*. We have no doubt they subsequently succeeded in manufacturing an orthodox spiritual *Medium*. Both ladies occasionally dressed in Bloomer costume,[17] the elder wearing spectacles, pantalettes of black crape, and an umbrella.

The remaining boarder had no greater peculiarities than those of general speechlessness, the habits of staring out of the window for hours together, bolting his food whole, and remaining locked up in the bath-room for many consecutive hours, when he was generally understood to be trying the cold-water cure. He always came out very leaden in aspect, and resentful of inquiries as to how he felt. We believe he was a Vermonter, and had been a schoolmaster.

With these companions, then, we diurnally assembled at the Vegetarian table. The conversation, in which our landlord took the lead, was generally of a mild and *ismy* character. The effect of the diet may be thus described:

A strong disinclination to do any thing; an unnatural meekness of disposition; a tendency to *boils*; and a generally-sublimated and windy estimation of our own importance and destiny, were the primary results. We experienced a sort of tranquil dissatisfaction with the world in general, and a desire to set it to rights through the medium of writing letters to the *Spiritual Telegraph*, *Water-Cure* and *Phrenological Journals*,[18] which papers formed part of the weekly literature of our Boarding-House. We read the matrimonial advertisements in the last-named periodical, and began to speculate on the propriety of taking for a wife some young lady with cold gray eyes, sandy hair, a large waist, severely rational principles, big feet, and strong faith in the Maine Law.

We shudder to think of our condition, and gladly turn to our rescue. Mentioning, in confidence, our intentions to a friend, he, struck with alarm and horror at the state of mind to which we were reduced, at once resorted to vigorous measures for effecting our deliverance. Sitting listlessly one evening in the front parlor, engaged in the study of entomology, as manifested in the dissection of large worms by the green-coated boarder (he was partial to such operations), we were summoned forth. Our friend proposed a moonlight sail upon the Hudson—we agreed. A boat was in waiting, into which we stepped, and for a couple of hours danced merrily over the silvery surface of our beautiful bay. We became hungry—he produced ham sandwiches; thirsty—he proffered champagne. Our readers will spare us the particulars of our fall.

We have a general impression of our legs doubling up considerably, and of the trees behaving in a remarkable manner as we crossed the alternate moonlight and shadow of the quiet Battery to our Boarding-House, at about 2 in the morning; of being assisted up-stairs by our friend and the landlord—the latter in scanty drapery and out of temper; of subsequently going to bed with our hat on. On the following morning we quitted the Vegetarian Boarding-House. Nor have we, since, encountered our landlord or any of his guests. We learn, however, that with his lady, he has relapsed into Spiritualism, and is making a good thing of it.

CHAPTER XXII

The Medical Students' Boarding-House

HOW many of our readers can recollect the ideas generally entertained with regard to Medical Students before the existence of Dickens' *Pickwick Papers*?[1] Were they not supposed to be pale, studious, intellectual, interesting young men?—often figuring as heroes in Annuals, *Forget-Me-Not's*,[2] and the like feeble-minded literature? Such is the testimony of our memory on the point. But the *Real*—in the shape of Mr. Bob Sawyer, and Mr. Ben Allen—ousted the *Ideal* as effectually as did Cervantes' knight the paladins of fictitious chivalry.[3] Albert Smith's lively *Punch* papers only deepened the Pickwickian impression,[4] and a sentimental Medical Student is now as rare a character in books as in reality.

It might not be difficult to decide why they should be the rackety generation they certainly are. "Croaker rhymes with joker," says Goldsmith's Good-natured Man,[5] and those whose professional studies necessarily bring them into contact with the more lugubrious aspects of life, may plead that they are half justified, on the Emersonian principle of *compensation*,[6] in going to the opposite extreme. We have known sextons and undertakers of decidedly jolly temperament; nor are turnkeys of a particularly misanthropic turn of mind—except in melodramas. And perhaps it is time enough for Medical Students to assume the conventional gravity incidental to their vocation when they formally undertake its responsibilities. At all events, it must be admitted that whether in Paris, London, or New York, it would be difficult to find a *faster* class.

Our Empire city has three medical colleges, and, of course, a large proportion of doctors in *embryo* forms part of its population. Being gregarious in their habits, these mostly contrive to board together, hence their claims to a chapter in our Physiology. One Establishment in the Fourth Avenue is said to accommodate upwards of ninety of them, and must unquestionably be the scene of many unique and diverting peculiarities, but, unfortunately, we have never dwelt within its walls. Our present subject, though in the same quarter, is much smaller, twenty boarders forming its average number of occupants, of whom, during our stay, upwards of fifteen were Medical Students.

A common-place, four-story house, its outward appearance, or internal management differed in no particular from other third-rate tenements devoted to the same purpose. It was a *cheap* establishment. Medical Students are not choice as to locality, or diet, preferring to consecrate their money, whether much or little, to active diversion, rather than to milder gratifications. They are, too, necessarily, very much of an out-o'-doors population, attendance at lectures *demanding* the hours of from 9 to 1, and from 2 to 5; while their evenings are *supposed* to be spent in the dissecting-room. We italicize two words in the above sentence, as it doesn't follow that the demand is always complied with, or the supposition a correct one. We, in common with the non-professional boarders, and landlady, saw quite enough of them indoors.

She was a brisk little widow with fiery red hair, but otherwise rather good-looking, and very good-tempered—unless provoked beyond endurance. Her characteristics might have been summed-up under the heads of approbativeness, love of money, and veneration, of which qualities the first-named often neutralized one another, and the third was entirely monopolized by her uncle, who though not an inmate of the Establishment, was a frequent visitor. We believe he claimed the title of a *Veteran* of some sort; in virtue of which he used to attend meetings at an English tavern, there to drink large quantities of beer, and pass resolutions that portions of the United States government lands ought to belong to him and his companions. Now far be it from us to mention the *corps* irreverently, but this we will say, of him, individually, that he was an unpleasant, snuffy, selfish old man; nor could we ever learn any reason for according to him the deference and respect claimed as his due—beyond that of his having accidentally shot a donkey in mistake for an enemy on a dark night, he being sentinel at the time. (For this patriotic act a grateful country had bestowed a pension upon him.) But of him hereafter. We "return to our (black) sheep"—the Medical Students.

He who bore the bell, as leader (for among half a score of men there will always be a dominant spirit), was a Londoner, who had dwelt, perhaps, ten years in New York. A middle-sized, thick-set, black-whiskered, vulgarly good-looking young fellow, his expatriation was rendered necessary by a little resurrectionist operation performed in the burying-ground attached to his father's Dissenting-chapel—in consequence of which he was looked upon as a sort of professional martyr. We have no intention of separately describing the entire fifteen, but this gentleman played so prominent a part in the Establishment that the above detail becomes necessary. In conjunction with three others, he occupied the front basement; which, as in the Artistic Boarding-House, served as a general *rendezvous* for the fraternity, who found coming in at the area door, or windows, an easy and congenial mode of entrance.

It was a very curiously-furnished room. Over the mantel-piece (which, being of wood, had been drilled into innumerable holes by the agency of red-hot pokers), was displayed an *injected* human heart in a glass case, and a collection of every variety of pipes, from *nargilehs*, *chibouks*, *calumets*, and *meerschaums*, to well blackened and odorous *dhudheens*.[7] A rickety book-case, containing perhaps twenty dog's-eared, torn, and occasionally lidless medical books, and surmounted by a skull and cross bones, occupied the space between two windows. On the opposite wall, over one of the beds (the inmates slept double), appeared single-sticks, foils, masks, boxing-gloves, and what might be termed street-trophies, as a fragmentary barber's pole, a gilt pestle and mortar, a bell-handle with a yard or so of wire, and a big board formerly in use as a play-bill poster—appertaining to which we have a story to tell, presently. A few anatomical plates and pictures of ballet-dancers, a three-stringed guitar, a banjo, and tambourine, an indefinite number of rough coats, and hats of various degrees of seediness—for Medical Students are not particular as to dress—and an atmosphere redolent of stale tobacco and spirits, may complete these interior details. Our first glimpse of them was upon an occasion characteristic enough to deserve narration. One of the Students—a "new man," from the Far West—had complained of a rush of blood to the head, possibly produced by over-indulgence in whisky punch, at a little jollification in honor of his novitiate; and was undergoing phlebotomy.[8] The patient sat, pipe in mouth, in a chair, with his extended arm grasping a huge *shillelagh* (in order to develop the veins),[9] while the practitioner, with his coat off, and a wet towel bound round his head (for the purpose of sobering him), operated with a broken-bladed pen-knife. Everybody was smoking and—with the exception of the sick man—drinking. They bled him until he fainted, and subsequently rolled him into a corner, humanely pillowing his head with a couple of boxing-gloves.

A vivacious, noisy, and, for the most part, dissipated set, our fellow-boarders' notions of pleasure seemed mainly to center in boisterous animal indulgences. Only when money and credit were at a low ebb were they, not comparatively quiet, but less tumultuous. At other times the "carryings on" in the basement, and indeed all over the house, were, as the landlady said, "orful." They held harmonic meetings, and prolonged them far into the small hours of the morning. They got up boxing-matches in the garrets. They danced infernal dances accompanied with shrieks and howlings. They chased each other up or down stairs by threes and fours, sometimes jumping whole flights, and descending with a crash at the bottom. They wrote autographs all over the windows and looking-glasses with *the* diamond ring of the party. They removed hinges off chamber-doors, that they might "come down with a run" on the heads of the occupants. They brought home fragments of the human form in their pockets, for or from dissection. We have a distinct recollection of a young gentleman volunteering to show us an *eye*, over the supper-table. (He had it in his breast-pocket, wrapped up in a cabbage-leaf and a fragment of the *Herald*.) The same ingenuous youth always used a little-finger bone as a tobacco-stopper; and on one occasion, created some excitement in an omnibus by accidentally allowing the great toe of a *leg* once appertaining to an old lady, to protrude through its brown paper envelope.

Such professional luxuries, by-the-by, costing money, Medical Students (who are remarkable for getting rid of it very rapidly) sometimes resort to singular expedients for "subjects." We strongly suspect that our friends' scientific ardor impelled them to kidnap stray cats and dogs for surgical experiments; as also to bribe the youth of the vicinity to supply them with these victims at the rate of ten cents a head. One evening we counted no less than three ragged juveniles, who, severally, entered the basement, two bearing a bag or sack (which appeared agitated by lively convulsions); while the third (a tow-headed varlet of tender years) held a newly-weaned puppy by the back of the neck. We suppose this to have been the identical animal which, skinned, and painted of a brilliant red, was, two days subsequent, discovered in the *ewer* of an old lady boarder, when it nearly frightened her into fits, and whom the Londoner wanted to cup and electrify, as restoratives. A similarly reprehensible joke was also played off at the expense of the cat of the Establishment, whom, after stupefying with ether, the Students partially shaved, painting the denuded portion of the body (including the tail) in black and yellow stripes, zebra fashion. Mrs. — became so incensed at this, and at a subsequent attempt to cleanse the animal by means of the shower-bath, as to give them all notice to quit—but they wouldn't go. And when the "Veteran" endeavored to enforce their departure, they, after hypocritically agreeing, made him deplorably drunk on rum and water, burnt-corked his nose and eye-brows, smashed his hat in, tore his coat up his back, carried him up-stairs and deposited him on the parlor-table; in which position he was discovered on the following morning by the servant when she went to lay the cloth for breakfast. Two of the more active participators in this frolic *did* leave the next day, and the "Veteran," after taking four-and-twenty hours to sober himself, tracked them to a little tavern; and persuading the landlord to turn the key of their room, started for the police. Yet, on his return, it appeared that the Students must have overheard his intentions, for they had escaped by means of the window and lightning rod; previously cutting the carpet of the room and the bed furniture into strips with their pen-knives, as a *souvenir* for the landlord. We believe the "Veteran" had to pay damages.

Our Students, anticipating the privileges accorded by a diploma, would sometimes obtain patients among the poor of the neighborhood. (Most ignorant persons have a distrust of hospitals, entertaining the idea that they will be forced to submit to surgical operations within them.) Their practice, as may be imagined, was marked with occasional eccentricities. We were present when an Irish bricklayer applied to be cured of some mysterious disorder, the predominant symptom of which he described as "a smotherin' of the harrut." A Seidlitz powder being administered to him in two doses—the contents of the blue paper first, and the white afterwards[10]—the consequent effervescence took place internally with extraordinary effect. The pupils of the patient's eyes almost entirely disappeared, he gave vent to a howl such as might be supposed to proceed from an insane jackal undergoing the process of being flayed alive, leaped into the air, and rushed from the house. The practitioners used his hat for a spittoon during the remainder of the evening. On another occasion one of them took out a Dutchman's entire set of teeth (they needed it), and it was not till he called several times—at last, with a *posse* of friends armed with clubs—that he could get an artificial set to replace the loss. He had rashly paid in advance, and the money had been immediately devoted to a general "bust."

It was upon this joyous occasion, if our memory is not at fault, that the playbill board came into the Students' possession. One of the party getting helplessly drunk at an unprecedentedly early period of the evening, his friends resolved to convey him in triumph to his residence—(he was not one of our boarders). So they first stole the said board, and then placed him upon it at full length, in which position he was borne aloft on the shoulders of four Students, an equal number preceding; each one performing upon some musical instrument—a banjo, tambourine, guitar, or tin trumpet—(captured by the Londoner in single combat with a fish-vendor); while half a dozen others brought up the rear as a protective guard against the police. Fortunately they had not far to go, for the populace, taking it for some political demonstration, manifested the most inconvenient enthusiasm; and on arriving at the recumbent one's Boarding-House, remained cheering outside and demanding "a speech" for some time.

Practical joking, indeed, was quite the order of the day and night, nor did the Students spare each other. They put bad eggs in one another's boots, cold fishes in each other's beds (on winter's nights); and once reduced a boarder's room to a state of most extraordinary disorder, during his absence, by rehanging the pictures upside-down, setting the bedstead on end, reversing the position of the table, prostrating a chest of drawers, blockading the windows with chairs, and scattering the washing utensils promiscuously on the stair-case. These proceedings were effected in retaliation of the occupant's having brought home, and not invited the Students to partake of, a dozen bottles of Leslie's *Bitters*[11]—which they subsequently purloined, and after drinking the contents, concealed the bottles in the stove-pipe which crossed the dining-parlor, where they were discovered in consequence of the flue smoking horribly.

New men from the West and South—(young fellows come to New York from all parts of the Union to study medicine)—were always extensively victimized. As most of these were very ignorant (some could scarcely write their names), frequent brawls ensued. One, originating in the connection of the knob of the basement door with a voltaic battery,[12] for the purpose of administering a severe shock to a big Tennessean (he rolled down the cellar-stairs and almost broke his neck) had like to have terminated awkwardly. Arming himself with a revolver and bowie-knife, he lay in wait in the passage, only abandoning his watch when he discovered the birds had escaped through the window.

Notwithstanding such little incidents, they were, for the most part, friendly enough. Some had pledged themselves in a ghastly sort of Damon-and-Pythias spirit to claim each other's skeletons,[13] according to priority of death. In money matters they were liberal—when they had the means to be so. They wore, and sometimes *pawned*, each other's clothes. Altogether they might be considered a very agreeable set of young men—to get away from. How women could live in the house we can scarcely imagine, yet among the four or five non-professional boarders there were two of them. As for the land-lady, had she not been new to the business and distrustful of refilling her house with quieter tenants, she, assuredly, would not have retained such.

Our sojourn might have comprised about a month—during which time we probably enjoyed about three nights of unbroken sleep. Finding we couldn't get along very well on such a limited allowance, we left; subsequently chancing upon an incident so horrible, yet so characteristic, that we shall risk shocking the reader by narrating it. If peculiarly sensitive, we, herewith, give him premonitory warning *not* to read it.

Happening, then, to meet one of our late fellow-boarders, he informed us that he had just been attending a *post-mortem* on the body of one of his friends who had committed suicide, adding that he had his intestines (he used another word) in his pocket—*would we like to see them?*

CHAPTER XXIII

The Boarding-House Frequented by Bostonians

Is a trim, sober-colored edifice of moderate dimensions, in an unfinished street on the North river side of the Sixth Avenue. It has trees in front of it, and is within five minutes' walk of the cars, of which convenience, however, the boarders avail themselves much less frequently than similarly-located New Yorkers would do—in fact, only when necessitated by haste or foul weather. Bostonians have faith in exercise, and, unlike our faster population, don't rush into a vehicle when they want to get from one block's end to the other.

Its mistress claims Massachusetts as her birth-State, a *mésalliance* with a New Yorker having proved the immediate cause of her expatriation from its much-loved capital. She will tell you calmly (now that years have brought resignation) how the change disgusted her, at first, and how long it was before she got used to it. Nor has she, since her marriage, revisited the "City of Notions."[1] Her time, she says, is too much taken up. Such is her sense of responsibility for the well-being of the Establishment, that she can not conceive of the possibility of its getting along—even for a week—during her absence. So, though believing in her birthplace to that extent of which only a Bostonian is capable, she endures voluntary banishment, devoting her energies to the production of a social atmosphere akin to that in which she was nurtured.

Her husband is a matter-of-fact, business-like man, his wife's senior by years, and inferior by education—both of which circumstances she is very well aware of. He has some clerkish employment in Wall-street, and is supposed to be in receipt of so good a salary as to render it probable that keeping a Boarding-House is (strange as it may seem) more a matter of inclination than necessity on the part of his lady. Perhaps she has resolved upon realizing enough to return to Boston, carrying her husband with her, there to dwell *en permanence*; perhaps the avocation suits her, as affording scope for her natural industry and thrift. If you question Mr. —, he laughs, and tells you his wife likes it.

In person, she is a dark-haired, dark-eyed woman of forty, keen-looking rather than handsome, of robust figure, and always attired with a sort of decisive neatness repellent of *crinoline* and the like vanities. You would hardly mistake her for a New Yorker, nor would she be flattered by such a supposition. Her self-possession is less demonstrative, chillier, and more indicative of latent self-esteem than that of metropolitan dames—for whom she entertains an unqualified contempt. She maintains considerable reserve towards strangers, is apt to form hasty and severe opinions of them, and to hold on to such with great tenacity. Her reserve once broken down, she becomes loquacious—especially on the subject of Boston.

If you hail from that phoenix of moral and intellectual capitals, she may condescend to put you on probation for her liking—if not, you may be a very good sort of person, but it behooves you to stand off and reverence your betters. Mrs. — knows her value, and that of the place of her nativity. Dispute the latter—disparage it in the slightest degree—put in a word in favor of New York (or any other city) in comparison—she listens to you, not with indignation, but compassion—much as a missionary in Kaffirland might be supposed to do if a savage were to arrogate the superiority of a girdle of ox-entrails over the decencies of broadcloth.[2] Finally, our landlady talks nasally, retaining (like most persons of eastern origin) certain provincialisms of speech, and is a Unitarian of the iciest and most intellectual description.

The house resembles its mistress in cleanliness and prim nicety of appearance. Irish servants, Mrs. — declares, don't suit *her*, either on the score of religion or efficiency. She has engaged a couple of English girls, and being informed of their home badge of servitude—*caps*, would have perpetuated it, but that the younger of the two (who is pretty, and has nice hair) rebelled. They, with their mistress—she personally superintends the cooking—do every thing. The meals are served to a miracle of punctuality, baked meats preponderate, beans always appear at Sunday's dinners, and Mrs. —, assisted by her husband, or the oldest boarder, presides at table.

As indicated by the title prefixed to our Chapter, the majority of the boarders are Bostonians, the exceptions being four New Yorkers, and a middle-aged Englishman with his wife and daughter. The landlady's son—a lubberly youth of sixteen—is, also, decidedly metropolitan, both by birth and instinct. He spends most of his time in engine or porter-houses, and has frequently deserted the paternal roof (after emptying his mother's pocket of such loose change as might happen to be there), returning in a penniless and ragged condition. The boarders allude to him as a "hard" boy, generally.

They—the Bostonians—average from nine to a dozen in number. All are engaged in business down-town, some as clerks in banks, or wholesale stores; one, a tall gentleman in a curly black wig (connected with an insurance office), is married, and his wife, with that of the Englishman, her daughter and two single ladies, constitute the female population of the Establishment—none of whom are New Yorkers.

There is a stiffness of manner prevalent among these gentlemen which is eminently characteristic. They seldom go to extremes of fashion in costume, preferring sober colors and quiet patterns. The cut of their clothes is rather English than Parisian. Some wear narrow-brimmed hats, all-rounder collars and little gaiters, and are prone to attenuated umbrellas. Very few sport moustaches, clean-shaven chins are not uncommon, and while one "does the English" with luxuriously-pendulous whiskers (after the style of John Leech's "swells"),[3] another displays a perfect specimen of the old-fashioned mutton-chop order. You will discover, in fact, on acquaintance, that they entertain a species of cold regard for Anglicisms, and, therefore, instinctively annex such as do not conflict with Bostonian sentiment.

They are a precise and exact race, punctual at meals, not accustomed to make allowances for deficiencies (accidental or otherwise), and very tightly buttoned up in their own opinions. Being away from their birth-place they find it necessary, in their daily avocations, to relax a little (as a Roman citizen might have done in his travels among barbarians) and therefore feel it incumbent upon them to be more than usually Bostonian—in their Boarding-House.

New York, they will tell you, is a very good sort of a place for making money, but that is all. It mustn't pretend to any thing else. They are Bostonians and know better. The relative merits of the two cities form the argument of unceasing discussion over the supper-table, some indirect or openly contemptuous remark generally provoking the New Yorkers to the championship of their metropolis; and, though in the minority, they do not always have the worst of the controversy. Yet some of their opponents possess a hard, dry humor which is very telling in debate. They all pull together, of course; the younger Bostonians—though, perhaps, secretly alive to the greater attractions of the Empire City—holding it a point of honor to stick to their party. We have known one of them to break off in the midst of a strenuous defense of the anti-smoking ordinances of Boston, to stroll up Broadway, cigar in mouth—being sublimely unconscious at the time of any incongruity of conduct.

Some of the Bostonians are dreadfully well-informed. It is appalling to think how much they must have read. Nothing comes amiss to them. Art, literature, politics, history, science, religion—they have them all at their fingers' ends. If they are particularly strong on one subject, above all others, it is arithmetic, as applied to valuation. Like Jews, they seem to have been born with the faculty of knowing the exact worth of every article in existence. You had better not venture any observation, to these gentlemen, on any subject on which you're not thoroughly well-posted. It will be tossed from one to the other and you turned inside out in a twinkling.

We have often thought that that King of Castile,[4] who said that he could have helped Providence to a notion or two on the subject of the Creation, ought to have been a Bostonian. The Chinese make maps representing their own country as occupying the center of the earth, others being depicted as little insignificant spots in out-o'-the-way corners—and this idea appears to exist in the minds of the inhabitants of the American Athens.[5] (Sparta would be the better denomination.)[6] It is the moral and intellectual center of the universe. Other capitals are to be judged only by its standard, according as they approach to or diverge from it.

This localism of character, like that of Englishmen, is rather latent than obtrusively manifest, as though it were superfluous to claim that superiority which ought to be universally admitted. But only *question* it, and see how quickly it blazes into assertion. The Bostonians of our Boarding-House could always be "riled" into controversy by encomium on New York.

Drop but a word of our forthcoming park,[7] they are down upon you with Boston Common,*[8] inquiring, with an aspect of calm pity, whether you're aware that it contains no less than *forty-eight acres!* If this doesn't knock you over, they state how long it has been in existence. Allude to New York Bay, the view from Greenwood or Hoboken Heights,[9] they prefer those of Dorchester and the look-out from the summit of the Bunker Hill Monument.[10] Commend Broadway, they incline to the opinion that much prettier women are to be seen, any day, in Washington-street.[11] Talk of our prominent editors, preachers, and business men (as Greeley, Raymond, Beecher, Chapin, Astor, Grinnell, etc.),[12] they first trump your remarks with the names of Boston notables (coming out very strong about Amos Lawrence[13]—who appears to have been the incarnation of Boston virtue pinnacled on money-bags), and then claim the majority of the former as of eastern origin. In nothing will they allow, not the superiority, but *equality* of New York with Boston.

They cut sarcastic jokes at our expensively inefficient police, dirty streets, blockaded side-walks, post-office, fires, municipal corruptions, and spasmodic attempt at reform—not without reason. They sneer at our claims to intellect. They declare our conscience—especially in the matter of *abolition*—is in our breeches-pocket. They object to our persistence in fraudulently representing New York as the metropolis of the United States; and think Jenny Lind, Grisi, and Rachel very ill-advised in having come here before they had secured the stamp of Bostonian approbation.[14] Altogether they set us down as a fast, flashy, ill-governed, temporary, rowdyish, hybrid, money-getting and money-squandering community, who might be a great deal better if we'd take example of—Boston.

To all this and more, the New Yorkers in our Boarding-House have much to reply. Admitting that Boston is the better-ruled city, they still affect to discover spots sullying her cold effulgency. They take objection to the ultra-intellectuality of her exclusive circles, pronouncing it decidedly uncomfortable. They assert

* We have heard it asserted that every Bostonian always carries a bit of his native Common in his pocket. Our faith in this statement is not implicit; we therefore confine it to a note.

that righteousness may be so fringed with conceit as to render it a very unattractive garment; and sometimes worn as a cloak or mask, to be laid aside at pleasure. New York, they acknowledge, has a *penchant* for agreeable sins, and commits them openly, while Boston locks the door; but whether spiritual pride be not worse than self-indulgence, admits, they argue, of some question. Society in that metropolis, they furthermore assert, does not possess the great cosmopolitan heart of England, the outward conservatism of which it apes; but breathes rather an isolated atmosphere, and is content to reproduce under new forms the old narrow-mindedness and intolerance of its Puritan ancestors. As for minor social questions they declare that New York doesn't pretend to be well-bred, but that as good-nature is the essence of politeness, so the assumption of superiority is, necessarily, in bad taste. Finally, they maintain the existence of a very large world lying beyond the shadow of Boston State House.[15]

These, like most discussions, generally terminate in confirming either party in their own opinions. The Bostonians are the cooler disputants. We recollect fewer manifestations of hot temper on their side, the worst being provoked by a New Yorker's quoting Fanny Fern's depreciatory mention of their capital as "a band-box"—for which remark no Bostonian ever did, can, or will, forgive Fanny.[16]

In these controversies a bank clerk—a cool, gentlemanly individual of five-and-thirty—stands pre-eminent. He is an opera-goer, and sometimes takes the landlady and the daughter of the English boarder to the Academy,[17] where he talks learnedly of music—previously stealing his opinions from the *New York Times*, which (as every body knows) is the highest of all possible authorities. The younger lady, a blue-eyed girl of sixteen, admires, but is rather afraid of her companion. If he entertain any reciprocal feeling, it has only become demonstrative on one occasion, when perceiving her annoyance at some attentions on the part of the landlady's son, he, to the amazement of all present (it was on a summer evening, immediately after supper), seized that ingenuous youth by the ear, deliberately led him to the door, and there dismissed him, too much astonished to attempt resistance.

The English boarder is a cheery, little, bald-headed man, with scanty whiskers, and gold-rimmed spectacles, a doctor by profession. His wife, a plump, matronly person, has attained great popularity among the gentlemen by volunteering to replace missing shirt-buttons. She suffers immensely from heat and mosquitoes in summer, and her particular mission seems to be that of mending stockings. They are both very fond of their daughter, and anxious that she should marry well, but, consider her "far too young to think of such things" at present. She doesn't share that opinion.

The two unmarried lady-boarders—we apologize for our involuntary discourtesy in introducing them after the gentlemen—are from the crowns of their neat bonnets to the soles of their stout walking-shoes unmitigated Bostonians. (They affect a disdain of those exquisite gaiter-boots so dear to the hearts of New

York belles, and their sometimes style of *chaussure* might justify a sensitive man in suing for a divorce, did his wife wear such.)[18] They attend lectures, meetings, Sunday-schools, Bible-classes, etc., etc. They are intellectually religious, and religiously intellectual. They can (and *will*) talk with you on any subject, from cosmogony to pollywogs. Lastly, they are more clever than lovable, for without wishing to disparage mental excellence, it is certain that highly intellectual people are not always agreeable ones; and that men will rather dispense with the former in their wives than with capacity for affection and sympathy.

The remaining lady-boarder (wife to the tall gentleman) is only noticeable as being much afflicted with the toothache, and accustomed to employing the intervals between each attack in assaulting a big accordion to the tune of "Poor Dog Tray."[19] We occupied the next room, and having always considered that air an eminently sniveling one, its performance, in conjunction with our being engaged in correcting the proofs of a book demonstrating that the world would come to an end on the Fourth of July, 1855, had such an effect on our spirits that we were goaded into improvising opposition harmony with a comb and piece of whity-brown paper. After two forenoons' practice upon that exhilarating musical instrument, the lady gave in, or only performed during our absence.

CHAPTER XXIV

The Boarding-House Whose Landlady Is a Southerner

Only rich Southerners travel; and such as are induced by business or pleasure to seek northern cities naturally prefer the accommodation of Hotels rather than Boarding-Houses—the St. Nicodemus, as every body knows, being especially favored by their patronage. Yet, as, among our list of Establishments, we have cognizance of one whose general characteristics savored of the sunny South; whose landlady prided herself on being "no Yankee," and whose boarders hailed mainly from the other side of Mason and Dixon's line,[1] we accord it a Chapter.

The house—a Union Square one—was, like its mistress, handsome, and of imposing exterior. You could scarcely contemplate either without being impressed by the assumption of aristocratic dignity, the consciousness of *position*, as it were, common to both. The lady had the gayer aspect: for the house, though a stylish four-story one, with a bit of garden in front, a flight of stone steps leading up to a columned and pilastered portico, an ornamental balcony fronting the first floor windows, rich mouldings and cornices decorating the entire *façade*—was yet of a sober brown tint. Whereas no horticultural *fête*, no promenade on Broadway when the Spring fashions come forth in all their glory, could display brighter colors than Mrs. — affected. Perhaps she rather overdid the *modes*, as is not uncommonly the case with Southern ladies. (However, in New York, they can plead the example of the aborigines.) But in a tall, good-looking widow, with large, brown eyes; black hair (and plenty of it); a straight, *decisive* nose; and smiling, but *willful* mouth, who could object to it?

We have called her a widow, such being her nominal condition. In reality, a husband from whom she had separated seven years ago, after less than half that period's matrimonial experience, was extant in California. Report intimated general misconduct on his part, crowned by conjugal infidelity, as the cause of the rupture; and, also, that his lady had subsequently cow-hided him in the streets of his native city in retaliation of certain slanders directed against her fair fame. And, recollecting *how* she looked on the occasion of discovering that the cook—an obese Irishwoman—had gone to a ball in one of her silk dresses, we can very well believe it.

Why our landlady had quitted Georgia for New York, unless in consequence of the inharmonious climax to her wedded life, we know as little as why she kept a Boarding-House. Possibly she was poor, and her pride sustained less mortification in seeking subsistence in a distant city than in remaining where her former position afforded scope for unfavorable contrasts. She had followed her present employment five years, ostensibly with success, yet, as events proved, surrounded by a constant environment of debt and difficulty.

On becoming an inmate of her Establishment, our expectations of the internal arrangements sustained some disappointment. We had, naturally, shaped them in accordance with the stylish exterior and dressy landlady, but intimacy rather lessened our regard for either. As Mrs. —'s presence suggested claims to patrician refinement which her manners and faults of temper militated against; so her domestic economy was unsatisfactory. Not that the house, or table exhibited any striking deficiencies, both being handsomely furnished, but a general *untidiness*—thoroughly Southern in its way—and originating in want of system, pervaded every thing. It was even perceptible on our introduction to our chamber, a spacious two-windowed one, with dusty curtains, a heap of ashes and cinders in the grate, a marble fire-place (ornamented with tobacco-stains), and a ewer and basin, respectively containing three-days-old water and slops. Our landlady (who had not disdained to pilot us thither, though, usually, she made over this duty to a servant), called up a sullen housemaid, and rated her severely, but we subsequently found "shiftlessness"—to use the pet word of Mrs. Stowe's *Aunt Ophelia*[2]—rather the rule than otherwise.

Beds were left unmade till sunset, the water supply being deferred to an equally late period; and *then* poured into unrinsed ewers. Fires were so hastily constructed that they went out almost immediately—inciting chilly boarders to do the same. The bath-room was always out of order. You discovered yourself unprovided with towels after facial lavation—which is always an aggravating circumstance. Meals were served at unequal intervals—always half an hour after their nominal time—and the cookery, though of an ambitious order, fluctuated in merit, occasionally proving a dead failure. We have known blood to follow an incision in a shoulder of veal, at dinner, and all the vegetables to come up flavored with soot. You had frequently to *ask* for water, the pitchers being unfilled. And all these nuisances, individual and combined, though subject to violent abolition at certain crises, appeared to be part of our normal condition, as we always got back to them. Mrs. — changed her servants very frequently, and once—in spite of the inherent dislike of all Southerners to "free niggers"—tried a kitchen-full of darkeys. But the colored gentleman who waited at table "sassed" her on a question of propriety (we believe he was discovered applying his mouth to a bottle of sherry belonging to one of the boarders), and he and his companions had to quit in consequence. And we entertain no doubt that had our landlady possessed the power—pretty woman, and generally indulgent as she was—the back of *Beauharnois* (that was our waiter's name), would have smarted for it. She acknowledged as much to us, over the supper-table, concluding the conversation with the sentiment that "a nigger *would* be a nigger anyhow." Which seemed, indeed, a self-evident proposition.

Perhaps the fault of general mismanagement lay not entirely on the servants' side. Mrs. — scarcely treated them in a consistent, not to say judicious manner. They appeared to have no recognized department assigned to them, individually. A housemaid would be set to nursing the baby of a lady-boarder; the cook called upon to arrange the dining-parlor, or to open the hall door. Their mistress' favor or ill-humor was accorded very capriciously. The "boy" *Beauharnois* (he was always called *boy* in the Establishment), obtained a three days' holiday after the Fourth of July, on the condition that he should find a substitute; which he did in the shape of a fat, greasy, idiotic, yellow man, who spilled soup on the carpet, was seized with paroxysms of sneezing while handing dishes, and cut his fingers to the bone in the endeavor to dissect a canvas-back duck. (He was removed from the table howling, and subsequently sent our landlady a bill for medical attendance, which *Beauharnois* compromised.) Had it been represented to Mrs. — that a more uniform sway might have produced pleasanter results, she would have resented the advice. In common with most Southerners, she believed that no adequate service could be obtained without the exercise of unlimited authority.

Her Establishment was an expensive one, the terms being rather higher than the average of similar Boarding-Houses. Some of the lodgers did not pay up very regularly; others got in debt, and left without paying at all. Of these last, a flashily-dressed gentleman of, perhaps, five-and-thirty, was a choice sample. Though not good-looking, he would have passed for it with most persons, in virtue of his hawk-nose, glossy moustache, and carefully-dyed and trimmed beard. He always wore clothes of the most fashionable cut, and rich vests; sporting also a profusion of jewelry, even to the coxcombry of displaying rings *over* his gloves—(as our landlady did, by-the-by). He had champagne at dinner, and was very liberal in passing the bottle to fellow-boarders; as in giving them cigars of choice brands and excellent quality, each being separately enwrapped, as a thing of rare price, in a dried tobacco leaf. To Mrs. — he was especially attentive, accompanying her to the Opera; and, occasionally, to that odd-looking church in the vicinity, which appears as if the architect, unable, from lack of funds, to finish both towers after the original design, had despairingly extinguished one of them beneath a quadrangular cone of slate-colored timber. The boarders—and, in particular, the young men—thought him at first, a knowing, pleasant fellow, and were ambitious of his companionship; but in time grew shy of him. It was whispered that his "plantation in Arkan*zaw*" might be apocryphal, that "some of the fellows" had lost a good deal of money in his company, and suspected him of being the proprietor of a faro-bank,[3] to which he had introduced them. A little incident growing out of this brought his stay in our Boarding-House to a sudden termination.

There came to it, on his way to Europe (and the Crystal Palace Exposition of 1851),[4] a young Kentuckian, a former acquaintance of the landlady's. He had intended no longer stay than the few days elapsing between his arrival and the departure of the next steamer. On the second night, having drunk deeply of town pleasures, under the guidance of our dubious Arkansas planter, he found himself cleaned out of something like $5000—being the entire sum intended to meet the expenses of his projected tour. Of which circumstance, after shame had kept him silent for the better part of a week, he informed Mrs. —. She counseled communication with the police, which he, from some wild notion of *honor*, would not agree to. So she privately telegraphed to his relatives; and on the fifth morning subsequent to the fleecing operation, a stalwart, six-foot-five-inch-high uncle of the victim arrived. Why the swindler had not shifted his quarters we are at a loss to conceive—perhaps he anticipated the youth would pocket his loss uncomplainingly, perhaps leaned in trustful reliance on legal or political friendship in New York. Any way he *stayed*, and had not risen at the time of the uncle's arrival, upon which that gentleman waited upon him in his bed-chamber.

What took place in that interview was never precisely ascertained. There were rumors that the Kentuckian opened the proceedings in a very Turpin-like man-

ner,[5] by placing the muzzle of a revolver in the immediate vicinity of the sharper's head, and presently compelled him to produce from a small *port-monnaiè* (which he wore in his breast, secured by a strong steel chain),[6] the greater part of the sum of which his nephew had been despoiled. Certain it is that we met the defeated black-leg with a very ghastly face, as he hurried down stairs, two hours afterwards, and that he incontinently decamped, leaving only a new valise filled with bricks, old newspapers, odd cards, French lithographs, a broken dice-box, and a book of "Confessions of a Reformed Gambler."[7]

This stalwart uncle, by-the-by—he stayed a fortnight at the house, and subsequently accompanied his nephew to Europe—was a true gentleman, possessing a *naïve* courtesy and good humor, very pleasant to contemplate. Only on one topic did he exhibit any sort of prejudice—the inevitable one—*Slavery*. "He had always been taught," he said, "to think all Abolitionists d—d scoundrels, and he was going to believe it."

Apropos of the London Exposition, our Establishment comprised a boarder who, just returned from a week in Europe, had started with the intention of seeing it, yet never touched English soil. He was a thin, tall Texan, who had gone out "on a spree" in one of the Southampton and Bremen steamers,[8] and being oblivious from intoxication on arriving at the former port, had held on to the latter, where he got rid of all his money, finally returning (on credit) by the same vessel. He complained greatly of a pious Dutch interpreter who wouldn't translate verbal improprieties to *filles-de-joie*,[9] but endeavored to convert them. Also he had got certain Londoners on the return voyage to fudge him notes relative to the Exhibition, that he might not be laughed at on his return to *Corpus Christi*.[10] We guess he was awaiting the arrival of funds to enable him to perform that journey.

But three lady-boarders ornamented the Establishment, two of whom were Southerners—one appertaining to a Northern husband. The other was a fair-haired, fat, little woman, very lazy, very stupid, very ill-bred, and very despotic in her mode of addressing servants. She attired herself, if possible, more extravagantly than Mrs. —, and was suspected of a mysterious habit, denominated, in Southern parlance "dipping"—in other words, of *chewing snuff*—(we can depose to the fact of her smelling like a spittoon, as we sat beside her at dinner). She nourished the most absurd ideas of her importance in consequence of a remote connection with the "first families of Virginia."

The "Old Dominion" was more pleasantly represented by her companion,[11] a quiet, lady-like, and rather reserved person, of youthful appearance, though not particularly. Her manners were less familiar and more ceremonious than is common with New Yorkers. She was highly accomplished, and played the piano exquisitely—when the other hadn't got it out of tune.

As dissimilar as their better halves, the husbands deserve a word of notice. The first we studied as a good type of the most obnoxious animal producible on this side of the Atlantic—a thoroughly *low* Southerner. We shall not mention his birth-State, as it might appear invidious. A coarse-haired, vicious-faced individual, of uncleanly, though expensively-dressed exterior (he always looked as if he had just put on a new suit of clothes for the express purpose of rolling underneath a bed), his total ignorance of any thing like decency, propriety, or morality, was absolutely startling. He swore habitually, conversed pruriently, jested obscenely, chewed unceasingly, expectorated promiscuously. All his opinions were in extremes, and backed by wagers, or appeals to physical force. Withal, he possessed the most perfect faith in the inherent, inevitable superiority of all Southrons over persons hailing from other points of the compass.

—Yet he found admirers. For, on his boasting, one morning, of having squandered a couple of hundred dollars overnight in places of *un*equivocal resort, two boarders, of Northern birth, admitted, "with a foolish face of praise," that "*it took a SOUTHERNER to spend money!*" We thought them just the prettiest samples of the *genus* denominated by John Randolph and the *Tribune* "dough-face" we had ever encountered.[12]

Husband the second was a brisk, business-like New Yorker, "a Northern man with Southern principles"—hence, we presume, his presence in the Establishment. He had an office in Wall-street, and anticipated coming in for an inheritance of land and slaves in Virginia on behalf of his wife. He would prove to you scripturally, politically, and every sort of way, the blessedness of the "peculiar institution." *He* was one of the admirers of the brute before described.

Yet if the worst-bred man we have known claimed Southern origin, so also did the best, and with him we shall conclude our Chapter. He was a handsome young Louisianan, very frank and good-humored. We have a suspicion that some college escapade had brought him to New York—chiefly founded on his getting us to make, from a daguerreotype, an outrageous caricature of a professorial-looking gentleman, with a rigid face and a white-choker, whom we presume had officiated as his tutor. (He had it lithographed, and sent two hundred copies to his fellow-students in South Carolina.) We never saw him appear to other than advantage. His easy courtesy, quiet self-respect, and invariable regard for the feelings of others, a hot temper never provoked him to violate. Once, however, we saw him severely tried. It was when the Social Nuisance recently delineated ventured on some jokes—about as delicate as blows from the fist of a pugilist—at the expense of Northern women. One—wife of Doughface No. 2, an amiable little lady, only noticeable for having a baby which was always cutting its teeth—was present, and looked hot and disconcerted. Whereupon young Louisiana took up the cudgels in the defense, and in three or four trenchant sentences utterly demolished the offender. The Nuisance was subsequently boasting, after his usual violent manner, of practically resenting his discomfiture, when his antagonist tapped him on the shoulder and inquired if he were talking of *him*. Our friend looked so unpleasantly resolute and menacing that the Nuisance's "chivalry" sunk to zero in a moment. He blurted out a very energetic denial, and embraced an early opportunity to sneak out of the room.

We must not forget to add that the Nuisance's wife had a strong admiration for the young Louisianan—which, as she cordially detested her husband (who beat her) was, perhaps, not unnatural. She used to question him as to his relatives and position in life with very little delicacy; and invited him to accompany her on Broadway promenades, or to theaters, which last she greatly affected. He dodged these advances towards "passional attraction" with considerable ingenuity, and without unnecessarily wounding her self-love—until the occasion of the landlady's birth-day. Then he utterly offended this Southern Mrs. Potiphar (not *à la* Curtis, but *à la* Genesis),[13] by bringing home a handsome *bouquet* for Mrs. —. Nuisance's "lady" took it so to heart, that in disgust at the Louisianan's want of taste, she compelled her husband to find another Boarding-House. We heard that she eloped from him subsequently.

Our Southern Boarding-House is no longer in existence. The landlady failed in business, obtained a divorce from her husband, married again, and is now resident in New Orleans.

CHAPTER XXV

The Boarding-House Whose Landlady Is from "Down East"

A DINGY-LOOKING, four-story, frame-house in the east-Chatham district standing all askew, and of such narrow frontage that it appears to have been squeezed into undue longitudinal development by the neighboring tenements, one of which is a recently erected manufactory. The street itself is a very up-and-down-hill thoroughfare, boasting a Presidential name; the bad smells, children in gutters, tumble-down old houses, and new ones of bright red brick.

Exteriorly the particular Establishment we write of is unpromising; on entering you snuff an atmosphere suggestive of cooking-stoves, confined air and mice. Yet the rooms are clean, for the landlady prides herself on the performance of fortnightly scrubbings-out, which always come off on Saturdays. On these occasions she and her servant are in a damp and draggled state for fourteen consecutive hours—commencing at 5 A.M.; her husband goes out for the whole day, and the boarders are expected to dine in the back kitchen.

Mr. — is a Jerseyman by birth, a New Englander by parentage. He was once—as his wife will take care to inform you—"in the ministry," but lost office in consequence of outraging the feelings of his parishioners by daring to get married without having previously solicited permission of every man, woman, child, and old woman among them. In early youth he ran away from college, turned barber, spent four years on a whaling voyage, tried farming, and kept school. He now fluctuates, Micawber-like,[1] from one employment to another—from commission agencies of Patent-Hydrostatic-Fire-Proof-Pump Companies, to peddling Histories of Coney Island in innumerable serial parts, with steel-plate engravings. In these pursuits he has so much success as, generally, to lose his expenses. He is always frightfully "hard up," but contrives to meet the demands of his landlord and butcher in some wonderful manner, utterly undiscoverable.

Probably he, with his wife and family, came to New York on some wild expectation akin to his illustrious prototype's dealings in "coals,"[2] which, miscarrying, precipitated them into the Boarding-House business. If, at that time, they had any idea of its proving a small Ophir or Lilliputian California,[3] twelve years of practical experience has effectually undeceived them. Mrs. —'s efforts (her husband always calls her "Miss," but we shall not adopt that Down-East peculiarity)—have but enabled them to rub along after a very shifty, desultory manner.

She was, formerly, one of her husband's pupils, and is, now, a shrewd, sharp, Yankee-woman, never at ease but while working, very neat, loquacious and ungraceful, and equally proud of her pies, husband, and self—as reflecting his importance. A minister's wife, she thinks (indissolubly identifying Mr. — with his former vocation), can have but few equals, and no superiors. She wears short dresses, utterly repudiates *crinoline*, and tucks her hair away behind her ears. From her pronunciation you would suppose her afflicted with a permanent stoppage of the nose, and constantly engaged in unsuccessful attempts to force a passage by projecting her words through it. Emphatically, she is a bustling, pains-taking New Englander, with a dry relish for domestic drudgery, but as destitute of womanly graces as a codfish is of whiskers.

The couple are very well matched, however, for there's as much sentiment in Mr. — as in a candle-box. His only pleasures—so far as we could discover—consisted in hearing his wife talk *of* him to the boarders, and setting the younger members of his family sums in arithmetic.

They are seven in number. The eldest, a newly-married young woman of, perhaps, two-and-twenty, has a husband employed on the city cars. He boards with his father and mother-in-law, and sometimes has squabbles with the latter in consequence of her habit of occasionally borrowing $5 bills from his *port-monnaiè* without mentioning it. The second, a saturnine youth, one year his sister's junior, is a journeyman watchmaker—suspected of having money in a Savings Bank, and of concealing his book, that his mother mayn't get it. The third takes after his father, has been employed as bar-tender in a porter-house, ticket-collector at a theatre, lottery-office clerk, house-painter and glazier, with intervals of "agencies" and bill-collectings. He is a scampish, good-looking fellow, and his mother's favorite—of which position he avails himself in pawning her dresses, when desperately put to it for a "raise." The fourth, a girl of sixteen, is only remarkable as being an enthusiastic admirer of the popular novels of "Silenus Gobb, Junior,"[4] the whole of which, it is believed, she knows by heart. The fifth, a lad of twelve, possesses a faculty of non-abashment perfectly wonderful in its intensity, and is president of a club of boys (established for no definite purpose) which meets in the back-kitchen on certain evenings, and is occasionally squirted at through the key-hole by the elder brothers. The sixth, a pretty girl of twelve, devotes her entire physical strength and existence generally to the youngest of the family, a large baby, which can never be got to sleep under any possible circumstances.

The meals—served in a dark back parlor which is scowled upon by a tall rear building—are of the cheap and dyspeptic character heretofore described in connection with the "Mean" Boarding-House, with some few exceptions. As in the "Dirty" Establishment, pork predominates. To say that all meats are overcooked, is simply stating the fact that the landlady is a New Englander, which equally includes the facts that she has a firm conviction that grease ought to form three fourths of human nutriment, and that bread and cakes, which she manufactures herself, can't be made without soda, saleratus, and cream of tartar.

But we can only do justice to the culinary arrangements by inserting the following "Rules," discovered among a heterogeneous medley of MS. in the chamber of a literary gentleman, who left without settling for his last month's board. Whether designed as a slight token of regard for the landlady, we know not, but have little doubt that her Establishment supplied the quarry from which the composition was wrought. As his successor, we plead the right of discovery in making use of it.

RULES

ELUCIDATIVE OF YANKEE BOARDING-HOUSE COOKERY

The production of Dyspepsia, Liver Complaint and bad complexions being the principal object of this Science, it is advisable on all possible occasions to be prodigal of those valuable ingredients, Pork-Fat and Saleratus.

Soup.—Gives a fashionable air to a repast, and may at any time be extemporized from the bones and scraps of yesterday's dinner. The condiments of rice, pork-fat and pepper will be found necessary. The last is indispensable.

To Roast Beef.—Procure a certain quantity of that description of animal food known as "Boarder's beef," being careful to select it from the corpse of a quadruped which has not suffered butchery by the hand of man, but had the advantage of dying a natural death, and during whose long and useful career plentiful exercise has compensated for inadequate nourishment. Bake for not less than seven hours in an oven. If, at the expiration of that time it prove horny enough to turn the edge of a knife, it may be considered properly *done*—and your boarders' appetites also, when they taste it.

For Gravy.—Melt down superfluous bits of pork, and fragments from boarders' plates, and mix with scrapings from the pan which has been used in baking. Add flour and tepid water, and serve in a lukewarm state.

To make Fish-Balls.—Procure slabs of vociferously-scented codfish. Soak potato-remnants in hot water. Mix with pork-fat. If you have been engaged in lighting the fire, blacking the stove, or getting coal from "below," refrain from washing your hands before commencing culinary proceedings, as additional flavor will be gained. Carefully close all windows and ventilatory orifices during baking, that the scent produced may stimulate appetite. N. B.—Any "Down East" family omitting to have Fish Balls for Sundays' breakfast—preparing them over night—can by no means expect to get to heaven, at any price.

For Good "Satisfying" Biscuit.—Take "seconds" flour and saleratus, mix and form your biscuit. Bake until the top crust is nearly brown, being careful that the interior retains its original doughiness. Serve hot, as an incentive to indigestion. N. B.—A capital "filling" pudding can be manufactured of the remnants.

Meat Pie.—When meat is "a little gone," or, for other reasons, unfit for baking, it can always be rendered available in a pie—the never-failing resource of good house-keepers. N. B.—Use plenty of pepper.

Pastry.—May be purchased at little expense, when stale, from the nearest baker's. Re-warming is an easy process, and, by means of it, the fiction of hot "dessert" can be kept up for any length of time.

The inmates of the Establishment, during our time, were as follows: Two journeymen painters, a printer and his wife, a German of unknown vocation—who subsequently frightened every body by having the small pox—a young woman who practiced vocalization ten hours each day; and a very beery glass-blower. These, with the addition of the numerous family, sufficed to fill the house, even to the garrets.

Regarding her boarders as her natural prey and heritage, Mrs. —'s ruling principle appeared to be that of getting as much out of them, every way, as was possible. To the painters she suggested that they "might as well" bestow a spare evening in "touching up" the street door, persuaded the German to go on errands, got the tuneful young lady to immolate herself on needle-work, and secured the reversion of the glass-blower's cast-off garments for her offspring. Only in the case of the printer's wife did she meet with defeat. Having successively tempted her with the prospect of quilting, scrubbing out rooms, mending her (the landlady's) husband's pantaloons—and all in vain, she became quite "down upon" the young wife (who was soon to become a mother), and took her revenge by relating painful stories of the dangers attendant on maternity. Which, coming to the husband's ears, provoked indignant remonstrance, and a further question arising between him and the landlady as to the quality of the eggs served at breakfast, it ended in the young couple's departure.

These eggs, by the way, were *not* the productions of either of three singularly wretched fowls, who picked up a precarious livelihood in adjacent gutters and roosted of nights in the back-kitchen. Such as *they* laid were sold elsewhere for the landlady's profit. Under an economical, though fallacious supposition, that a male bird was an unnecessary expense, Mrs. — condemned them for some time to a life of celibacy. This didn't answer, so a rusty-looking Shanghai, with a discordant crow and bald places on his thighs—as if he had scratched off his feathers in getting through a grating, or out of a cage—was added to the ornithological department. The older boarders had a tradition that the family had attempted to keep a cow in the back yard—where she certainly could not have turned round, so limited was the area. An extraordinary appetite, on the part of the animal, for *starch*—as contained in shirt-fronts, collars and wrist-bands, when hung out to dry—induced the abandonment of the idea.

We have but few incidents to relate in connection with the Boarding-House whose landlady is from Down-East. It is true that the glass-blower—a man with bushy whiskers and no perceptible forehead—sometimes remained in bed, in company with a bottle of rum, for three days together. We recollect passing his room-door, one night, and seeing the rain pouring in upon him from the open window, while he half sat, half reclined, singing in a maudlin manner the following ridiculous verse—apparently a hybrid composition of sacred and profane melodies:

"Jerusalem, my happy home! O how I long to see
The great Menad-ge-ree that went to Milwaukie;
And from there they went to Chicago, to see what they could see—
And from there back into Buffalo, up the Niag-a-ree.
With a fine ole-d English gentleman,
One of the oldest kind!"

He used to have rows with the landlady on a subject alluded to in a former Chapter as especially productive of such—coals—which he laid in himself, charging her with annexing them to her own use. She generally told him that he was "a mean man" and a nuisance. We've no doubt the incriminations of both were correct. All drunkards *are* nuisances.

There came, as boarder, on the removal of the printer and his wife, a saffron-colored Chinaman, awaiting the departure for his native country of the patron whom he had accompanied to New York. He was a good-humored fellow, with a tail artificially lengthened by plaited silk, which he generally wore twisted round his head. The painters occasionally treated him to beer and spirits, but never prevailed on him to drink to excess. Yet the slightest encouragement stimulated him to the wildest exhilaration, when he would laugh, shout, dance and shriek in a manner which excited the greatest indignation on the part of the landlady, and the liveliest delight on that of her boarders. Once, he was induced by general solicitation to indulge in opium—the drug being stoutly maintained as inherently congenial to the celestial stomach, but the effect proved so startling as to render a repetition undesirable. *Ching*—so he was called, after making many diabolical grimaces while chewing, sunk into a sort of muzzy stupor, to presently awake in a state of frantic excitement, when he screeched like a vulture being plucked alive, and asserted that his head was growing so big that the room wouldn't contain it! Nor until he was half-drowned under the tap in the back-kitchen, did he master the delusion.

Our stay in the Establishment scarcely exceeded five weeks. It was brought to a close in consequence of our meeting the landlady's second son attired in our best coat and pants, at the High Bridge, Harlem,[5] on a Saturday afternoon. We had long felt dubious as to our shirts being our own exclusive property—and this little incident decided us.

CHAPTER XXVI

The Boarding-House in Which Englishmen Predominate

ENGLISHMEN—being constitutional grumblers (which we consider a respectable quality, inasmuch as it indicates dissatisfaction with every thing *that may be made better*), are prone to indulge in this national characteristic to considerable extent when necessitated to become inmates of Boarding-Houses. The system militates against their inherent exclusiveness, inducing involuntary apprehensions that they may be brought into contact with persons whom they won't be able to get along with, and—what is worse—who will be slow in admitting their inevitable inferiority. (For every Briton, whether consciously or not, has a thorough conviction that he is the natural superior of every body.) Wherefore they not infrequently endeavor to dispense with these substitutes for homes, preferring a lodging at an English tavern or a furnished room elsewhere. But speedily discovering that living at restaurants with any degree of gastronomic satisfaction, is not to be done at a lesser expense than would suffice to procure a greater average of decency and comfort at that Yankee institution—a Boarding-House—they presently yield to necessity. We have, however, encountered Britons of lively and inquisitive temperament, who rushed into Boarding-House life with ardor, as to an experience proffering them opportunities of deep insight into the various peculiarities of social life on this side of the Atlantic. Probably they formed a high estimate of American character in consequence.

The first care of the Englishman whose necessities or inclinations impel him to this mode of existence, is to discover an Establishment which combines the advantages of satisfactory diet, economic charges, and distance from the scene of his daily labors. He is desirous of this hardly-to-be-expected combination of excellencies for three reasons. Firstly, he has a truly English regard for good living. Secondly, he (we, with our usual good nature, select a respectable type of the species), is at once prudent and proud of his pecuniary integrity. Lastly, he loves exercise, and exults in a rapid walk down-town, where he "chaffs" fellow employees on their effeminacy in using omnibuses. As might be expected, these lofty requisitions have to undergo considerable modifications ere he fixes upon a Boarding-House which, he thinks, will do.

It—we, as usual, draw upon personal experience—is situate on the eastern side of the city, some distance up the "Broadway" of that quarter. A plain, four-story, red brick house, with green blinds, and shaded by ailanthus trees. The landlady's worser half (she is English by birth) kept, during life, a London coffee-house, and emigrating to this country some fifteen years ago, died in consequence of an injudicious attempt to vote the Whig ticket in an Irish ward.[1] Upon which, after a decent interval, she married her present husband, who is a New Yorker, and became known to her in his capacity of physician to his predecessor. It was, perhaps, in order to relieve his wife of any unpleasant reminiscences in connection with this circumstance, that, immediately on effecting matrimony, he relinquished practice, being generously content to rely upon his wife's exertions for a livelihood.

She is a light-haired, round-faced woman, still good-looking, very industrious, and eminently cockneyish in opinions, behavior, and pronunciation. She has no living children, her only relative in the United States being the mother of her former husband, between whom and the present a strong antagonism exists. We verily believe that the old lady—who boards in the house, insisting on paying up, regularly, every Saturday night—only remains in this country (towards which she professes the greatest contempt and aversion) in order to "serve out"—as she would phrase it—the successor of her son. Which fell purpose she follows up with that sleepless animosity and implacable malignity of which only old ladies are capable. The cause of offense would appear to lie in the fact of the marriage, and her low estimate of the character of Mr. —. He is, she says, "a regular bad 'un," and "not worth his salt." In the latter of which opinions we perfectly coincide.

Mr. —, indeed, confines his business operations to playing at billiards, attendance at pugilistic encounters, trotting-matches, rowdy political clubs, rat-hunts, and badger-drawings.[2] To the furtherance of these amiable pursuits, he is accustomed to extract loans from the boarders, under the pretext of temporary pecuniary embarrassment on the part of the Establishment—generally telling them they can "take it out" in food and lodging. His success, however, is but infrequent, as the old lady always forewarns new comers of this peculiarity, accompanying the intelligence with an emphatic *veto* on the behalf of her daughter-in-law. Mr. — strongly objects to this, as calculated to degrade him in the eyes of the boarders, and it is said that his outraged delicacy once prompted him to an attempt at throwing the old lady out of window. But she, defying him and arming herself with a fire-shovel, until Mrs. —, who, though a quiet woman, is by no means afraid of her husband, came to the rescue, it was, happily, not carried into effect.

The average number of boarders might be from twelve to fifteen, of whom, perhaps, two thirds were English born; the remainder (with one solitary exception) being Americans. We will give the Britons the precedence in description—first, however, devoting a few brief lines to the prevailing domestic economy, as differing from other Boarding-Houses.

Englishmen carry their own customs everywhere. They drink pale ale in the Sandwich Islands,[3] and would willingly devour imperfectly-cooked beefsteaks in Jerusalem—if they could get 'em. Hence, though fifteen years' residence in the United States had modified some of our landlady's culinary Anglicisms, others remained in full insular perfection.

For breakfast she supplied soft-boiled eggs, bacon, herrings, and strong black tea—seldom coffee, and never steak. For dinner, alternate joints of boiled or roast—literally *roast* and not *baked*, as Mrs. — at first, with pride, informed us, though we fear the comparatively smaller trouble of the inferior process subsequently induced her to adopt it—and puddings. Pies appeared but rarely, being then of massive construction, thickly crusted, and embedded in big earthen *sarcophagi*, every way unlike the thin, circular comestibles familiar to American tables.[4] Tea—as the final meal was generally designated—proffered a frugal display of dried toast, stacks of bread and butter piled like planks in a lumber-yard, occasional shrimps or watercresses, and no preserves. Our landlady's former London coffee-house experience was a little evident in these arrangements.

To such fare, then—served in cleanly manner, if in no great style—did the boarders assemble, Mrs. —, her mother-in-law, or one of the guests presiding. This latter was a character. A little, bald, dimple-faced Briton, he had but recently arrived, thus finally carrying out an inclination which seemed to have haunted him from his earliest youth—he was then upwards of sixty. We should suppose, from his own representations, that his enthusiastic admiration of the United States had instigated some hundreds of his countrymen to precede him. "There was no kings," he had said, "in Amerikey, and no taxes, so hevery-think" (he was a Londoner) "*must* be hall right." A dread of crossing the *h*ocean—how conquered we are uninformed—seemed to have hitherto deterred him from emigration. He was sick during the entire passage, and brought with him upwards of seventeen coats, under the impression that he should find it difficult to supply himself with attire in a new country. His intended destination appeared to be Iowa, where he had a son and daughter, but the heat and mosquitoes (he was bitten till his face resembled something between a cullender and a gravel-pit[5])—not to mention a narrow escape from being knocked down and run over by a fire-engine—had effected such a change in his opinion of American institutions that he was not unlikely to return. Pending the settlement of this question, and the recovery of his baggage, which had been forwarded to Cincinnati by some ingenious bungling on his own part, he put up at our Boarding-House. Having known the landlady in the old country, and, indeed, abetted her exodus to the new, he was on a friendly footing in the family, allowed to carve at table, and very much joked by the boarders on the subject of a presumed passion for the old lady.

Foremost among these jokers, and the moral antipodes of their object, was a loud-voiced gentleman of five-and-thirty, diurnally engaged in the wholesale provisions trade. He, during fifteen years' experience of American life, had found nothing whatever worthy of British admiration. Over the breakfast, or tea-table (for, happily, he didn't appear at dinner), he would, on the slightest encouragement, launch out into a flood of deprecation of the "Benighted States"—such being his invariable appellation for the country honored by his residence. Militia companies, the non-universal preference of beer as a national drink, New York firemen, policemen, and newspapers generally, Target Excursions, oysters,* and Collins' steamers,[6] were the objects of his especial derision. On the latter subject he might be considered a monomaniac. We remember his nearly getting into a fight with one of the American boarders in consequence of something very like an exultation about the fate of the *Arctic*.[7] He invariably wore straps to his pantaloons, an "all-rounder" collar,[8] square-toed boots, and a narrow-brimmed hat. He revered Mrs. Trollope, and was a subscriber to the *European*,[9] which extraordinary journal† may be considered an attempt to establish a permanent weekly *raw* upon the sacred person of the American Eagle. You could always provoke his liveliest indignation by commending the *Sun* newspaper. As a fellow-boarder, he was an unmitigated nuisance.

Not more so, however, than another, a little, low Londoner, whose ignoble face was fringed with sandy whiskers, who considered the *ne plus ultra* of existence to be in connection with the *Coal 'Ole, Evans*,' and cockney *casinos*,[10] who boasted acquaintance with third-rate London actors, and was popularly supposed to obtain a subsistence by acting as "agent" in selling drilling-machines, the patentee of which he subsequently swindled to a considerable extent. He had no control over himself with respect to beer and bad puns, and would bore you, by the hour, with stories of 'Arry Widdicombe,[11] and similar notables with whom he professed intimacy, and had, probably, seen once or twice—from the galleries of theaters. When possessed of money he generally got drearily drunk in English taverns, and came home very loud and disputatious. There were traditions afloat that a little autographic mistake—the substitution of another person's name for his own—had necessitated his expatriation; as, also, that the one at present assumed by him was fictitious. Mrs. —'s mother-in-law regarded him with a degree of animosity only second to that she felt for the "master of the house"—

*It may be worthy of remark that newly-arrived Britons invariably denounce American oysters, while United States citizens declare that English bivalves taste like bad half-pence. Can there be a difference of construction in the national palates? Or is it possible that *both nations* are prejudiced?

†Now—alas!—defunct.

or Americans generally. He was deeply in arrears for board, and had experienced expulsions from other tenements for that reason.

The British lion found better representatives in other boarders. One, a tall, manly-looking Yorkshireman, blunt in speech, but possessing sterling sense and education, was a good type of the class so well portrayed in Mrs. Gaskell's *North and South*.[12] He had quitted Manchester life for twelve months in Canada, but finding farm labor unsuited to him, sought New York, and was now thriving apace as a cotton-broker. "The old country," he said, "though the comfortablest in the world—*if you had money*—was rather crowded."

In which opinion a youth of nineteen, who sported a glazed cap, a suit of dark, sailor-like blue, and a perpetual cigar, coincided. He had just returned, *viâ* California, from Australian diggings, where he had sold revolvers, and engaged in riots against the authorities. At present he fluctuated between two projects, going to Kansas or joining Walker. We shouldn't be at all surprised at hearing of his heading a *filibuster* republic some day.[13]

We have to regret that the English Boarding-House afforded us but few lady-portraits, and those of no very prominent characteristics. A bashful young lady who colored up if you looked at her, and was distressingly disconcerted when you passed the salt at dinner; her mother, whom we always suspected of being the original of Punch's "Unprotected Female"[14]—she had such a painful facility of getting into scrapes—these were rather outlines than strongly-defined individualities. Yet one peculiarity of the last-mentioned lady deserves chronicling. She invariably asked every healthy-looking individual whether he didn't come from the old country, and received negative answers with evident surprise and incredulity.

The rest of the English boarders were only remarkable for having arrived in this country in a state of extreme ignorance with respect to its institutions, manners, and customs. Some—not all—knew as little of the United States as a Polar Bear does of playing the Banjo. Their general impressions appeared to have been, that each citizen of this republic passed his time in chewing tobacco and expectorating while seated in a rocking-chair, wore short pantaloons, thick boots, a straw hat, and a bowie-knife, conversed in the style of Halliburton's Clock-maker,[15] and maintained a negro for the purpose of daily flagellation—as a pleasurable mode of excitement. Which ideas—though rapidly ignored by their owners—afforded considerable entertainment to the American portion of the boarders.

They agreed pretty well, in general, though sometimes a strong remark of uncomplimentary nature towards Mr. Bull would lead to a conversational skirmish,[16] in which nationality ran high on either side. The Britons came out very strong—as they would have called it—when war was talked of in connection with the Crampton difficulty;[17] receiving the ironical suggestions of the Americans—about getting naturalized forthwith, or journeying certain miles into the interior—with great indignation. The hidea of a Hinglishman turning his back on his country! Didn't you wish you might get it? Eh?

We have alluded to the existence of a solitary boarder appertaining neither to Old England or Young America. This was an Irishman, and however Yankees or Britons might antagonize, it was at once whimsical and edifying to remark how they united in one common sentiment of dislike to the Celt. There were personal reasons for his unpopularity. He was an ugly man with no perceptible eyes, and a face like an imperfectly shaved ape. He seldom washed himself, and smelt of horse-medicines in which he dealt. Every body was at feud with him, especially the young Australianized-Briton, who extemporized an imitation brogue in his presence; and finally drove him from the house by the persistent utterance of the mysterious sentence, "*Smug him for a Guy!*" This he repeated in measured accents when alone in his victim's company. After enduring it for some time—rendered the more annoying in consequence of his utter ignorance as to the meaning*—the martyred Celt left, previously forgetting to settle for his board.

We had occasion to imitate the former proceeding shortly afterwards.

* The tormentor subsequently informed us that the phrase was plagiarized from the street boys of London, who thus suggest the propriety of stealing (or *smugging*), any person of peculiar ugliness on the Fifth of November, as a substitute for the effigy of that eminent practical Roman Catholic, Guy Fawkes.[18]

CHAPTER XXVII

The "Pension Française"

FRENCHMEN, and especially Parisians, possess but little of that desire for domestic privacy characterizing Englishmen and Germans. They are an out-o'-door population, the streets, shops, *cafés*, theaters, and places of public promenade being necessary component parts of their existence, and *home* only represented by a furnished chamber in which to pass the night. Bachelor life in the French capital is almost exclusively of this order, and any one who has resided in that most attractive and mercurial of cities will at once call to mind how common a spectacle is that of a whole family—father, mother, and children—dining at a public restaurant, not once, but as a general custom. We should fancy it about as well calculated to develop home-virtues and domestic felicity as our Boarding-House and hotel-system—but that by the way. Eminently social as the Frenchman is, he prefers taking his meals in places of public resort, and as, in Paris, he can get them at every possible scale of prices, generally does so. And if this *is* discontinued on his getting married, he then aspires rather to an *Establishment* than a home. *Home*, and the love of it, appear to be peculiarly Saxon institutions.

When, therefore, a Frenchman expatriates himself—which he never does willingly, as he firmly believes with that most exquisite of cockneys, M. Beauvallet,[1] that there is not, never was, or will be, any thing equal to Paris—he naturally endeavors to resume, as nearly as circumstances will permit, his abnormal mode of life. But though New York has its restaurants, they do not afford as many courses at as low a price as those of the *Palais Royal*,[2] nor proffer to their guests the inclusive privileges of bread *à discretion* and a bottle of *vin ordinaire*.[3] There are a score of places where he can get a perfectly Parisian dinner—but at a cost which, if he be poor, as is commonly the case (for he wouldn't be in the United States were he rich), makes him shrug his shoulders and *sacré* with true Gallic energy.[4] For a very little money goes a great way in Paris, and people retire from business on a sum which a Broadway store-keeper would think moderate if paid but for one year's rent. Rent too, even for a single room, is an important item in the expenses of our Frenchman. Like the Englishman spoken of in our last Chapter, he finds that he can board for an extra dollar or so over the cost of his lodging. So he goes into Boarding-House life accordingly.

Not, at first, into our *Pension Française*. He is painfully conscious of his ignorance of the language, and desirous of acquiring it, for which purpose he has procured a phrase book, a French and English dictionary and a copy of *The Vicar of Wakefield*[5]—which work appears to occupy the same position with respect to neophytes in our tongue that *Gil Blas* and *Telemaque* do to beginners in French.[6] With the same praiseworthy object he becomes an inmate of an American Boarding-House. But he doesn't get along very well. The Irish servants avail themselves of his helplessness to neglect him, or to bring him what he doesn't want, at dinner, the landlady is embarrassed by his gesticulations and evident misery, the boarders aggravate him with broken English (thinking he'll take to it more kindly when mispronounced), and he's not allowed to smoke all over the house and in bed. Which combination of inflictions, finally drives him into a *Pension Française*.

The particular one we select as a type of the class, is in a street leading eastwards from Broadway, not many blocks above Stewart's store.[7] Three or four signs ornament its exterior, and an ever-present and powerful odor of cookery—in which garlic predominates—hovers about the portal. Ascending the steps and pushing back the unfastened door, you pass from the hall into the front parlor, where two or three men with hair cropped *à la* States prison, the bushiest of beards, and the most stiffly-waxed of moustaches, play dominoes and smoke cigarettes all day long. If you're a stranger to the place, Madame or her husband will shortly appear.

She is a brisk little woman of forty, with a voluble face, and a profusion of minute, barrel-shaped curls, projecting on either side of her head from beneath a very gauzy cap of original construction. Ordinarily, in the morning, she is loose-waisted, short-skirted, and wears an apron—retaining, indeed, the latter peculiarity all day. Educated in France, though born in Louisiana, she has traveled considerably and visited most European capitals. You will find, on conversing with her, that she understands three languages, and possesses a knowledge of French literature sufficient to set up any Fifth Avenue belle as an immense authority. We regret to add that she doesn't like Americans—making, however, an exception in favor of Southerners. "They," says she, "are gentlemen."

Monsieur — is a little, good-humored man, with a thick moustache, which looks as if recently inked, the hair being black but unlustrous, and inclining to gray at the roots. He is as polite and active a man as exists in New York, we are sure. No boarder, though of never so ancient standing, recollects rising before he, M. —, had made his appearance, and come home at what unholy hour you will, there is M. —, poring, by the light of a shaded lamp, over a great book, to the pages of which, from time to time, he confided mysterious entries. By birth we believe him to be a Swiss, by adoption an American, in age, somewhere about fifty.

The house is a spacious and not very cleanly one, divided into many apartments, partitions having still further economized its original dimensions. We should say there were about twenty rooms, generally comprising their full complement of boarders. Three quarters of these are single men, employed as working-jewelers, lithographers, engravers on metal, etc., crafts where some degree of taste and delicacy of hand is necessary. At least half of their number have been influenced by political opinions in seeking this country, and the ones as yet unspoken of are escaped exiles from Cayenne.[8]

To Americans and Englishmen the word *banishment* has but an indefinite sound, as rather appertaining to fiction, or the politics of other nations, than at all likely to be brought within the range of their own personal experience. We know little of the sad reality, and though it exists within our midst, are not very curious about it. Yet, however cosmopolitan the world is growing, few there are who have eaten the bitter bread of exile without feeling the truth of Danton's saying,[9] that "a man does not carry his country at the sole of his shoe." Our Frenchmen have sorrowful knowledge of this.

To be cut off from all dear and familiar associations—to find yourself a stranger and an alien in a distant land—to have the acrid element of politics mingling in the current of your life, and tainting all its pleasanter influences—to rage impotently at the ban that lies betwixt you and home—to know the heart-sickness bred of hope deferred—this, and how much more of misery in slow and wearisome detail, is Exile. There need scarcely be superadded to it, as is but too frequent—Poverty.

Our banished men are of little note, and we will not pause to inquire whether they fought at the barricades against the drunken and murderous soldiery of Napoleon *le Petit*,[10] in his bloody *coup de etat*, whether they simply cried *Vive la Republique*, or whether they were but suspected of wishing success to either fighters or criers. They were condemned to Cayenne for some, or for no cause. Heroes like the big or little Bonaparte can not be expected to be particular as to whose hearts and lives they tread upon in their strides to a throne—as the Reverend Abbott will tell us.[11] But if you want to learn how Frenchmen can curse, just mention the name of the present ruler of their native country.

The domestic economy of our *Pension Française* is of a hybrid character, partaking equally of American and French peculiarities. For instance, the first meal of the day is decidedly a New York breakfast, consisting of steak and coffee—rather than a Parisian *dejeuner*[12]—which would come off three hours later, and might comprise pretty nearly every thing, inclusive of fowls, cock's-combs, truffles, cray-fish, lumps of sugar, salad, *vin ordinaire*, rum, and radishes. But the *diner*, which is served at 6 P.M. (no public meal occurring in the interim), is certainly French. It commences with very greasy soup, contains courses of fish, flesh, and fowl—the former in various disguises, and the latter so bony of construction and gambogian in hue as to excite a suspicion that they must have died of starvation and yellow-fever combined[13]—and concludes with *cafè au naturel*, and, occasionally, brandy. (Frenchmen, by the way, generally contrive to ruin their digestions quite as effectually, and almost as rapidly, as Americans.)

These gastronomic performances take place in the rear parlor, a spacious room, looking into an angular court-yard, and a distracting confusion of trees, sheds and buildings. Maps and lithographic portraits ornament the walls, and over the closed-up fire-place are seven pictures, starting, as appears on either side, from the same level, and each hopping centrally until the odd one has triumphantly surmounted the clock, which is large, and has its internal arrangements mysteriously sunk in the flaccid room-papering. There is, too, a big screen, stuck all over with caricatures, scissored from *le Charivari*, or *Journal Pour Rire*,[14] and some older ones of Napoleon the Third, before his assumption of that title. And wherever his evil face and thick moustache appears, be sure a halo of penciled epithets—as *scélérat*, *polisson*, *monster*, *coquin*, *liberticide*[15]—surrounds it. A sketch of the Count Goggleowski,[16] as he appears on Broadway—from the *N. Y. Picayune*[17]—is also here. Some of the exiles—especially one or two of Polish origin—are particularly "down on" the Count, why, we know not.

We suspect that Monsieur and Madame share this room, nocturnally, with a fat and formidable old lady, claiming to be Monsieur's mother. We further suspect a big sofa—underneath which one's legs won't go, in consequence of the space being filled with beams and sacking—of affording her the means of repose. She is—we say it with all respect—an awful old lady. She takes snuff in large quantities, is fearfully polite, ravenous after victuals, and always looking sharp after the boarders' payments. We incline to the belief that both Monsieur and Madame sympathize with this feeling, to some extent, good-humored as they appear. French people, after a certain age, often become avaricious. The passion develops itself, not in the American manner—scheming and speculative daring—but rather in parsimony—the shrewdest, tightest-griping, meanest, but most courteous close-fistedness.

Our old lady came to the United States twenty years ago, under a wild idea of realizing an immense fortune by means of a certain invention (either blacking, varnish, or pills), and retiring to Paris on it. She has resented her failure ever since, and will "fix" you, as a purchaser of the aforesaid blacking, varnish, or pills, on the slightest encouragement. She does the marketing, sells cigars and *liqueurs*, smells of onions, and is supposed to have a great deal of money hid away somewhere in an old stocking. She distrusts all bank notes, and invariably converts them into specie as soon as possible. It is advisable, in case of your offering her that accommodation, to scrutinize the bills she gives you rather minutely.

Of the boarders we have not much to say. They are, with the occasional exceptions of the exiles, cheerful fellows, possessing that *gaiete de coeur* common to all Frenchmen when there's nothing to depress them—in which case they assume an aspect of intense misery only conceivable in wet cats and their countrymen. All have that surface politeness which the self-will of the American and the self-esteem of the Briton ignore—and which has been so felicitously compared by Punch to an air-cushion, inasmuch as "there's nothing in it, but it eases jolts wonderfully." Chief and jolliest among them is a fat, cross-eyed lithographic-printer, who smokes a short clay pipe, sings Beranger's songs,[18] and gets very sentimental on the subject of his mistress when he's drunk—which invariably occurs on the evening upon which he receives his weekly wages. He carries her portrait (somewhere in the immediate vicinity of a red flannel shirt), and tells you how the original was desolated at parting. Notwithstanding which he makes love to every available female, including Madame and the Irish servant-girl. So ardent, indeed, have been his addresses in the latter quarter that on more than one occasion the Celtic virgin has found it necessary to shriek for assistance. Upon which Madame calls him *un diable* and *mauvais sujet*,[19] and insists on his apologizing, which he does volubly in his native language. Once, in consequence of the death of a relative, he inherited a legacy of three hundred dollars. On fingering the money he immediately abandoned work and went on a fortnight's "bust," returning at the expiration of that time without a cent, and with *delirium tremens*.[20] And though Monsieur and Madame have a sharp eye for the main chance, they nursed him very tenderly until he got well, subsequently tolerating a very irregular payment of arrears.

Perhaps it is as well that we should not go into any very minute detail of the furnishings of the upper apartments—or the want of them. It may be, as Madame can't expect the Irish girl to wax and polish her floors after the French fashion, she objects to the use of soap and water—which we're somewhat inclined to consider a national characteristic. The degrees of comparative dirtiness might be thus stated: Frenchman, dirty; German, dirtier; Irishman, dirtiest. There's scarcely a European nation but could bear some improvement on the score of cleanliness.

With which complimentary remark we quit our "*Pension Française*."

CHAPTER XXVIII

The German "Gasthaus"

Your German is not, in general, a Boarding-House animal. He prefers renting a single room for two-fold reasons—firstly, from motives of economy. (As he can subsist, exclusively, on *sour-krout*, tobacco, and *lager-bier*, he finds the practice of this virtue comparatively easy.) In the second place, he invariably plays upon some musical instrument—usually a noisy one—which practice landladies of Boarding-Houses ordinarily object to. Therefore if obliged to make a contract for the supply of his daily necessities, he does it, as it were, under protest, and only temporarily. Yet there are German Boarding-Houses, and were many more before the conversion of Castle Garden to its present purpose.[1] We select one as a sample of the class. As few besides *poor* Germans board—prosperous ones soon finding a home of their own—it will, of course, be an humble Establishment. By far the greater proportion of the needy, too, contrive to lodge, singly, or in twos and threes, with some fellow-countryman. Premising, then, that our Chapter claims to depict only the lower (though not the *lowest* aspect) of Teuton life in this city, we proceed.

Every body knows Greenwich-street—for which excellent reason we shall not inflict a description of it upon the reader. It is there—as, where else should it be—that our German *Gasthaus* is located. An old-fashioned building, the by-gone respectability of which is not entirely effaced by its decayed fortunes and the accumulated neglect and dirt of three quarters of a century—such a one, indeed, as Diedrich Knickerbocker might, in his school-boy days, have known as a stylish and newly-erected mansion.[2] Its front is now so weather-stained and grimy that the original bright red brick-work is invisible, its roof is broken and leaky, its parlor converted into a *lager-bier* saloon. Between the windows of the lower story are various signs notifying this fact to the German public, which inscriptions, together with long lists of the names of Western cities (our *Gasthaus* has a "forwarding agency" for the sale of railroad tickets), are all in that mediaeval type which, in our eyes, renders a German newspaper an anachronism, and make us feel cotemporaneous with Faust and Guttemburg.[3] The three or four rickety wooden steps of the stoop are generally occupied by as many children—little, tow-headed, blue-eyed, coarse-featured urchins, as Teutonic in appearance as though they had just stepped out of the pages of the *Fliegende Blätter*.[4] Entering the "saloon," you observe a plain bar-counter fitted up with bottles, etc., sundry barrels of *lager-bier*, a cheap Yankee clock, and some coarsely-executed lithographs—mostly on revolutionary German subjects, as the execution of Blüm,[5] barricade scenes, and the like. Near the windows there will probably be a group or two of short, and very hairy men, talking over little tables and *lager* in the most guttural of accents. But the landlord claims our attention.

He is a stout, middle-sized man, with a broad, good-looking face, light, curly hair, short beard, and shaven upper lip, always in his shirt-sleeves, and seldom out of temper. Most in-comers—for whom he always has a word of greeting and a remark on the subject of the "vedder," address him by the abbreviation of some Christian name—Hans, Gus, or Franz, as they please—he answers to each indifferently. He is also a member of a German militia company, and looks very portly and martial on parades and target excursions. Generally, he is popular with his customers, in spite of a sharp eye towards dollars and dimes—and especially so with the ladies. But not more so than his wife is with the gentlemen.

She is equally bulky in appearance, but dark-haired, and very talkative—so much so that conversation with her rapidly glides into a monologue, in which you play the part of listener, and, if unfamiliar with the German accent, a helplessly-confused one. Ordinarily she dresses in black (perhaps in memory of two former husbands), with large carpet slippers; and sits in her chair in a rather masculine position. As industrious and pains-taking as her husband, she is a jolly, hearty woman, with a proportionably large appetite, a laugh and joke for male boarders, and a ten-widow power of tongue. Give it scope, she will tell you stories of German student life, or repeat whole poems of Schiller, Goethe, or Uhland,[6] with the same zest that she displays for the sausage of her native country; nor does she appear conscious of incongruity while discussing both at the same time.

Herr — and his wife have been engaged in their present business for upwards of fifteen years, and are supposed to have made money enough to retire on a farm, did they so choose. But if Germans can be content on little, they are tenacious of *certain* profit—so, though times are harder of late years, our landlady and her husband still keep a *Gasthaus*.

It may accommodate upwards of twenty boarders, the average number being, probably, less. There are very few married couples among them, and two thirds consist of newly arrived immigrants, who intend remaining in the city, but will, on the first eligible opportunity, find private lodgings. Meantime it is our business to photograph them.

Were one to drop in at our *Gasthaus* between the hours of 12 and 1 P.M., and to pass behind the screen which partially conceals the interior of the back-room, the Establishment would be visible under its most Germanic of aspects. Dinner is then in progress. Two tables are spread at either side of the room, at which the boarders assemble, sitting very close together, for other guests contract for their mid-day meal, and, sometimes, chance customers are present. The room is full of persons, noise, and culinary odors of the most powerful description. Evidently the Teutonic stomach is no squeamish one, as the viands provided testify. Huge dishes of baked pork swimming in grease, rank cow-beef, half-warm *sour krout* (the nastiest edible, we think, claiming that name), dishes of prunes and dried apples, and soup apparently derived from cabbages, stale beer, and moldy beans, constitute the fare provided. And judging from the rapid manner in which every thing disappears down the throats of the company, the meal is very much to its liking.

The newly arrived immigrants, fresh—or rather *stale*—from five weeks' experience of salt-water and steerage life, are the most active of trenchermen. Many of them still wear the queerly-fashioned habiliments which served them on the voyage, and a more motley and picturesque group it would be difficult to imagine. Long green-baize coats, with curious red worsted embroidery illustrating their capes and pockets; scanty coats of strange colors, and fitting so tightly that you involuntarily fancy their owners have grown into them and couldn't take them off if they tried; pantaloons like collapsed balloons, or the skins of mammoth sausages; brightly braided and long peaked caps; ugly-shaped and shapeless hats; shoes looking as though the feet wearing them had been dipped in ink and permitted to dry; list slippers, leather slippers, gorgeously-beaded slippers, and compressive, knobby, corn-suggesting boots—all these are here, and much more than we can depict or describe.

Among the wearers are grim, wiry-haired, bristly-bearded old men; stumpy, harsh-speaking young ones, with moustaches so stiff and prickly in appearance that you fancy they might draw blood if heedlessly touched; women who in their youth could never have looked pleasant or feminine, and who now have faces as hard as those drawn by Albert Dürer,[7] and as wrinkled "as a wet cloak ill-laid up"; young and buxom *frauleins*, and unlimited children. These last have to wait until their seniors' appetites are satisfied, which ordinance they submit to with some impatience, making rushes at each chair as the sitter vacates it.

Directly any individual has "got through" with his dinner, he commences smoking, with or without the accompaniment of *lager-bier*. (Indeed the fragrance of the herb Nicotina is omnipresent on the premises.) Pipes by far outnumber cigars, and you might venture a guess, with a tolerable certainty of its proving correct, that the smokers of the latter are those who have been longest in this country. And the concourse thinning rapidly, very soon only some few old men, women, and children remain, if in summer, to sun themselves at the open windows of the bar-room, if in winter, to draw closer to the red hot stove.

At early morning and evening the same scene, with some modifications, is repeated. But the two rooms, both front and rear, present an especially lively spectacle on Saturday nights, for then, after supper, the boarders give themselves up to unrestrained enjoyment. If there are no professional musicians among them (a very wild supposition, by-the-by), in all probability every man, woman, and child performs on some favorite musical instrument—so there's no lack of harmony. Generally, too, one street-organ relieves another, outside. Hence the amount of cotillions, waltzes, polkas, schottisches, marches, gallopes, mazourkas performed, might astonish any body but a German. They sing, too, of Fatherland, and the Rhine, of Wine, and Beer, and Maidens, and swill immeasurable *lager* in honor of that quintette of agreeable institutions. They exult in remarkable choruses, two favorite ones being that of the "leathery" *Burschen* ditty translated in Longfellow's *Hyperion*,[8] and a mysterious refrain attached to a song immortalizing the achievements of a certain Doctor Eisembach, which appears to run thus:

"Swiddy, widdy, wim, *pum*, PUM."

—each word increasing in vehemence upon repetition. Occasionally, too, they indulge in that harmonic bacchanalization known to the initiated as a *Salamander*—which consists, to the best of our recollection, of the following performance: Rising alternately, each individual elevates his *lager*, sings a little, and drinks a little; on *repetition* emptying his glass and turning it upside down in proof of having done so. Upon which every body thumps on the table, stamps with his feet, drums with his fists, makes as much noise as is possible, and otherwise keeps time, laughing and shouting uproariously. Above and around all these proceedings a dense and ever-prevailing fog of tobacco-smoke hovers, shrouding the company as completely, as, on a certain Homeric occasion, the clouds did Jupiter and Juno on Mount Ida.[9]

The house closes regularly at 12. We shall not follow our friends into their dormitories, which are uninviting enough, preferring to devote the remainder of our Chapter to a few additional particulars of the Germans generally.

Sunday—in the United States and England the dullest, most stupid, and often the most irrationally passed day in the week; either a stolid resting-place from a routine of utilitarianism and money-getting, or an irksomely-endured interval of puritanic privation from all pleasures, however harmless—is a great day with the Germans. In summer they invade Hoboken and Staten Island in innumerable holiday groups, or crowd the decks of the little steamers that ply on the broad bosom of the beautiful Hudson, to Bull's Ferry, Fort Lee, and the like easy distances.[10] These are economic enjoyments, as they mostly take their edibles—and often drinkables—with them. The only excesses committed are in dancing and *lager*—and, as every body knows, *lager* is a beverage that does not intoxicate. Returning at eventide they throng the musical taverns, the *Volks' Gartens*,[11] the

Germanic precincts of the Bowery,[12] where music, tobacco, and *lager*—necessary component parts of Teutonic existence—are to be had in their full perfection.

Altogether they are a hard-working, honest, good-humored *solid* race—the best raw material which Europe sends hither to be ground into American citizens.

CHAPTER XXIX

The Irish Immigrant Boarding-House (As It Was)

The charge of a perverse conservatism of character which renders its possessors very slow in doing away with open and acknowledged evils is often brought, and with some show of justice, by Americans, against Englishmen. Yet if the conduct of New Yorkers may be taken as a sample of national feeling, we are equally liable to the same reproach. Abuses worthy of the rottenest despotism that ever produced barricades in the streets of a European city have flourished (and do yet flourish) in gloriously diabolic vigor in our metropolis; every body knowing of, but few caring to do aught but contemn their existence.

But the legalized villainy that grew rich by transforming the raw material of self-helpful labor that reached our shores into paupers and criminals, has succumbed—at last. So far we may plume ourselves. Yet how many inhabitants of Blackwell's Island,[1] tenants of States Prisons, and miserable street-outcasts, owe their degradation to that most iniquitous system?

The profession of Immigrant Boarding-House Keeper is not, however, entirely extinct, though shorn of its more odious features, and every way possessing less opportunities of preying upon the stranger. Ignorant as Irishmen may be, they are scarcely blockheads enough to walk from the admirably-conducted *dépôt* at Castle Garden to such a sty as we shall presently describe. Those who have Western destinations—the majority—are at once forwarded thither by the most expeditious and economical routes. Those who, unwisely, prefer remaining in New York, generally find private lodgings. Some few improvident single men may fall a prey to the sharks whose rapacity was formerly so fully glutted, but for the most part they may be compared to the ogre-giant in *Pilgrim's Progress*,[2] who sits at his cave's mouth grinning and biting his nails in impotent spleen, because he can not come at his former victims.

We have, therefore, appended a retrospective qualification to the present Chapter's title. Our book would be incomplete without a type of a class of

Boarding-Houses formerly so numerous. Without further prelude we proceed to depict one.

A plain, brick edifice, in one of the river-side streets of the lower portion of the city; its ground floor fitted up as a low groggery, its proprietor's name (which is as Celtic as his countenance) and calling displayed in attenuated yellow letters on a black board over the doorway. On pushing your way through the crowd of immigrants, "runners," carmen, "dock-loafers," and blackguards generally,[3] which constantly overflowed from the bar-room into the street, you observed that the place was furnished with some half dozen decanters, thrice that number of tumblers, a few cigar-boxes, pipes, and matches, and a saucer full of "free" tobacco—for the gratuitous use of customers. Two or three barrels of the coarsest and commonest description of spirit distilled from Indian corn, and colored to represent brandy, rum, or whisky, comprised the store of liquors. Cheaply-colored lithographic portraits of Washington, O'Connell, the vitriolically-patriotic Mitchel, and President Pierce, a copy of "Emmett's Speech"[4]—all of which had apparently served as a rendezvous for several generations of flies—a Connecticut clock,[5] and a chair or two, completed the picture.

The landlord, a thick, squat, muscular fellow—he had risen to his position from that of "runner"—possessed a countenance equally indicative of cunning, rapacity, and brutality; its general expression being the more odious for the mask of *blather* and *blarney* ordinarily assumed by its owner, when desirous of giving Nature the lie in persuading you that he was a very good fellow. He had been an adopted citizen of the United States, and his tenement a "Licensed Immigrant Boarding-House" (paying ten dollars every twelve months to the city government) for some years.[6] Hence he was legally required, "under a penalty of $50, to cause to be kept conspicuously-posted" in the public rooms of his house, "in the English, German, Dutch, French, and Welsh languages, a list of the rates of prices charged for board and lodging"—which enactment he manifested as much care in obeying as did the municipal authorities in compelling him to do so.

He was unmarried, though a plump, coarse-featured young woman of half his age arrogated the position and title of his "lady"; four or five unwashed, unkempt urchins having sprung from the connection. "Mrs." — had also two brothers, who officiated as "runners" to the Establishment.

Few New Yorkers require to be told what a "runner" attached to our Immigrant Boarding-Houses is like. Their city is unfortunately prolific of the raw element of which such scoundrels are composed. Big-fisted, double-jointed "shoulder-hitters," who pride themselves on traveling through life "on their muscle"; demi-savages of civilization, and far more dangerous than the real, inasmuch as they possess greater scope for evil—whether as professed pugilists, election bullies, recruits for filibusterism, or "runners" for Immigrant Boarding-Houses, the stock is identical. And as the turning out of our citizens in considerable numbers, to do honor to the funeral of one of the class is yet within the memory of the present generation, it is to be presumed we entertain a due respect and admiration for them.

We believe that those attached to our Immigrant Boarding-House confined their operations to what might be termed the legitimate branches of their craft, as swindling, bullying, and despoiling such of their luckless countrymen as could be decoyed into the place. (There are darker accusations against the fraternity which we shall only allude to.*) Like most of their tribe, they were eminently successful.

Immediately beneath the bar, and only accessible to the landlord or his agents (one of whom officiated as bar-tender, under the designation of "steward") was "the baggage-room," a small, damp, rat-haunted cellar, always kept securely locked—ostensibly for the better preservation of the boarder's property, in reality to keep it from him, in case of default in or demur against the payment of any sum the landlord might think proper to extort—according to law. And behind the bar, in a dirty, low-roofed chamber, used as a parlor dining, and general sitting-room, at all hours of the day, and nearly all hours of the night, the boarders congregated.

Old immigrants and young, babies, boys, girls, men, women, married couples, grandfathers and grandmothers. Paddies in the caped and high-waisted frieze coats, the brimless *caubeens*, the knee-breeches, woolen stockings, and rusty *brogues* of immemorial tradition.[7] Paddies with the "hanging-bone" gait, the forelock (to be pulled in token of subjection), the low brow denoting the serf of fifty descents, the shillelagh and inevitable *dhudeen*. Paddyesses whose arms were only less thick than their waists or speech; withered old women, who seemed to have come into the world predestinate street-vendors of apples and peanuts; children considerably dirtier and much less wholesome-looking than the bad potatoes they couldn't get enough of at home—in short every variety of those

* Such as catering for houses of ill-fame, and supplying them with victims at so much a head. German "runners" appear to be peculiarly liable to this charge.

strange birds whose necessities or whose inclinations induce them to wing their way from the parent nest across the Atlantic—were here. And perhaps it is well for us that they *do* wing their way hither, as "our Model Republic," to quote the words of one who told us many wholesome though unpalatable truths, "would find it very difficult to get along without them."

The upper portion of our Immigrant Boarding-House was divided into innumerable rooms, or rather closets, each one being filthy and noisome in the extreme, infested with all manner of vermin, and holding as many straw-mattresses, ragged quilts, and dirty blankets as sufficed for the nocturnal requirements of the boarders—eight or ten of whom, without regard to sex or age, were crowded into spaces fit only for one or two. Decency was, of course, entirely out of the question, the only object being to stow away as many sleepers as possible.

Thus lived, and sometimes died, when cholera or ship fever happened to break out among them (in which case Potter's field obtained a few tenants,[8] and the city paid expenses) the inmates of the Immigrant Boarding-House, until, under every variety of fraudulent pretext, they had been robbed of as much money and time as could be wrung from them. Exorbitant charges for board and cartage, in open defiance of municipal regulations, payments enforced by ruffianism, detention of property, and, if necessary, perjury—these were but the commonest experiences of the poor Irish immigrant, and too often those of the German and Englishman also. Finally, he was defrauded of the last few dollars in his possession by a forged railroad ticket, which deposited him at some three or four hundred miles *less* distance than he had paid over fare for. And there we leave him.

It is known that before the devotion of Castle Garden to its present excellent purpose, there were upwards of a thousand persons engaged as Immigrant Boarding-House keepers, agents, "runners," etc. Granting the improbability that among these *some* were honest, fancy the hordes of victims required to sustain such a brood of harpies!

CHAPTER XXX

The Chinese Boarding-House

FEW, if any of our readers, whose daily peregrinations have not made them familiar with the slim figures, the yellow-soap-colored complexions, the pig-eyes sloping angularly into the low, flat foreheads of such inhabitants of the Flowery Country as we have among us.[1] Behind little stalls, or holding trays containing bad cigars and cheap confectionery, they haunt our public places; or squat despondently under some authorized covert, relying on charity as stimulated by a printed or written placard, worn tabard-wise on the breast.[2] Few New Yorkers, we say, but have observed them. Yet how many of us have cast a stray thought in such direction as where do they eat, drink and sleep? and how are they lodged? We are as little interested in the matter as in the internal affairs of China itself, and know still less.

For that Celestial Empire,[3] in spite of Hue, Bayard Taylor, Ida Pfeiffer,[4] and similar enterprising and intelligent travelers, yet appears half fable-land to us. We have indistinct impressions of a large and densely populated country of impracticable conservatives, employed in the culture of tea and silk; addicted to lanterns, pagodas, opium, banqueting on puppies, birds' nests, and kittens, and to infanticide—not to mention the production of dwarf trees, elaborately-carved and utterly-useless articles in ivory, and similar branches of idiotic industry. We know they are partial to dragons, both in a pictorial and theologic sense (and shouldn't be surprised to learn that that mythologic monster yet survived in the interior); that the women have little feet, and the men shave their heads with chisels; that they try to frighten their enemies, in war, by making diabolic noises and painting hideous visages on their shields; and that they are now simultaneously engaged in a murderous revolution and a war with Great Britain,[5] wherein it is to be hoped that large numbers of them will be rapidly improved off the face of the earth—and this is about all. Charles Lamb's immortal story of the Origin of Roast Pig might be an authentic page from Chinese History for any thing we can tell.[6]

So, too, we know little of the luckless Celestials of New York, unless a stray newspaper paragraph have enlightened us. But, reader, accept our convoy, and you shall visit a Chinese Boarding-House—perhaps two.

Down Broadway—for you, of course, live up-town—as far as the City Hospital;[7] and then crossing to that sinuous thoroughfare which cork-screws its way southward to the Battery (and which we always think of in connection with those New Amsterdam cows whose meanderings,[8] as recorded in Diedrich Knickerbocker's History, originated the plan of the future city)—we proceed until in sight of that colossal edifice comprising the largest publishing establishment in the United States, if not in the world.[9] And then, turning into a mean street, in the center of which the mire and filth of three months have accumulated mound-high; where low groggeries, Sailors' Boarding-Houses, "slop-shops," and rag-and-bottle establishments line either side of the way; we will dive down a narrow alley just wide enough to admit one at a time, beside a Dutch grocery, in the rear of which is a low, timber-built tenement. A frowzy Irishwoman presiding at an adjacent apple-stall, after the usual Celtic repetition of our question, and the look of distrust (intimating that she *may* conceive it her interest to deceive us)—has assured us that "it's the Chaynee Boarding-House"—so we will enter.

Up the rickety stairs then, being careful to avoid hat-concussion by the way. The house has but two stories, and we soon stand in front of a low unpainted door, which, without waiting for Celestial permission, we open. Pah! what an atmosphere!

A horrible odor! and of a mysteriously compound character, utterly unlike any thing which has heretofore offended your nostrils. The breath of men rendered foetid and poisonous by the exclusion of ventilation, the reek of strange cookery, the vapid, bitter taste of opium, the fumes of stale tobacco, and, perhaps, other unguessable abominations, make you gasp and sicken, as though plunged into a plague pit. You have a strong inclination to break half-a-dozen panes of the hermetically closed-up windows—but repress it, take a seat and cigar, put a bit of tobacco in your mouth—any thing to change the predominant flavor—and look around you.

It is a queer sort of apartment, two of its sides being fitted up with beds arranged like berths in the steerage of an emigrant ship, one above the other, only more roughly put together. Each shelf is calculated, apparently, to hold from one to three persons. There are odd toys, fans, and incongruous-looking articles you would be puzzled to imagine the use of, on the walls, and some cheap prints. A Chinaman is cooking something at a stove in the center of the room—you wonder the fire don't go out in such an atmosphere. Six or seven others are present, and we'll now take a look at them.

Flat-faced, high-cheek-boned, squint-eyed, swarthy-hued, stunted, fragile-looking mortals, of such hideously, yet pitifully repulsive aspect, that one feels humiliated in admitting their claims to brotherhood with humanity. Miserably clad, too—mostly in loose woolen frocks, with their long plaited *queues* of coarse black hair gathered in a circle on the top of their heads. They steal sidelong glances of impotent curiosity at the strangers. One, however, is attired in European costume and speaks a little English. To him we address ourselves.

He informs us that upwards of fifteen occupy that apartment, and that he "boards" them for $3 per week, renting the floor from the keeper of the Dutch grocery below. That they are very poor, and get their livings by peddling cigars, working in wholesale tea-warehouses, or mendicancy, with occasional employment about the docks and shipping—though in the latter he adds, they are liable to be ill-used by the Irish or Germans. That they came to this country in the capacity of ships' stewards, cooks, or sailors, their average experience of it dating from one to four years. He himself has been here five, and rather prefers New York to Canton. Finally, he wishes to know whether we don't want men to load or unload a vessel.

Responding with a mild negative and extemporizing a pretext for our visit, we venture another question or so. Do they all live in that apartment? He nods, and points to the shelves and closets. It is plain that they do, using it for culinary and other purposes. Are they ever sick? Oh, yes—four of them have died in that room within that number of years, the expenses of their funerals being defrayed by contributions among themselves. They kept them during their sickness, too. Poor Chinamen!—What sort of food does he provide for his boarders? (We ask this with a glance at the culinary Celestial, and a latent suspicion that he might, on his over-night's return home, have kidnapped some lady's "sweet pet" of a lap-dog with the intention of practically testing the justice of the epithet.) But the answer is, chiefly rice, always tea, sometimes coffee, and never bread.

We express our obligations, and proceed to another and a delicate question. Are there any ladies among them? Our informant don't or *won't* understand us. But we have noticed the door of a closet at the further end of the room partially open, and a more than usually ugly Celestial countenance protruded therefrom. We take a step in that direction under the pretense of admiring a singular bird-cage—like something between a pagoda and a dog-kennel—the door closes suddenly! The Chinamen look as if they considered their domestic arrangements as none of our business, and have evidently arrived at the conclusion that we are rather ill-bred persons. We mentally acknowledge that our action has afforded them grounds for the supposition, make our adieu, and depart, in the full conviction that we have looked upon a real Celestial lady.

It is very bad liquor we shall get in the Dutch grocery, nor is the atmosphere particularly pure—but any thing after the effluvium above, is a change for the better. So while sipping at, or spilling on the saw-dusted floor, a half glass-full of fiery spirits, we endeavor to extract some information from the landlord on the subject of his lodgers. But he's sullen and incommunicative, and evidently disposed to suspect the existence of some covert object inimical to his interests. He don't know whether there are many Chinamen lodging thereabouts. Has heard so. Perhaps there's a hundred or two of 'em, altogether, living in New York—he shouldn't think there was more. Some lives in Gold-street.[10] *His* are decent, peaceably-disposed men, who never interferes with you, if you never interferes with them; and pays their rent regularly. What is their rent? Well, he don't see as he's bound to tell you. He guesses you don't want to take board there, do you? And that's all we got out of him.

We will try this bushy-whiskered, hairy-necked sailor, who, with his low-crowned, black-japanned hat perched on the very back of his head, is ventilating himself at the street corner, and both gnawing and smoking a cigar at the same time. Ay! *He* knows. He's seed the *Johnnies* goin' into that there doorway next block, 'side o' the grog shop with the name of — over it. There's a — of a lot on 'em too. We pause to inquire in the "grog-shop," and the proprietor, an unnaturally civil-spoken Irishman, volunteers to accompany us up-stairs.

Into a room of much the same aspect as the last, but this time looking into the street. Possessing, too, an equally abominable atmosphere, and tenanted by at least double the number of Chinese. Some, engaged over a pack of cards, are evidently gambling (it is scarcely noon), others cooking, and four or five eating. As brutalized in appearance, as miserably-clad and sordid-looking as their recently-visited countrymen, there is little to be seen to tempt our stay. We put a few questions to an atrociously hideous little Chinaman—who replies in a fierce, snapping manner—and incontinently take our leave, glad to breathe the air of even that foul quarter again.

The number of Chinese at present in this city has been much over-rated. It can scarcely exceed one hundred and fifty. *How* they live has been shown, and it may be worth more than a passing thought, that here, in our midst, exists a class of wretched and degraded beings, thoroughly pagan in faith, in vices, in ignorance and misery.

CHAPTER XXXI

The Sailors' Boarding-House

In that quarter of the town containing the two preceding Establishments, and within five minutes' walk of the latter, stands the tenement now claiming our notice. Like the Irish Immigrant Boarding-House, its exterior is that of a low tavern, and of equally repulsive aspect. A fancy marine title over the door, and an American flag stuck out of an upper window—as attractions for sea-faring men—indicate the purpose to which it is devoted.

The landlord claims a Portuguese origin, but his fleshy, aquiline nose, protuberant lips, and small eyes, are unmistakably Hebraical—to say nothing of the remorseless wrinkles of his evil face. He has made a voyage or two in some unknown capacity, and assumes the *bonhomie* of a sailor, denying his lineage with many oaths, if rallied thereon, and boasting that he has eaten as much salt pork, in his time, as any of his guests. His wife does not attempt to repudiate her "peoples." She is a large, oleaginous, black-haired, hook-nosed woman, who invariably wears ear-rings, and perfumes a room with the odor of fried fish. Their mutual offspring—Jews are almost as prolific as Irish—comprise something less than a dozen of dark-eyed, nasal, and turgid-lipped children, of whom the eldest, a slim youth of fifteen, assists his father in the bar-room.

The tenement resembles the Immigrant Boarding-House in internal arrangements, and, like it, is provided with a strongly-barred cellar for the storage and "safe-keeping" of lodgers' baggage. The sleeping chambers are equally ill-furnished and uncleanly. Only the bar-room and lower floor present any thing characteristic or worthy of notice. We will peep therein at night, when the peculiarities of the Establishment are visible in all their glory. We shall assume that the landlord's jackals (or "runners") have succeeded in inveigling a house-full of newly-arrived sea-men into his den, there to be fleeced at pleasure.

It is a long, low-roofed apartment, extending from front to rear, crowded with individuals, and as full of tobacco-smoke as any assemblage of *Burschen* appertaining to a German university. The chairs and benches surrounding it are filled with sailors and females, the former enjoying themselves with a zest which would appear only to be known to them and to school-boys during holidays. They hail from various points of the compass: here you may listen to the harsh guttural of the German, there see the light hair, blue eyes, and rough, frank, jovial look, characterizing the English tar; further on, note the keen, ready-witted physiognomy of the American. Perhaps the British are in the majority. Most of them appear cleanly dressed, for "Jack ashore" has a great idea of rigging himself out smartly, and if he have no money to receive at the conclusion of a voyage—which is sometimes the case—he can always "make a raise" by means of the landlord, that disinterested Israelite advancing it on the certainty of repayment out of Jack's next trip, a month's wages of which he knows he can secure before his departure. Which sum, indeed, besides every dollar possessed by his guest on debarkation, he will probably obtain; for no Guinea negro on the Slave-Coast is more completely bought and sold, or less the master of his own actions, than Jack in the hands of his crimping landlord. Such reflections, however, do not trouble our tars at present, as, clad in trim blue jackets and trousers, with black tarpaulin hats stuck, *à la* ladies' bonnets, at the very back of their heads, they abandon themselves to the pleasures of the hour. All are smoking, many laughing, and not a few telling yarns of an extent and nature demanding in the listener the gullibility of Marryat's *Pacha*.[1] And more than one "old salt" has been *doubling the Horn* with such hearty good-will as to be "half seas over."[2]

At one end of the room two fiddlers are uniting in the production of harmonic discord sufficient to drive Ole Bull frantic.[3] A third has succumbed, either to professional enthusiasm or to the amount of liquor injudiciously bestowed upon him by his admiring audience, and now lies in a corner, his countenance decorated after the style of a New Zealand chief by an artistic performance in burnt cork.[4] His two friends have, also, sympathizingly relieved him of a pocket full of copper coin; it being the custom at the conclusion of each dance to bestow voluntary contributions on the orchestra.

To this accompaniment half a dozen persons of either sex are dancing. The figure, an abnormal one, is kept up with energy worthy of the Fifth Avenue, when in full performance of the *German*. Stamping, capering, jigging to and fro, hands across and down the middle—such is the order of the night—till the sanded floor vibrates again, and the glasses on the table tinkle with sympathetic excitement. The male dancers are all sailors, their partners being coarse, fat, vulgar-looking young women whose bloated features indicate confirmed habits of drunkenness. They have very hoarse voices, wear necklaces and large brass earrings, call each other *sisters*, and affect bright red or yellow dresses. Three of them reside constantly in the house, and are important adjuncts to the landlord in one great object—pillaging his guests.

A seaman's life ashore, unless he have sense and thrift enough to seek one of the well-managed and orderly houses especially instituted for his benefit, is invariably characterized by reckless extravagance and dissipation. As a natural sequence, he is victimized every way—even more atrociously than the Immigrant *was*. Overcharges from the landlord, robberies on the part of "the ladies," money borrowed at usury, watches or clothes pawned for the means of "spreeing"—these comprise the outlines of a tar's experience among the land sharks. Finally, when despoiled of every thing, he is made over by the arch-crimp, his landlord, to the mate of some vessel needing "hands," put aboard when helplessly drunk, and thus shipped off for another voyage. And if he survive the revolting barbarities to which he is commonly subject at sea—of which let Liverpool police-courts and our own newspapers testify—he only quits his "*hell-afloat*" (Jack's own epithet for the majority of American vessels) to land at some foreign port, after the expiration of months or years—there to repeat the same experience.

The keepers of Sailors' Boarding-Houses are not required, by law, to take out a license. Perhaps our legislators know why they are thus favored. *We* don't.

CHAPTER XXXII

The Boarding-House Which Gives Satisfaction to Everybody

* * * * * * *

* * * * * * * *

* * * * * * *

* * * * * * * *

* * * * * * *

* * * * * * * *

* * * * * * *

* * * * * * * *

* * * * * * *

* * * * * * * *

* * * * * * *

* * * * * * * *

CHAPTER XXXIII

Of Different Sorts of Boarders

At length, Reader, our Physiology draws towards its conclusion. Not that we have exhausted the subject—to do that would necessitate the devotion of a particular chapter to every Boarding-House in the city of New York; for not one of them, as has been already intimated, but possesses its own peculiarities. Such a task might be achieved only by a Briareus or Alexandre Dumas.[1] It suffices us to have selected types of the more prominent, and, to the best of our judgment, noteworthy Establishments.

Yet there are particulars remaining which should form part of our subject, though not conveniently admissible, or only cursorily alluded to, within the preceding pages. Our book has necessarily included a considerable variety of boarder character, yet we find some very recognizable types of it still unportrayed. To remedy which we write the present Chapter.

For instance, what person familiar with New York Boarding-Houses but has encountered, and what proprietor or proprietress of such Establishments but has, at some time, been victimized by one of that obnoxious tribe popularly known as *Shark* Boarders? We shall, in a final Chapter, have occasion to speak of many grievances incidental to the vocation, but this—exposure to the meanest kind of robbery—is one to which *all*, from the landlord of the palace hotel on Broadway to the poor old maid who starts a "Hand-to-Mouth" Establishment in the hope of obtaining a meager subsistence—are liable, and perhaps the direst. Samples of the *genus*, both male and female, have incidentally illuminated our pages, but were we to chronicle all the diversities of the species, our volume would suffer literary Elephantiasis.

The Shark Boarder is of every aspect, and in no wise to be detected from outward appearance. Now an individual of imposing address, dashing exterior, and presumable opulence; now—though less frequently—a quiet, unassuming, and, ostensibly, respectable person, who is always expecting to receive money which experiences unlooked-for delays in reaching its destination. We have known

Sharks under the disguise of clergymen, or of Bostonians; we remember one who passed himself off as a Shaking Quaker; another who went about seeking what she might devour, as the abbess of a Spanish nunnery. Proteus, the Bravo of Venice, the author of Junius' Letters, or any other generally indefinite personages that may be mentioned, were nothing to them.[2]

In many cases the Shark Boarder pays liberally and promptly on the outset, with a view to future credit. If of the male species, he generally endeavors to ingratiate himself in the good graces of the landlady. Weak-minded women—there are such, even among mistresses of Boarding-Houses—are his especial prey. Ladies such as those presiding over the Establishments described in Chapters the Fifteenth and Seventeenth, could scarcely be expected to resist the fascinations of flattery, dyed moustachios, half a yard of pendant watch-chain, and a flashy style of dress and conversation. This description of Shark possesses his female counterpart, who, were a museum of Social Ichthyology established might be labeled in it *as very dangerous—especially to young gentlemen boarders.* Our "Tip-Top" Establishment has afforded a choice sample of the species, which is uncommonly prevalent in hotels and stylish Boarding-Houses. Ordinarily, the lady Shark is handsome—or has good-looking daughters.

A considerable number of these pecuniary vampires exist in New York, who are *known* NEVER to pay their way, decamping surreptitiously when it becomes

evident that their exactions will no longer be submitted to, or impudently remaining till expelled. Of course, they are encumbered with very little baggage. We have a story of one of the fraternity which may be worth the telling.

There came to a Private Boarding-House a quietly-voracious young man who affected extreme piety, and told the landlady, on his arrival, that he was desirous of a room where he should be undisturbed in his devotions—which ought to have put her on her guard. He professed to have employment at some Bible or Tract publishing institution, where it was generally understood that the "young men" sung hymns during their dinner hour, and always "asked a blessing" when they put on a clean shirt-collar. The landlady formed a favorable opinion of her new boarder, which only began to decline on his getting in arrears. This commenced at the second week, and continued till the date of his expulsion, nearly two months afterwards. She could neither obtain payment or get him to quit.

When dunned, he *wept* and invented excuses, telling her how his pocket had been picked at the Tabernacle[3]—how his feelings had impelled him to give his wages to a missionary who "came up in the office"—how his grandmother had written from some remote Western locality, stating that she had been compelled by pecuniary distress to pawn her entire wardrobe, with the solitary exception of one unmentionable flannel garment. Mrs. — clung to hope awhile, tolerating her boarder until the servants complained of the pious youth's accidentally finding his way into their rooms nocturnally. He then received a strong intimation that his apartment was wanted. Still he *wouldn't* go. He appeared, as usual, at meals—the landlady didn't like risking a row before her boarders—but having no latch-key, was accustomed, at night, to ring softly; stealing up-stairs, on gaining admission, to bed. Finally, the other boarders took the matter in hand, and having locked and bolted the street-door, placed themselves at an upper window to await the result. Eleven o'clock came, and with it a gentle application at the bell. Looking out, they beheld an indistinctly-seen figure apparently engaged in an attempt to pick the lock—upon which figure the contents of a couple of ewers were immediately discharged. But imagine the astonishment of the party when, instead of seeing their victim slink off with the air of a detected pick-pocket, they observed him clutch the bell-handle, and pull it with frantic vehemence, again and again, accompanying the act with vigorously-bestowed kicks on the lower panels of the door. Flesh and blood could not stand this. The boarders in a body rushed down-stairs, and fell, with fist and foot, upon the author of the clamor. Not until he had been severely pounded did they discover that it was—NOT the Shark Boarder, but a highly estimable gentleman—quite the model man of the Establishment! Yet, still worse; during the *mêlée*, as subsequently appeared, the Shark had arrived, and slipping in unobserved at the open door, had gained his room. He left, however, very early next morning, and for good, taking with him a pair of pants belonging to another boarder, two coats, a watch, and a copy of the Rev. Mr. Splurge-on's sermons[4]—which lively volume had been loaned to him by the landlady.

We have, several times, during the progress of our work, had occasion to allude to *Pet* Boarders. Who has not some knowledge of this species? We have yet to encounter *one* Establishment in which Pet Boarder-ism does not, in some degree, exist. It would appear to be an inevitable, though highly objectionable appendage to the Institution. In strength and potency it admits of the greatest diversity, from open, recognized despotism, to the mild, insidious, covert authority which is rather felt than seen, and only detected by the narrowest scrutiny. A comparatively rare case, such as we have described in Chapter the Fifteenth, would be at once observable, but not so with others. You may live twelve months in a Boarding-House, utterly unconscious of the existence of a Pet, albeit every meal you have partaken of during that time has been especially provided with a view to pleasing his appetite. We say *his*, never having discovered a lady Pet—unless merely admitted as a partaker in her husband's privileges.

Some live by it. Admitted on the express agreement that they shall undertake what in theatrical parlance is denominated "general utility business"—as carving at table, leading the small talk, and, so to speak, ingeniously blending the parts of family-man and head-waiter—they may be termed gastronomic *dead-heads*, and though not occupying a very dignified position, are otherwise unobjectionable. Some glide into office from indolence, abetted by stress of circumstances, and are, finally, married by their landlady. We have heard stories of the system being so formally recognized that preliminary stipulations were entered into as to what the Pet was to "eat, drink, and avoid"; dishes of rarity and price being *tabooed* to him, and he expected, in no case, to send his plate up twice for pie. But under such controlment he is, manifestly, scarcely entitled to his denomination. The true Pet Boarder is he who *pays* and *rules*, openly or in secret, over the appetites of his fellows. Mildly facetious gentlemen—not "funny" ones, for landladies, in common with their sex, are rather afraid of *them*, as they don't know but that they may be induced to laugh at something that's not proper—clergymen, and stupid, respectable, *old* gentlemen are very apt to become Pet Boarders. An infallible instance of their position is the appearance of some exclusive dainty in their immediate vicinity at table, of which nothing is said to the other boarders. If you ask for it and *pass it on*—as we always did (on high moral grounds), be sure that both the Pet and landlady will hate you intensely. We have an anecdote illustrative of this phase of Pet Boarderism.

We were once sojourning in a stylish Establishment where there was a Pet Boarder—a faint, fair man, of *Carkerish* aspect with respect to teeth.[5] He used to carve at table, and always took care to reserve for himself the daintiest bits. We resolved to punish him by plagiarizing the conduct of the sculptor Chantrey on a similar occasion,[6] and lay in wait for a good opportunity. In due time it chanced that one small, special delicacy was placed before him. He, very graciously, assisted those nearest to him to the inferior parts, proffering some to us—which we declined, until, having disposed of all but the very choicest portion, he was about to transfer that to his own plate, when we begged to be allowed to change our minds, and—received the plate from the hands of the waiter. The Pet's face was awful to contemplate. He had the additional satisfaction of seeing us send our plate away after disposing of a few mouthfuls of its contents.

All Pets, when known to be such, are detested by their fellow-boarders—and deservedly so.

Of *Disagreeable* Boarders we have exhibited some, perhaps too many, samples. But besides those who are obnoxious in their own peculiar and private capacity, there are numerous publicly offensive ones who, like the *Shark* and *Pet*, appear inseparable from the system. Inevitably comic gentlemen, for instance, who enjoy *clique* fun over the dinner-table, laugh loudly at one another's bad jokes, and talk indirectly *at* fellow-boarders. Argumentative individuals who seize upon every opportunity for controversial fisty-cuffs, lose temper, get red in the face, and *shout* at one another. Politicians generally. People who pride themselves on their dignity, and try to "look down" those whom they *must* meet, three times a day, at the same table. Vulgar people who rush into the opposite course of extreme familiarity with every body. Husbands who are absurdly jealous of their wives, and pick a quarrel with you if you pass a lady's plate, or tell her that it's fine day. Old maids of the keep-your-distance-and-know-your-betters order, who have preternaturally good noses for snuffing out moral taints in the most innocent words and actions, and are, constitutionally, down on humanity. Solemn old foozles who think a laugh betokens want of respect for their dignity, and resent the mildest difference in opinion with a heavy malignancy of which only stupid people are capable. Unmitigated pious people who *will* have "grace" said before meals, who sit in judgment on their fellow-boarders, and look eternal sulphur-and-pitchforks at you if you talk of theatres. In short, all persons who ride their hobbies without regard to the corns of their neighbors, may be classed under the head of Disagreeable Boarders. Lovers of scandal deserve a worse title, but that is a plant indigenous to Boarding-Houses, and until the advent of the Millennium we despair of seeing it eradicated. We believe—as we hope—that the Institution will be extinct first.

We have known a few instances of *Mysterious* Boarders. One (heretofore alluded to in our pages) was an old lady who took her meals in her own room, having made a special contract to that effect with the proprietress of the Establishment. She never went abroad, but spent her entire time in the indulgence of a raven-like predilection for obtaining surreptitious glimpses of the boarders, as they ascended to, or descended from their chambers. For this purpose she lay in wait constantly, at all hours of the day and night, generally keeping the door of her apartment open to the extent of about two inches, and invariably closing it with a bang when you had passed—as if she resented your existence, and took that way of informing you of the fact. It was a singularly disconcerting practice, placing you in the position of one who took a liberty—in walking up-stairs. Its effects on a newly-arrived boarder were peculiar. He became low-spirited, thought of his sins, and was haunted by a lively apprehension of some indefinable retribution impending over him. He passed the door at midnight with a shuddering conviction that a Spectral Eye was watching him through the key-hole. Finally, he waxed resentful, bought a pair of creaking boots, and when the door opened softly behind him, had to repress a strong inclination to shriek out, or to throw up one leg, or to jump several feet into the air, bringing his heels into violent concussion on descending, or similar saltatory proceedings. Sometimes the Mysterious Boarder glided to the stair-case, and called, over the banisters, in a spectral voice to the servants. She was peculiarly restless just before dinner. Passing her door at that period—especially if you encountered the servant bringing up her dinner, and so got caught, as it were, between two fires—was always a nervous transaction. It affected us to that extent that had there been a fire-escape, or a rope-ladder handy, we should have preferred that mode of descent to the stair-case. Only on two occasions do we recollect the Mysterious Boarder's quitting her own apartment for the lower story. She remained invisible on the first. The boarders were assembled at the breakfast-table, when the door of a small room at one end of the apartment (occupied by the landlady) suddenly opened to the width of two inches, and, in the midst of a dead silence, a Voice demanded of the company, generally, "*Has MY PAPER come yet?*" The second instance was far more appalling, and experienced by us, individually. We had come down late to breakfast, and were, subsequently, luxuriating over one of "Byles'" exquisite letters to the *Tribune*,[7] in the front parlor—all alone—no person being visible in either that or the rear room. When, happening to raise our eyes over the top of the page, to our infinite horror and astonishment we beheld the Mysterious Boarder *glowering* at us. She was dressed in black, wore spectacles, and had a white handkerchief tied round her head, the loose ends of which projecting upwards at the top, gave her a strong resemblance to a large, horned owl. Solemnly advancing, she seized the *Times* and slowly retired, her spectacles still fixed remorselessly upon us. Incontinently we dashed down the *Tribune* and fled.

The landlady, when questioned, informed us that she—the Mysterious Boarder—was an estimable person, and possessed a fine mind. We did not question the fact, but should have been glad to have seen it direct its owner to some more cheerful mode of entertainment. By the boarders, generally, she was known by the *soubriquet* of "Grace Poole"—after the twin Mystery in Jane Eyre.[8]

We knew another Mysterious, or rather Incomprehensible Boarder. He labored under two extraordinary hallucinations—the one that womankind, in general, adored him and were bent on persecuting him to the death with their addresses—the other that Nature had intended him for a Cortez, a Pizarro, or a Walker.[9] Now, as he was by no means a handsome or intelligent individual, being, indeed, rather common-place—not to say ignoble—in appearance, the opinion he entertained of his merits was, moderately speaking, a cool one. And when he burst into tears over the dinner-table, while bewailing his unappreciated talent for conquest, and demanded, with much excitement, "a hundred thousand men," that he might carry the Stars and Stripes throughout the length and breadth of South America—it became very unpleasant for his neighbors, one of whom we happened to be. Furthermore, his faith in his own powers of fascination induced him to write an excessively ungrammatical love-letter—wherein the personal pronoun was invariably represented by a small i—to a handsome lady-boarder; and, subsequently, to favor her with a visit at her country-seat. We believe that he was rather "hard up," and that the landlady good-naturedly allowed him to remain for six weeks or so without demanding payment for his board. She experienced some difficulty in getting rid of him. He was discovered in his room on several occasions at remote intervals after his nominal departure, and, more than once, came down to breakfast as heretofore. He also contracted a habit of calling on the boarders—especially one—a clerical gentleman—and negotiating small loans in the hall—incidentally displaying a large cheese-knife, which he carried under his coat during such transactions. We don't know what became of him.

Another, and a still more eccentric instance shall conclude our Chapter—which is already protracted beyond its legitimate limits. There came, as boarder, to a certain Establishment, a Strange Gentleman of foreign aspect, who stipulated for private gastronomic arrangements, and owned a large hairy dog, which he used to beat, regularly, for a quarter of an hour after each meal—breakfast, dinner, and supper. This, he said, he did *for exercise*. On the second evening of his domiciliation he asked the land-lady's permission to unbolt a trap-door leading to the roof, in order to enjoy the fresh air, which, the doctor told him, was good for his stomach. She according it, he spent two hours on the top of the house, and then began to pull down chimney-pots, and to hurl them into the street. Two policemen and some of the male boarders subsequently secured him, just as he was preparing to descend (attired only in shirt and boots) the interior of a chimney, having already forced his dog to precede him! He proved to be a lunatic, recently escaped from the confinement in which his friends had placed him.

CHAPTER XXXIV

Retrospective and Valedictory

There is an old story of a certain painter, who having depicted a man in the act of overcoming a lion in single combat, submitted his performance to one of the latter species for Criticism, which was accorded in the simple remark, that had the artist been a lion, the relative positions of the parties represented might have been different. We apprehend a somewhat similar judgment will be passed upon our volume by the proprietors and proprietresses of New York Boarding-Houses. If the writer, they will say, had experience of *keeping*, instead of *boarding*, at our Establishments, this "Physiology" would not have contained half so much matter derogatory to our calling, and infinitely more at the expense of our boarders. Now, without wishing to disparage leonine or landlordial censure, we have a word or two to say in anticipation of such (inevitable) objections; as, also, in conclusion.

In the first place, we would profess that our book is pretty honestly written. If we have described obnoxious landladies, our pages have included equally objectionable boarders; nor are we conscious of invidiousness in the portrayal of either. The keepers of Boarding-Houses are, as a class, neither better nor worse than the majority of persons who rely upon their own exertions for a livelihood. Charges of meanness, of selfishness, of a rapacious advocacy of their own rights and a notable indifference to those of others, may, as often, and with as much justice, be brought against boarders as landladies. We have known some of the latter every way superior in mind, morals, and manners, to those who met at their tables, and whose whims and exactions they—to a certain extent—were obliged to tolerate, in virtue of their position: we have encountered others of the meanest, most mercenary, most offensive description. Of which our Physiology may testify.

The vocation is a singularly unhappy and irksome one, involving much risk and responsibility, and possessing no uncommon facilities for realizing pecuniary profit. If Boarding-Houses had existed in Job's day,[1] and the Arch-Enemy had clapped that respectable patriarch into one, as landlord, for a month or so, we have no doubt that he would have adopted Mrs. J.'s advice and done the "cussing" incontinently. Nor are the general relations between a landlady and her boarders too conciliatory. Our readers will scarcely have failed to remark, in their own experience, as in our volume, the spirit of antagonism commonly prevalent. Very frequently boarders and landladies get to regard each other as natural enemies. The fault, we take it, lies—as faults usually do—equally on either side. In boarding, as in other matters, we are—all of us—prone to think rather of what is due *to* than *from* us; hence boarders become aggressively selfish, and landladies—discovering how little sympathy or consideration is felt for them—passively so. In most cases the former are more unthinkingly than intentionally unjust; albeit we have, certainly, observed some instances of exaction on the part of boarders thoroughly *Shylockian* in their infernal selfishness.[2] We knew a "lady" to originate a row in a Boarding-House in consequence of a temporary delay in lighting her fire, when the mother of the proprietress lay dying! Our general experience would indicate that the gentler sex are less considerate towards one another than male boarders. We never yet encountered a lady who professed herself satisfied with her Boarding-House. Men may be hasty, but hardly so exacting. If the reader doubt this assertion, we emphatically refer him to the proprietress of any Boarding-House with whom he may be acquainted.

Landladies are, from the nature of their position, inevitably cognizant of most of the little meannesses, jealousies, and faults of their boarders—for in no place does an individual exhibit himself more completely in his true colors than in a Boarding-House. It has just enough of the freedom of home to induce a conviction that one may act as he pleases, but none of its restraining sanctity and responsibilities. (We have witnessed a stormy altercation over a breakfast-table in consequence of a boarder's disappointment in not getting a penny roll.) Unless of unusually secretive disposition, you can't live for any length of time in one of these Establishments without having all your failings "reckoned up" *sans* mitigation. And never flatter yourself with the idea that they are not *talked about by your fellow-boarders*. You might as well suppose that what you say of them will not be carried to their ears. That unluckily-constructed Sicilian confessional which repeated penitents' whispers in a place of public resort was not better adapted to the diffusion of mischievous information than are Boarding-Houses.[3] The evil is inherent, inevitable.

We have often thought that the most appropriate simile we could hit upon for a Boarding-House is afforded by what Showmen denominate "a Happy Family"; where a number of animals of incongruous, antagonistic, and conflicting natures, are confined in a single cage—it being gratuitously assumed that they have conquered their instinctive aversions to each other's society. And, to be sure, they stand on their good behavior when in public. But, who shall speak of the desire the dog must possess to strangle the cat; the inclination the owl must have to lunch off the mice; the intense longing existing in the sable bosom of the raven for the gratification of taking out one of the guinea-pig's eyes. Let Dickens's Raven—from whom we borrow the last illustration—reply.[4] As with the "Happy Family" so with the inmates of a Boarding-House. In an indiscriminately-got-together community, where, like our national democracy "one person's as good as another, and a good deal better"—it is in the nature of things for people to conflict—and conflict they do, accordingly.

There is only ONE way of avoiding Boarding-House squabbles—a strictly-acted-upon system of *Non-Intercourse* with fellow-boarders. In which case you'll only be considered "stuck-up," and detested in consequence. Which is, comparatively, easy of endurance when contrasted with other risks.

We are inclined to believe that ill-bred persons fare best in Boarding-Houses. Just as, were a lady of education and refinement and a Zooloo-Kaffir to sit down at one common ordinary,[5] in all probability the latter would come off best in the eating department. Exacting people are hated—but they get what they want, and, generally, have their own way.

Our objections to the Institution of Boarding may be all summed up in one sentence. That, as our virtues are much more dependent on our surroundings than we are willing to admit, when the check of *home* is removed (and a Boarding-House is, emphatically, NOT a home) all sorts of evils are liable to rush in. The good that exists in these Establishments does so in spite of the system, which is inherently mischievous. But it were useless to rail against them. We have to accept the Institution as we do our existence—and make the best of both. It is part of our anomalous social state, and so long as it is next to an impossibility for those who desire to live at once privately, decently, and economically, to find a suitable dwelling in this city—so long as there's scarcely any medium between mansions far beyond the reach of men of moderate incomes and miserable tenement houses—so long as a large proportion of our citizens entertain the idea that an inordinately extravagant style of house-keeping is absolutely *necessary* to secure position; and that attempting comfort in an humbler sphere is rather contemptible than otherwise—so long as young men *can't afford* to get married, and young ladies object to the "trouble" of household ministry—in short, so long as New York aspires to become a *Brummagem* Paris (and does it very clumsily),[6] Boarding-Houses will, undoubtedly, continue to exist. Of their general effects on individual and metropolitan character we have no doubt. Charles Dickens half charged Americans with "an inaptitude for social pleasures."[7] Granting that there may be some grounds for the accusation, has not this universal *barrack* system something to do with its existence?

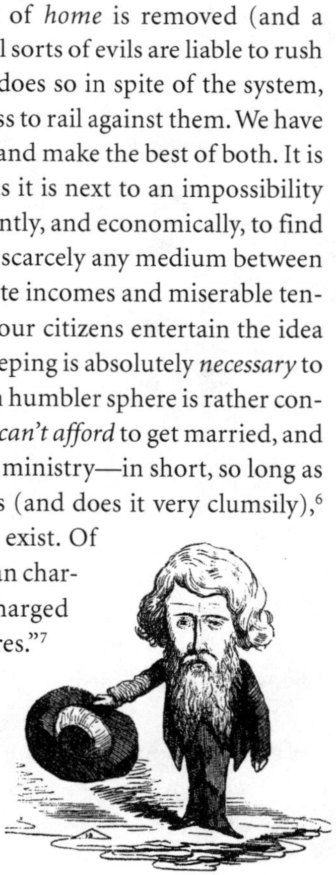

Reader, our task is done. Hoping that we part friends, with all good-will we bid you FAREWELL.

EXPLANATORY NOTES

EPIGRAPH

1. *Le Diable Boiteux*: a 1707 novel by author Alain-Rene Lesage (1668–1747). The Frenchman Lesage based his work on an earlier volume titled *El Diablo Cojuelo* (1641), by the Spaniard Luis Vélez de Guevara, in which the lame, or *boiteux*, demon Asmodeus escorts a young Castilian student around Madrid—lifting the lids of the houses in the process, so as to expose the vices and follies of the people inside. Lesage substitutes Paris for Madrid, much as Gunn switches the setting for his own Asmodean observations to New York. The aim of all three authors is the same: to provide a narrative perspective that sees through household walls.

PREFACE

1. Layard: Austen Henry Layard, 1817–1894. The Parisian Layard was a pioneer in the emerging field of archaeology during the Victorian period. Working alongside fellow Frenchman Paul Emile Botta, he helped to uncover the ancient civilization of Assyria, located in what today are the northern plains of Iraq. A prolific writer, Layard published just a few years before the appearance of Gunn's *Physiology* three accounts of his experiences in the Near East. Gunn could have drawn on the English translations of two of these works, *Nineveh and Its Remains* (1849) and *Discoveries in the Ruins of Nineveh and Babylon* (1853), for an account of the Bedouins, an Arab nomadic tribe.

CHAPTER I — INTRODUCTORY, METROPOLITAN, AND ANTICIPATORY

1. Gascon: both a people and a dialect language, rooted in the Gascony region of southwest France. Gunn's "sage Gascon" might be the seventeenth-century historical figure Comte d'Artagnan, who, as a real-life Gascon and captain of the Musketeers of the Guard under Louis XIV, in part inspired Alexandre Dumas's 1844 novel, *The Three Musketeers*.

Tupper: Martin Farquhar Tupper, 1810–1889. English writer and poet, whose long-running serial *Proverbial Philosophy* (first installment, 1837) consisted of blank-verse moral musings disguised as prose.

2. Carlyle's *Past and Present*: Thomas Carlyle, 1795–1881. Scottish essayist and historian, who offered Victorian readers of works like *Past and Present* (1843) an ethical critique of modern industrial society.

3. Astor Library: John Jacob Astor, 1763–1848. At the time of his death, the German immigrant Astor was the wealthiest man in America—his fortune based in part on vast Manhat-

tan real-estate holdings. Astor's will set aside $400,000 for the creation of a non-circulating reference library in New York. That library opened its doors in 1849, and in time supplied a substantial portion of the collection of the New York Public Library.

CHAPTER II — OF LOOKING OUT FOR A BOARDING-HOUSE

1. *Gow Chrom*, in Scott's novel: Sir Walter Scott, 1771–1832. A popular Scottish author of historical romances, Scott achieved international celebrity before the appearance of his novel *The Fair Maid of Perth* (1828), which relates in fictional form the Battle of the Clans fought in the Highlands of Perth, Scotland, in 1396. Tradition records that the harness-maker Henry Smith, also known by the names Hal o' the Wynd and the Gow-Chrom, offered himself as a last-minute substitute combatant for one of the warring clans.

2. *Herald*, *Tribune*, or *Times*: three contemporary New York newspapers, founded, respectively, in 1835, 1841, and 1851. The New York *Herald* was among the first of the city's penny newspapers, whose lively, often sensational, coverage appealed to working-class readers. Both the *Tribune* and *Times*, meanwhile, maintained a more sober tone in their commitment to serious news reportage.

3. Greenwich and Hudson streets: parallel north-south thoroughfares in Manhattan. The reference is to the neighborhoods adjoining both streets in the lower sections of the island, known for their mixed residential and commercial character. In Gunn's day, this area had a high concentration of boardinghouses, and would have been seen as less than genteel—a working-class "downtown" counterpart to what Gunn describes as the privileged precincts of "up-towndom."

4. Hoboken: a city in New Jersey, located on the west bank of the Hudson River across from Manhattan. New Yorkers of the mid-nineteenth century could travel to and from Hoboken by ferryboat.

Williamsburg: a neighborhood in Brooklyn, opposite Manhattan across the East River.

5. sanatory: conducive to health; not to be confused with *sanitary*, meaning of or related to health generally.

6. Five Points and Cow Bay: notorious slum districts of nineteenth-century lower Manhattan.

CHAPTER III — OF BOARDING WITH A PRIVATE FAMILY

1. Herod: Herod I, or Herod the Great, 73 BC–4 BC. Under Roman rule, Herod served as king of Judea for thirty-four years, beginning in 37 BC. He is known in Christian scripture for the Murder of the Innocents. Informed of the expected birth of a new "King of the Jews," Herod sought to avoid the loss of his throne by ordering the execution of all young male children in Bethlehem.

2. Taylor's: an upscale Broadway hotel and restaurant in mid-nineteenth-century Manhattan. Although it began as a humble ice-cream saloon, Taylor's was by the time of Gunn's writing a fashionable establishment, especially popular with women.

3. Madame *Bluebeard* in the story: Bluebeard is the imposing nobleman of a French fairy tale, dating from 1697. Madame Bluebeard is his over-curious wife, who literally examines the skeletons in her husband's closet.

4. Hottentot: a quasi-anthropological label that dates to eighteenth-century European writings. It refers to a tribe of southern Africans who, in many Western eyes, served as a stereotype of mankind in its most "savage" state.

5. *tendresse*: French term, meaning tender feeling.

6. Godfrey's Cordial: a period patent medicine administered to children with colic. Poor mothers also were known to give Godfrey's to their underfed offspring—the opium in the cordial bringing temporary relief, if not a genuine medical remedy, to various ailments.

7. *hegira*: Islamic term, designating the departure of the prophet Muhammad from Mecca in September 622.

CHAPTER IV — THE CHEAP BOARDING-HOUSE ON A LARGE SCALE

1. the "great fire" of 1836: New York's Great Fire began on December 16, 1835, and raged for nearly twenty-four hours. It was and remains the city's most destructive conflagration; much of lower Manhattan's financial district burned.

2. Croton: beginning in 1842, a complex aqueduct system that brought fresh water to New York City from reserves in outlying northern counties. Many considered the opening of the Croton Aqueduct to be one of the great engineering feats of the age.

Schuylkill: a major waterway in Philadelphia, often taken as the city's signature river.

3. Sydney Smith: 1771–1845. English clergyman, author, and lecturer, known for his progressive views on the education of women, the abolition of slavery, and practical, as opposed to classical, learning. Gunn's Philadelphian would have resented Smith's work *Petition and Letters* (1843), in which the writer criticized the U.S. state of Pennsylvania for its temporary default on interest payments owed state bondholders—of whom Smith himself was one. Americans generally would have resented Smith's notorious remarks from the *Edinburgh Review* in 1820, when he condescendingly asked, "In the four quarters of the globe, who reads an American book?"

4. Sweeney's: a downtown Manhattan eatery, catering mainly to men.

5. like the dove to the ark: a reference to the Old Testament story of Noah, who sent forth from his ark a dove as a means to see if the waters of God's Great Flood had receded. Finding no resting place on dry ground, the dove repeatedly returned to Noah in his ark.

6. cockney: a member of London's working classes, often residing in the city's East End. A "cockney accent" characterized the language spoken by members of this class, whether inside or outside London; its distinguishing features included a strongly vernacular mix of tone and figure of speech.

7. *Solon*: 638 BC–558 BC. Noted Athenian statesman, lawmaker, and poet, famed for his support of democratic reforms and facilitating harmony among rival political factions.

8. Turkish opinion: traditional Islamic law outlawed the public ringing of bells, because of their association with Christian worship. Note that Gunn uses the terms *Turkish* and *Muslim* interchangeably, as was once common practice.

9. Argus: in Greek mythology, a giant with one hundred eyes.

10. Laodicean Christians: during the early Christian era, Laodicea was a prosperous, self-supporting city in Asia Minor. The Laodicean Church was one of seven churches directly addressed by St. John in the New Testament's Book of Revelation. St. John there takes the Laodiceans to task for their "lukewarm" faith—"neither cold, nor hot," as Gunn relates.

11. "flagrant weed": a colloquial Anglo-Irish term for tobacco.

12. avenging Fury: three goddesses of vengeance appear in Greek mythology. They were known for inflicting swift, merciless punishment on those who broke society's rules.

13. battle royal: traditionally, a formal fight involving three or more combatants; in recent times, a general term for a fight involving many people.

14. "Billingsgate": a district in the southeast of London. The city's Great Fire of 1666 began in this ward. Several decades later, the area became home to one of London's great fish markets. So shrill and colorful were the cries of fish vendors here that the term *billingsgate* itself became synonymous with profane, offensive language—presumably like that used by the landlady whom Gunn describes.

CHAPTER V — THE FASHIONABLE BOARDING-HOUSE WHERE YOU DON'T GET ENOUGH TO EAT

1. a dish of trifle or *blanc mange*: trifle is a rich Dutch dessert of layered ingredients, popular in England for many centuries past. *Blanc mange* is a sweet dessert made from thickened cream, sugar, and almonds.

2. as many hands as Briareus: in Greek mythology, Briareus was one of three hundred-handed giants, also brothers.

3. the *Courier*, *Enquirer*, and *Home Journal*: the *Courier* and *Enquirer* were two of contemporary New York's leading newspapers. Founded (under a different name) in 1846, the *Home Journal* catered to a more specialized audience of newspaper readers, those with a specific interest in literature, the arts, high-society coverage, and the world of fashion.

4. *Churchman*: a weekly New York newspaper from the period, aimed at the more exclusive members of the city's Episcopalian community.

5. Grace Church: a contemporary Episcopalian Church in lower Manhattan, attended by the well-to-do.

6. *eau de Cologne*, *frangi-panni*, jockey-club, or otto of roses: various perfumes and fragrances.

7. wristlets: elaborate lace cuffs.

8. Canal-street: a largely commercial street in lower Manhattan, running diagonally north-south just above Hudson Square and west to the Hudson River docks.

9. discommotion: a term of Gunn's invention, being the noun form of the transitive verb *discommode*, which means to put to inconvenience or trouble.

10. Longfellow, Holmes, Willis: Henry Wadsworth Longfellow, 1807–1882; Oliver Wendell Holmes, 1809–1894; Nathaniel Parker Willis, 1806–1867. Three of the leading literary figures in the United States during the middle years of the nineteenth century. Each contributed to the development of U.S. letters in several different genres. Yet their respective contributions came mainly in the forms of poetry, prose essay/lecture, and the newspaper sketch. Collectively, they are remembered for the polish of their finished productions, and thus for raising the general tone of American literature in the period.

11. Mr. Wallack Lester: John Lester Wallack, 1820–1888. Anglo-American actor, playwright, and theater manager, whose professional move to America in 1847 marked the start of a long and successful career on the New York stage. Wallack would open his own theater at Broadway and Thirteenth Street in 1861, and spent time off the stage in some of the same circles as author Gunn.

CHAPTER VI — THE DIRTY BOARDING-HOUSE

1. Bowery pit: founded in the 1830s, New York's Bowery Theatre was by the following decade one of the city's principal venues for working-class entertainment. Fronting the theater's main stage was a designated "pit" area, characterized by both its cheaper seats and the rowdy behavior of its audience members during performances.

2. "Red Rovers": bedbugs, identified by their reddish-brown appearance.

3. Daniel Lambert: 1770–1809. Englishman who achieved notoriety in the early nineteenth century for his extreme obesity. At the time of his death he weighed more than seven hundred pounds.

4. why the old English poets made the devil lord of insects: a reference to the Biblical demon Beelzebub, whom many read as the devil himself. Beelzebub translates literally as "Lord of the Flies," a name that suggests the poetic conceits of plague and pestilence.

5. *battues*: French term, from the singular form *battue*. A *battue* is a hunt in which participants beat on the surrounding woods and brush in order to drive fleeing animals in the direction of waiting hunters.

6. Lowell's *Parson Wilbur*: James Russell Lowell, 1819–1891. Celebrated New England poet of the mid-nineteenth century. The first of the satirical poems that would come to comprise Lowell's masterpiece, *The Biglow Papers*, began appearing in the *Boston Courier* newspaper in 1846; the series as a whole later was collected into book form, the first edition appearing in 1848. The poems themselves, rendered in Yankee dialect, ostensibly represented the folk wisdom of one Mr. Hosea Biglow. To the fictional pastor Homer Wilbur fell the responsibility of supplying learned commentary, the overly learned and stuffy nature of which enhanced the poems' humor and thus their popularity.

7. Giulio Cordara: Giulio Cesare Cordara, 1704–1785. Italian Jesuit and man of letters, known principally for his historical works and poetry. Gunn alludes here to Cordara's poem

on insects, in which the writer declares that insects held no place in the Biblical Paradise, but instead were created by God as a punishment for mankind after the Fall.

8. *Porgies*: plural form of *porgy*, a category of fish that includes sea bream and shad.

9. Flanders-brick: a traditional flat, Flemish brick of reddish color, common in Europe's Low Countries.

10. gutta-percha: a type of tropical tree found mainly in Southeast Asia. Gutta-percha is known for its inelastic qualities.

11. varioloid: a mild form of smallpox appearing in people who previously have been vaccinated or already have had the disease.

12. firkin: a small cask, usually for liquids, fish, or, as in this case, butter. A firkin of butter would contain about 56 pounds, or 25.4 kilograms.

13. cruets: a cruet is a small flask with flat bottom, narrow neck, and covering lid. Cruets are used to hold liquid condiments, such as salad oils and vinegar.

14. Tombs: before the Civil War, the Tombs was Manhattan's main municipal prison. Its official name was the New York Halls of Justice and House of Detention, but it became known in everyday speech as "the Tombs" because of its Egyptian burial style of architecture.

15. *Biddyness*: *biddy* was the slang term in Gunn's day for an Irish housemaid. *Biddyness* would suggest both a slovenly style of work and unkempt personal appearance—two of the stereotypes associated with the figure in question.

16. vitriol: sulfuric acid, frequently used in the processing of metals and manufacture of fertilizer and detergent.

17. *Sutteeism*: historically, the practice of self-immolation by widows in Hindu culture.

18. camphene: a potentially explosive chemical compound, used in the mid-nineteenth century as a fuel for lamps.

CHAPTER VII — THE "HAND-TO-MOUTH" BOARDING-HOUSE

1. the extension of Canal-street: major east-west street in lower Manhattan, cutting diagonally through the heart of today's Chinatown. The street takes its name from an actual canal that was dug in the early 1800s to drain a nearby pond. Although Canal Street's construction was completed in 1820, the neighborhood surrounding it remained saturated with water. Local property values and living conditions fell in consequence, while the street's eastern reaches came to be identified with the notorious Five Points slums.

2. harridans: a harridan is a haggard old woman.

3. *Sun*: New York's first penny newspaper, founded by publisher Benjamin Day in 1833 and appealing in particular to working-class readers.

4. James K. Polk: 1795–1849. U.S. president, serving from 1845 to 1849. A staunch Democrat, Polk supported the nation's internal expansion and prosecuted a short-lived war against Mexico during his single term of office.

5. Red Ash or Peach Orchard: high-quality coals dug from the Appalachian Mountains region, used in Gunn's day as fuel for home heating.

6. novels of G. W. Reynolds: George William MacArthur (G.W.M.) Reynolds, 1814–1879. Popular Victorian English novelist, best remembered for his serial work *The Mysteries of London* (1844–1846).

7. *Police Gazette*: *The National Police Gazette*, a New York newspaper founded in 1845, offered readers nationwide a signature brand of highly sensationalized news coverage. Crime and urban vice were at the center of its reportage.

8. noble Jean Paul: Johann Paul Friedrich Richter, 1763–1825. German writer, known for the humorous tales and novels that found much favor with readers in his day. Gunn probably refers here to Richter's work *Flower, Fruit and Thorn Pieces; or, the Married Life, Death and Wedding of Siebenkäs, Poor Man's Lawyer* (1796–1797).

CHAPTER VIII — THE "SERIOUS" BOARDING-HOUSE

1. Bleecker-street: major thoroughfare in lower Manhattan, running diagonally north-south between Ninth Avenue and Broadway, and providing a main artery through New York's Greenwich Village. The area north of Bleecker Street includes Washington Square, a center of fashionable residence for Gunn's "upper-tendom" in the 1820s and 1830s.

2. *Evangelist*: the *New York Evangelist* newspaper. Evangelical and Presbyterian in orientation, the paper in Gunn's day lent its support to a number of contemporary moral reform efforts, including antislavery.

3. Dickens' *David Copperfeld*: Charles Dickens, 1812–1870. English Victorian author, acclaimed on both sides of the Atlantic for the memorable characters in his fiction, as well as his literary portraits of London. *David Copperfield* is Dickens's popular novel of 1850, and features the moral self-development of the title character. Presumably, Gunn's "mildly-developed youth" would not be in need of such moral instruction as offered by the novel; nor would he approve of its collected characters, some of them less than upstanding.

4. Miss Murdstone: the cruel Jane Murdstone, a character from Dickens's novel *David Copperfield*.

5. Burton's: William E. Burton, 1804–1860. English-born actor, editor, and stage manager who emigrated to the United States in 1834. Until the time of his death in 1860, Burton owned and operated a number of theaters along the mid-Atlantic corridor, where he orchestrated performances of popular works—perhaps including, as Gunn suggests, stage adaptations of Dickens's novels—as well as more self-consciously "artful" productions of Shakespeare.

6. persimmons: edible orange-colored fruit, sweet when ripe but otherwise sharp and astringent when not fully ripened.

7. Presbyterian—Hard-Shell denomination: primitive, "old school" Christians, strongly Calvinist in doctrine and opposed to innovations in church institutions.

8. Hannah More: 1745–1833. English religious writer, known early in her career as the author of clever moral verse and drama, and later for more "serious" writings of a Puritanical strain.

9. Pandemonium: literally, "all the demons." An assembly hall of devils, as described at the end of Book I in English writer John Milton's (1608–1674) epic poem *Paradise Lost* (1667).

10. "a whitening of sepulchers": Biblical reference, Matthew 23:27, meant to suggest exterior beauty disguising inner decay.

11. Calvinistic: of or related to reformed Protestant Christianity, as embodied by the sixteenth-century French theologian John Calvin. Exiled in Geneva, Switzerland, Calvin wrote a number of influential tracts and treatises that revolutionized religion both in his own day and in the centuries to come. Calvin's followers, know as Calvinists, subscribed to a doctrine that saw God as dominant over mankind.

12. ultra-Garrisonian: William Lloyd Garrison, 1805–1879. Radical American abolitionist, who called for the immediate emancipation of slaves during the decades leading up to the U.S. Civil War. Garrison's supporters were known as "Garrisonians"; an "ultra"-Garrisonian would have subscribed to Garrison's views in the extreme.

13. the Maine Law: legislation passed in 1851 in the U.S. state of Maine. The law prohibited the sale of all alcoholic beverages (except under certain special circumstances), and quickly became a model for similar legislation in other states.

14. Temperance: a mid-nineteenth-century social movement, in both England and the United States, to ban the sale of alcoholic beverages. Temperance bore close ties to a broader contemporary effort among evangelical Protestants to reform modern, urban industrial society on moral grounds.

15. "author of the life of P. T. Barnum": Phineas Taylor Barnum, 1810–1891. Impresario of a variety of urban American popular entertainments during the middle decades of the nineteenth century. A successful showman, Barnum traded on the willingness of audiences to suspend disbelief in his sometimes outrageous spectacles. Among these spectacles might be included his own autobiography, which Barnum "wrote" and published in 1854 (the text in

fact was ghost-written by Rufus Griswold, a well-known New York editor and anthologist of American literature).

16. Michael: archangel mentioned by name in the Old Testament's Book of Revelation.

17. Model Artist exhibition: a risqué form of late-night popular entertainment, patronized by men about town in mid-nineteenth-century America's larger cities. The "artists" in question were attractive young women, either scantily clad in period costume or else appearing in the nude.

18. Christy's: the leading contemporary troupe of blackface minstrel performers, named for troupe founder Edwin Pearce Christy. Although often on tour, Christy's Minstrels spent long spells in New York, where for many years audiences gathered to witness Christy's "authentic" brand of African American music, dancing, and comical skits.

CHAPTER IX — THE THEATRICAL BOARDING-HOUSE

1. "'Chance governed all,' as in Milton's Chaos": in the orthodox Christian view of Creation, God created life *ex nihilo*, "out of nothing." In his epic poem *Paradise Lost* (1667), English poet John Milton offers an alternative view, one that borrows from the classical Greek writings of Hesiod's *Theogony*. In this interpretation, Creation comes from God's providing shape and form to *un*formed matter, also called Chaos.

2. Poe's Raven: Edgar Allan Poe, 1809–1849. American author, editor, and literary critic, primarily known for his emotionally charged Gothic poems and tales. Poe's widely read poem "The Raven," of 1845, features a vaguely threatening bird of the same name that comes tapping at the chamber door of the speaker-narrator.

3. tocsin: alarm bell.

4. Rabelais' inscription over the gate of the Abbey of Theleme, "Do what thou wilt": François Rabelais, 1494–1553. French monk turned Renaissance doctor/author, whose extended work *Gargantua and Pantagruel* (1532-) comprises a series of books filled with serio-comical adventures. Rabelais writes in the first of these of the Abbey of Theleme, a structure built by the giant Gargantua. Beneath the whimsical surface of the story, wherein the author satirizes the monastic institutions to which he once belonged, Rabelais propounds a philosophy of life based on the premise, "Do what thou wilt." This same saying appeared in the inscription on a gate outside the giant's Abbey, and for later thinkers laid the basis for a genuine thought system known as the Thelemic Law of Rabelais.

5. Shaking Quakers: a semi-mystical sect of dissenting Quakers, also known as Shakers. Religious worship among Shakers combines quiet mediation with enthusiastic outbursts of singing and dancing, hence the "shaking" of their name.

6. "John Knox and the 'Free Kirk' of his country": John Knox, 1514–1572. Scottish religious reformer, credited with introducing the Protestant Reformation to his native country. Knox also is known as the father of the Calvinist Church, or "Kirk," of Scotland.

7. Caledonian: strictly speaking, a geographical term used to refer to the Caledonia region of modern Scotland; loosely, also used to refer to any of the people or products of Scotland, particularly those associated with the Scottish Highlands.

8. Lady Macbeth: the domineering female lead in Elizabethan playwright William Shakespeare's Scottish stage tragedy, *Macbeth* (1603–1606?).

CHAPTER X — THE BOARDING-HOUSE WHEREIN "SPIRITUALISM" BECOMES PREDOMINANT

1. Jacob's ladder: in the Bible's Book of Genesis, a ladder leading to heaven envisioned by the patriarch Jacob.

2. William Penn: 1644–1718. Prominent English Quaker, who in the 1670s and 1680s became the proprietor and founder of the American colony of Pennsylvania.

3. Spiritualism: a scattered transatlantic religious movement, which reached the peak of its U.S. influence during the early-middle and late decades of the nineteenth century.

Spiritualists believed that certain "seers," or mediums, could channel the spirits of the dead, who in turn would make their presence felt by various physical signs such as tapping, rattling, and tilting tables.

4. Orestes Brownson: 1803–1876. American minister, author, editor, and religious and social reformer. Brownson engaged in a lifelong, and high-profile, religious quest that led him by turns from Unitarianism to Transcendentalism to Roman Catholicism.

5. hierophant: a kind of religious guide, tasked with interpreting spiritual mysteries for congregants.

6. Peter Funks: Peter Funk, a mythical swindler who appears in a number of New York sketches and stories during the decades before the U.S. Civil War. For contemporary readers and writers, the name "Peter Funk" became synonymous with various types of urban trickster figures.

7. "Schottische": a lively country dance, originating in the Bohemian region of Europe, which moved partners through a rhythmic sequence of alternating steps and hops.

CHAPTER XI — THE MEAN BOARDING-HOUSE

1. Chatham Square: an area in lower Manhattan, near the intersection of Bowery and East Broadway. In Gunn's day, the neighborhood was known for its high concentration of saloons and cheap residences.

2. the river: New York's East River.

3. Milesian: in Irish mythology, the people believed to be the final inhabitants of Ireland. Here Gunn uses the term to refer to the Irish generally.

4. "relict": archaic term for widow.

5. saleratus: baking soda.

6. "kickshaws": a kickshaw is the vernacular term for a fancy food dish, usually French.

7. a defunct *Mrs. Harris*: a fictional personage and benefactor. The allusion is to English author Charles Dickens's novel *The Life and Adventures of Martin Chuzzlewit* (1844), in which the character Sarah Gamp refers repeatedly to a dubious patroness, one Mrs. Harris.

8. drugget: a coarse cloth, often used as a floor covering.

9. Tipperarian: a person from County Tipperary, in the southwest of Ireland.

10. Smith O'Brien campaign of '48: William Smith O'Brien, 1803–1864. Irish nationalist, politician, and leader of the Young Ireland movement. In March 1848, O'Brien failed in his attempt to incite a national rebellion against British rule over Ireland.

11. Charles's *Cordial Gin*: a popular patent medicine originating in London, and imported into the United States during the middle years of the nineteenth century. The claims of newspaper advertisements notwithstanding, the Cordial's "medicinal" qualities relied heavily on the intoxicating effects of alcohol.

12. "Ben Bolt": a poem by American author Thomas Dunn English (1819–1902), subsequently set to music by the Philadelphia composer Nelson Kneass. It became a much-loved tune in America following its first performance in Pittsburgh in 1848.

CHAPTER XII — THE BOARDING-HOUSE WHERE THERE ARE MARRIAGEABLE DAUGHTERS

1. Mrs. Trollope's *Widow Barnaby*: Frances Trollope, 1780–1863. Socially conscious English commentator and novelist. Trollope depicts the title character from her 1838 novel, *The Widow Barnaby*, as cruel, crude, and selfish, making Gunn's comparison unflattering in the extreme. Like Gunn, Trollope specialized in observations of domestic life, American domestic life included.

2. Inspector Bucket of *Bleak House*: English author Charles Dickens completed serialization of his ninth novel, *Bleak House*, in 1853. The Inspector named here is a police detective who features in one of several of the narrative's interwoven plots.

3. Phrenology: a popular pseudo-science from the nineteenth century, which held that a person's character could be "read" according to the exterior shape and contour of his or her head.

Fowler and Wells: a brother-owned and -operated mid-nineteenth-century publishing firm, based in New York. Fowler and Wells specialized in publishing reform works, including texts that sought to promote and explain phrenology.

Amativeness: in phrenology, a measure of one's capacity for physical, sexual arousal.

4. Malakoff: Fought during the Crimean War, the Battle of Malakoff pitted the French and Russian armies against each other on September 7, 1855. French success in the battle proved decisive for them and their allies in the larger conflict.

5. Alexander Smith's *Life Drama*: Alexander Smith, 1830–1867. Scottish poet, whose volume *A Life Drama and other Poems* (1853) won admiration on both sides of the English-speaking Atlantic.

6. *Don Juan*: George Gordon, Lord Byron, 1788–1824. English Romantic poet, celebrated for both the adventures of his personal life and his contributions to literature. Begun in 1819, although still incomplete at the time of his death, Byron's rambling satiric verse narrative *Don Juan* was greeted with shock in some quarters upon its appearance, due to the work's reputed immoral content.

7. Walt Whitman's *Leaves of Grass*: Walt Whitman, 1819–1892. New York journalist, editor, and poet, best known for his expansive, innovative free-verse volume *Leaves of Grass* (1855).

8. daguerreotype: an early type of photograph, developed by Frenchman Louis Daguerre in 1839.

9. "Harp of a Thousand Strings": a popular burlesque sermon from the period, reprinted widely in American newspapers. Attributed to a folksy Western preacher, the piece provides a classic example of irreverent frontier humor.

10. Moses in the bulrushes: from the Biblical story of Moses (Exodus 2:1–10), recounting the early childhood of the Old Testament Israelite. Gunn puns here on *bulrushes*: the play on words involves neither the dictionary meaning of "bulrushes," or cattails, nor the basket of bulrushes in which the infant Moses was laid by a river's edge; rather, Gunn's "artist-boarder" literally depicts a pair of *rushing bulls*, or "*bul-rushes*," to represent "two rushing animals of the bovine species."

11. *Phyfe* correspondence: in the minds of many of Gunn's original readers, "Fortune-Telling And Seduction," to borrow the title from an article in the *New York Tribune* newspaper (February 7, 1855, 7), were closely connected in America's cities before the Civil War. Gunn here makes playful reference to this connection. As he suggests, it was not uncommon for men in the period to advertise for wives in the pages of metropolitan dailies; in turn, women seeking husbands would answer such advertisements, and so precipitate a meeting with their potential love match. What Gunn only hints at is that self-proclaimed "fortune-tellers," who already were providing (for a fee) female clients with dubious descriptions of their future mates, sometimes accepted cash payments from men in return for directing young women to them. The kinds of men who made these arrangements often aimed at seduction, not marriage, and accordingly provided the era's newspapers with an ample supply of stories involving breach of promise or worse—which is to say, sexual scandal. Gunn's "Phyfe correspondence" may refer to just such a scandal.

Madame Morrow: contemporary astrologist, who practiced her trade in a number of different locales along the U.S. eastern seaboard during the middle years of the nineteenth century. Arrested on more than one occasion for fraud, she and other practicing "Witches of New York" nevertheless continued to advertise their services in metropolitan newspapers from the period.

12. Doesticks: Mortimer Thomson, 1831–1875. American humorist and author, celebrated for his satirical newspaper writings. Thomson, a friend of Gunn's through fellow author Fanny Fern, wrote under the pseudonym "Q. K. Philander Doesticks, P. B." Just one of Thom-

son's literary works from the period is the above-named *The Witches of New York* (1858), a smiling examination of the city's practicing astrologers and other reputed clairvoyants.

13. Napoleonic axiom: Napoleon Bonaparte, 1769–1821. A leading general of the French Revolution, and later ruler, then emperor, of France. Among the many maxims attributed to Napoleon is this political statement, made before the French Legislative Assembly, "We should wash our dirty linen at home."

CHAPTER XIII — THE CHEAP HOTEL BOARDING-HOUSE

1. bagatelle-table: a gaming table, resembling a small billiards table.

2. Babel: the ancient city of Babylon. In the Bible's Book of Genesis, the people of Babel unite to build a tower to heaven. Angered by human arrogance, God punishes the Babylonians by denying them a shared language—resulting in a "confusion of tongues."

3. General Scott: Winfield Scott, 1786–1866. U.S. Army general who came to national prominence during the Mexican-American War of 1846–1848. Based on his success—both military and administrative—in that conflict, Scott later, and as a civilian, would run for the office of U.S. President on the Whig ticket of 1852. After a national campaign that brought him to Gunn's New York, Scott lost the election to the Democratic Party candidate, Franklin Pierce.

4. Teuton: a member of an early Germanic tribe; also, and more commonly, a general term for a person of German descent or citizenship.

5. Falstaff: a recurring character in Shakespeare's stage comedies and history plays, known for his brash talk and burly physical presence.

6. Samaritanship: an act of Christian charity. The name derives from the Samaritans, a people descended from an ancient group of Israelites, and who practice Samaritan*ism* as a religion.

CHAPTER XIV — THE BOARDING-HOUSE WHERE THE LANDLADY DRINKS

1. "the copy-book proverb, that 'Comparisons are Odious' ": a familiar literary maxim, often used by authors to counsel against comparing one's written work to another's (or even to one's own, earlier work). The phrase found its way into schoolbooks in Gunn's day; it particularly appeared in writing and spelling manuals that trained students to compose both accurately and in a neat hand.

2. *Monsieur Tonson*: a mythical figure from contemporary English folklore. In various vernacular poems and tales from the late eighteenth and early nineteenth centuries, a "*Monsieur Tonson*," or Mr. Thompson, represented a paradox of personhood: someone who at once did not exist, and yet would not go away.

3. panorama: a large-scale visual representation, meant to impress viewers with a total sense of a geographical place, scene, or setting. In Gunn's time, an age before cinema, panoramic exhibits provided a form of popular entertainment for which spectators would pay an admission fee.

4. pestilence in 1849: In the politically unstable year of 1848, Europe experienced a severe outbreak of the deadly disease cholera. By May 1849, the outbreak had spread across the Atlantic, and by June it had reached epidemic proportions in Manhattan.

5. *Pete's* on the *Points*: nineteenth-century dance hall establishment located in New York's Five Points slum. Owned and operated by Pete Williams, "Pete's" was a place notorious about town for the mixed-race dancing that occurred there.

6. *perruquier*: French term, for wig-maker.

CHAPTER XV — THE BOARDING-HOUSE WHOSE LANDLADY LIKES TO BE ILL-USED

1. *Viliken's Dinah*: "Villikins and his Dinah," a popular tune in Gunn's day, which sang the cautionary tale of an "uncommon nice" sixteen-year-old daughter of a wealthy London merchant.

2. *Uncle Tom's Cabin*: best-selling antislavery novel of 1852, written by American author Harriet Beecher Stowe (1811–1896).

3. "Tell's knocking the hat of Gesler off the pole": in European legend, the Swissman William Tell defies an Austrian tyrant named Gessler, whose hat—a supposed sign of his authority—sits upon a pole in Tell's native village. One version of the legend has Tell knocking Gessler's hat from the pole.

CHAPTER XVI — OF A TIP-TOP BOARDING-HOUSE

1. Madison Square: an area in lower Manhattan, whose landmark park (bordered by Fifth and Madison avenues, and 23rd and 26th streets) the municipality officially set aside as a public space in 1847. The neighborhood remained largely residential for the next decade, and quickly became one of the city's leading seats of fashion.

2. "lingering Peri-like at the portal": in Persian myth, the Peris are fairy-like fallen angels who must remain outside paradise until they perform an acceptable penance. Figuratively, they linger at paradise's door, or portal. Gunn most likely refers to English author Thomas Moore's version of the Peri myth, found in his well-received narrative poem *Lalla Rookh: an Oriental Romance* (1817).

3. Jonker Afrikaner: in the 1830s, the leader of the white, partially Dutch-descended "Afrikaner" people of South Africa.

4. *tournure*: French term, for figure, or personal bearing.

5. "a pecuniary *Jorkins*": Jorkins, an attorney from the law firm of Spenlow and Jorkins in English author Charles Dickens's novel *David Copperfield* (1850). Whereas Spenlow habitually declares himself willing to take decisive action, Jorkins serves as a restraining foil for his partner, predictably preventing action with his many reservations. A "pecuniary Jorkins" would be a person whose objections repeatedly prevent someone else from spending money.

6. Mrs. Siddons: Sarah Siddins, 1755–1831. Eighteenth-century English actress, believed by many to be the best tragic stage performer of the age.

7. Zenobia: a commanding third-century queen of the western Orient.

8. forfeit *philopœna*: a philopena is a traditional game, originating in Germany, that requires one person to give a gift to another. The rules of the game are as follows: two people, eating of the same nut, open a shell and find two (rather than one) kernels inside; upon their next meeting, the first of these people to say "philopena" may rightfully claim a gift from the other.

9. Tennyson: Alfred, Lord Tennyson, 1809–1892. Celebrated English Victorian poet, and for many years Poet Laureate of Great Britain.

10. *Hiawatha*: *The Song of Hiawatha*, a popular epic poem of 1855 by U.S. poet Henry Wadsworth Longfellow. Longfellow's subject matter and style for this work derived from the legends of the Ojibway Native American tribe, and to some extent sought to replicate the sound and speech rhythms of this particular indigenous people's language.

11. *Hood-like* Serenade: Thomas Hood, 1799–1845. English poet and humorist, known for his mildly comic handling of the romantic literary tradition.

12. the Dead March in *La Gazza Ladra*: *La gazza ladra*, Italian for "The Thieving Magpie," was a serio-comic opera of 1817 by composer Gioachino Rossini. The "Dead March" comes from the opera's overture, famous for the marching beat sustained by its use of snare drums.

13. Campagna: a small mountain town in the southern Italian province of Salerno.

14. *rencontre*: French term, for encounter.

15. Empress Eugenie: Eugénie de Montijo, 1826–1920. Spanish-born countess, who, upon her marriage to Napoleon III in 1853, served as France's last empress until the country's 1871 defeat in the Franco-Prussian War.

16. Racine: Jean Racine, 1639–1699. One of the leading French dramatists of the seventeenth century, who primarily wrote tragedies for the stage.

17. Amazon: in Greek mythology, a member of a tribe of warring women from Asia Minor.

CHAPTER XVII — THE BOARDING-HOUSE WHERE YOU'RE EXPECTED TO MAKE LOVE TO THE LANDLADY

1. "Tragic *Mews*": *Mews* is a British term, associated mostly with London, used to indicate a style of joint-use building—with a stable for horses below and living quarters (normally for stablemen) above. The pun referred to here jokingly suggests that horses housed in a mews are the source of the morning's breakfast sausages.

2. Miss Warner's novels: Susan Warner, 1819–1885. American author, New Yorker, and religious reformer whose writings often carried evangelical Christian overtones.

CHAPTER XVIII — OF ANOTHER MEAN BOARDING-HOUSE

1. St. John's Square: area on the lower west side of Manhattan, bordered by Varick, Beach, and Laight streets. Until the early twentieth century the site of St. John's Chapel, with its adjacent park and fine homes, the "Square," as Gunn calls it, had in his day entered into a period of decline. By that time, the neighborhood increasingly featured warehouses and low-end housing.

2. Slawkenbergian: in English author and clergyman Laurence Sterne's novel *Tristram Shandy* (1759), there features a satirical, "Slawkenbergian" story about a man whose nose was so long as to distract the people of his native Strasburg, Germany, from thinking of anything else.

3. Seven Deadly Sins: Christian belief identifies seven severe vices that epitomize man's inherent tendency toward sin and jeopardize his soul's afterlife. Among these seven deadly sins is gluttony, called here by Gunn Appetite.

4. *Lar*: one among many ancient Roman domestic deities, known in the plural form as Lares. The Lares were believed to protect both home and family.

5. the lady-*ghoule* in the Arabian Nights: the *Arabian Nights* is a composite volume of traditional Persian tales, collected over thousands of years, from various different authors, and believed to have been set down in manuscript form between AD 800 and 900. One particular tale concerns "The Wife Who Wouldn't Eat"; as her husband observes, the wife in question indeed does eat, waking at night to join a ghoul in the local cemetery—where the two of them feast on corpses.

6. *Adventures of Lazarillo de Tormes*: *The Life of Lazarillo de Tormes and of His Fortunes and Adversities*, Spanish novella published anonymously in 1574. The work follows the wide-ranging adventures of the title character, beginning with his early, resourceful climb from poverty and hunger.

7. Anthropophagi: in English folklore, cannibals distinguished by their peculiar anatomy: they had no heads, and their mouths were located in their chests.

8. Mr. Sparrowgrass: *The Sparrowgrass Papers; or, Living in the Country* (1856), a book by American author Frederic S. Cozzens, recounts the humorous exploits of an urban-dwelling Mr. Sparrowgrass as he sets up rural cottage residence outside his native New York.

9. *double-gangers*: in German, a *doppelgänger* is a living person's ghostly double; here as elsewhere, Gunn is poking fun at Scottish pronunciation.

10. "Stolen waters are sweet": from the Bible's Book of Proverbs 9:17—"Stolen waters are sweet, and the bread of secrecy is pleasant." Although often called the "Proverbs of Solomon"—Solomon being the son of David, ancient king of Israel—the book's actual authorship remains open to question.

11. North River: well into the nineteenth century, an alternate name for New York's Hudson River, which runs due north from the island of Manhattan. The North, or Hudson, River runs through the eastern portion of the state, and, where it empties to the south in New York Harbor, forms a natural geographical boundary between the neighboring states of New York and New Jersey.

12. bourne: the ultimate end point, as of a journey; a poetic term for death.

CHAPTER XIX — THE FAMILY HOTEL ON BROADWAY

1. the Cosmopolitan, St. Nicodemus, or other "traveler's houses": contemporary New York hotels.

CHAPTER XX — THE ARTISTS' BOARDING-HOUSE

1. Nootka Sound: a remote inlet along the western coast of Vancouver Island, in the Pacific Canadian province of British Columbia.

2. *burins*: a burin is a sharp-edged engraver's tool.

3. the poet of *Idlewild*: Idlewild was the name of New York poet Nathaniel Parker Willis's Hudson River home outside the city. Willis's work was popular with readers in Gunn's day, and appeared in book form as well as in newspapers and magazines.

4. Ixion's wheel: in Greek mythology, the ancient tribal king Ixion is punished by the gods for various crimes by being attached for eternity to a spinning, fiery wheel.

Sisyphus's stone-rolling: in Greek mythology, King Sisyphus is punished by Tartarus, lord of the underworld, by being sentenced to an eternity of rolling a large boulder up a hill.

5. Tartarean: of or related to Tartarus, the dark underworld of Greek mythology (also the deity of that same name) where lost souls were sent as punishment after death.

6. pictorial philo-progenitiveness: philoprogenitiveness means a fondness for children—thus a fondness for drawing children.

7. the hero of Tennyson's ballad: in his poem "The Lord of Burleigh" (1842), Victorian poet Alfred Tennyson portrays a sensitive English aristocratic who, in the guise of a humble landscape painter, meets and weds a village maiden—later to reveal his true identity.

8. Vandykish: Sir Anthony van Dyke, 1599–1641. Flemish artist who became the leading English court painter during the reign of Charles I. Self-portraits by the artist reveal van Dyke's signature short, pointed beard.

9. Catskills: a mountain range that runs to the northwest of New York's Hudson River Valley; the Catskills provided both the inspiration and subject matter for a number of nineteenth-century American landscape painters.

10. hecatomb of yellow-covered novels: in Gunn's day, cheap pamphlet novels often bore yellow-paper covers, and featured among their contents sensational stories involving the romantic exploits of dashing heroes and villains. A "hecatomb" of such novels is Gunn's poetic way of saying "many," a reference to the ancient Greek religious ritual of sacrificing one hundred oxen to the gods.

11. down East: a geographic area encompassing rural, coastal Maine, and running north to the U.S.-Canadian border.

12. an intellectual-Jack-Sheppardish physiognomy: Jack Sheppard, 1702–1724. A notorious thief of early eighteenth-century London, who ultimately was captured, tried, and hanged. Sheppard thereafter became a recurring character in English literature, featuring in Gunn's day in William Harrison Ainsworth's novel *Jack Sheppard* (1840)—with illustrations by Charles Dickens's longtime collaborator, artist George Cruikshank.

13. semi-Manichean system of philosophy: Manicheanism was a major early religion originating in third-century Persia, based on a dualistic understanding of life as a constant struggle between light and darkness.

14. *Haggises*: haggis is a traditional Scottish food dish, composed of a sheep's organ meats, oatmeal, and spices stuffed inside the animal's stomach, and then boiled before serving.

15. Mahlström: a maelstrom is a strong whirlpool; in Scandinavian legend, a Mahlström was a specific instance of this phenomenon located in the Arctic Ocean, off the western coast of Norway, and believed to seize hold of and destroy any sailing vessels that drew within a certain radius.

16. the *statuette* of the Fighting Gladiator: traditional artists' subject, most notably in statuary, depicting one or more of the professional fighters, or gladiators, of ancient Rome.

17. the White Mountains: a scenic mountain range in New Hampshire; like New York's Catskills, the White Mountains appeared often in nineteenth-century American landscape paintings.

CHAPTER XXI — THE VEGETARIAN BOARDING-HOUSE (AS IT WAS)

1. the Battery: waterfront area at the southern tip of Manhattan, overlooking New York Harbor. In 1855, city authorities opened a processing center for foreign immigrants at the site, some four decades before a similar center opened on New York's Ellis Island.

2. the Athenians in Scripture: in Biblical scripture (Acts 17), the apostle Paul visits the city of Athens to spread the teachings of Christ. He finds there a general mass of people given over to the worship of idols, and, among the learned, a variety of competing sects and schools of thought—all of whom, as Gunn says, are inquiring into "new things."

3. Unitarianism: Unitarian Christians believe in a "unitary" godhead, rather than a Trinitarian God manifested separately as a Father, Son, and Holy Spirit. Unitarians achieved prominence and cultural influence in the United States beginning in the early 1800s; during the decades before the Civil War, they often were involved in various contemporary reform efforts.

Transcendentalism: a liberal religious, reform, and artistic outpouring of the 1830s and 1840s, Transcendentalism emerged in the United States in direct response to what many of its New England adherents believed to be the cold rationalism of Unitarianism. Like their Unitarian counterparts, Transcendentalists frequently joined the ranks of contemporary reformers; unlike the majority of Unitarians, not a few Transcendentalists supported experimental, sometimes radical, causes.

Universalism: both a general religious outlook and an official creed that at once emphasizes God's spiritual harmony with all peoples and creatures, and recognizes as valid the beliefs of many world religions.

Swedenborgianism: Emanuel Swedenborg, 1688–1772. Swedish philosopher and Christian mystic, who derived a faith based on the supposed close "correspondence" between the natural and spiritual worlds. The writings of Swedenborg made a firm impression on a number of nineteenth-century American Transcendentalists; and, like the Transcendentalists, many so-called "Swedenborgians" devoted themselves both to social and religious reform, particularly, but not exclusively, in the United States.

Millerism: William Miller, 1782–1849. American Baptist minister and cult leader, whose followers (known as Millerites) made national headlines in the 1840s as they waited in vain for what they believed to be the world's imminent end.

Mormonism: an American-inspired religious movement, whose members belong to The Church of Jesus Christ of Latter-day Saints. Mormons claim to seek to restore Christianity to its earliest practices, and rest their beliefs on the sacred *Book of Mormon*, first published in upstate New York in 1830.

General Negation: a basic tenet of various religious mysticisms, all of which call in one way or another for a "general negation," or final denial, of earthly existence in order to foster a closer embrace of the spiritual realm.

4. Water-cure Establishment: the water-cure was a quasi-medical treatment, especially popular in both the United States and Europe during the nineteenth century. At hotel resorts, or "establishments," built and run for the purpose, patients—suffering from everything from headaches to more serious ailments—submitted to a regimen of drinking and bathing in what they believed to be restorative waters.

5. Icaria: an island off the coast of Greece, considered sacred to the ancient peoples of the surrounding Aegean Sea.

6. Phalanstery: an experimental reform commune founded on the writings of French utopian socialist Charles Fourier. Fourier's thought generated much interest and controversy in the United States during the 1840s and 1850s; his most ardent American supporters

even tried to implement his communal vision, opening (and then closing) several short-lived communities along Fourierist lines.

7. "Elder" at Salt Lake: the Mormon Church is based in Salt Lake City, Utah, in the American West; the Church's governing body consists of a number of regional "Elders," the "Elder" at Salt Lake being the highest-ranking of these.

8. Neal Dow: Neal S. Dow, 1804–1897. Sometime mayor of Portland, Maine, whose support for the Maine Law of 1851 strengthened the nationwide crusade against the manufacture and sale of alcoholic beverages.

9. Preissnitz: Vincent Preissnitz, 1799–1851. Eastern European medical therapist whose water treatments in Germany initiated the nineteenth-century vogue for hydrotherapy.

10. Salamanderish: salamanders are amphibious animals, noted for periodically shedding their skin and their ability to regenerate lost limbs.

11. ophthalmia: medical term, for inflammation of the eye.

12. Shadrach, Meshach and Abednego: in the Bible's Book of Daniel, three royal advisors who, because of their unwillingness to worship what they consider to be false idols, provoke the anger of King Nebuchadnezzar; as punishment, the king orders that the three men be confined to a flaming furnace.

13. Brahmins: in traditional Hindu society, high priests; more generally, members of the highest caste.

14. Queen Mab: a fairy figure in English folklore, memorably evoked by Shakespeare in his stage tragedy *Romeo and Juliet*. Gunn refers here to English poet Percy Bysshe Shelley's "philosophical poem" *Queen Mab* (1813), a biographical work wherein the poet, expressing his youthful sympathy for all his fellow creatures, renounces the eating of meat.

15. The Golden Age: in Greek mythology, an idyllic time at the dawn of mankind.

16. the celebrated "Moon Hoax" of Richard Adams Locke: Richard Adams Locke, 1800–1871. American-born journalist whose "Moon Hoax" of 1835 appeared in the sensational penny newspaper the *New York Sun*. In a series of articles, presented as plain fact, Locke managed to convince many of the *Sun*'s readers that recent scientific observations had revealed extraordinary intelligence about the moon.

17. Bloomer costume: a loose-fitting women's outfit named for American Amelia Bloomer, who conducted a high-profile campaign for female dress reform in the 1850s.

18. the *Spiritual Telegraph*, *Water-Cure* and *Phrenological Journals*: contemporary reform newspapers.

CHAPTER XXII — THE MEDICAL STUDENTS' BOARDING-HOUSE

1. Dickens' *Pickwick Papers*: English author Charles Dickens's best-selling comic novel of 1836; in Chapter XXX, readers meet the supporting characters Mr. Bob Sawyer and Mr. Ben Allen, two rough-and-tumble medical students who defy the studious stereotype.

2. *Forget-Me-Not's*: generic name for literary gift annuals, popular in the United States during the 1830s and 1840s, whose flowery titles matched their sentimental contents—poetry, prose, and engravings, bound in book form (often elaborately), and given as gifts.

3. Cervantes' knight: Miguel de Cervantes, 1547–1616. Spanish author best known for his classic early novel *Don Quixote* (1605), whose deluded title character believes that he is a chivalric knight on a romantic quest—fighting the likes of paladins, or high-ranking officials of the medieval Catholic Church.

4. Albert Smith's lively *Punch* papers: Albert Richard Smith, 1816–1860. English author, remembered mostly for his adaptations of Charles Dickens's stories for the stage, and for his early contributions to the well-known London journal of literature and humor, *Punch*.

5. Goldsmith's Good-natured Man: Oliver Goldsmith, 1730?–1774. Anglo-Irish author and physician. Gunn refers here to Goldsmith's much-quoted play *The Good-natur'd Man* (1768).

6. the Emersonian principle of compensation: Ralph Waldo Emerson, 1803–1882. Nineteenth-century New England author, lecturer, and public intellectual, identified then

and now as the leading Transcendentalist. In his essay "Compensation" (1841), Emerson argues for a universal balance between all of life's opposing forces.

7. "every variety of pipes, from *nargilehs*, *chibouks*, *calumets*, and *meerschaums*, to . . . *dhudheens*": an assortment of the world's tobacco pipes, representing, respectively, Persia, Turkey, Native America, Germany, and Anglo-Ireland.

8. phlebotomy: professional term for bloodletting, once a common medical practice.

9. shillelagh: Irish term for a cudgel, or club, usually made of oak.

10. Seidlitz powder: a medicinal compound powder (one powder wrapped in blue paper, the other in white) from the nineteenth century, consumed when mixed with tonic water as a remedy for indigestion.

11. Leslie's *Bitters*: a popular potable medicine, derived in part from alcohol.

12. voltaic battery: a battery apparatus capable of producing an electric charge by chemical reaction.

13. Damon and Pythias: Damon and Pythias occupy the central roles in a legend from Greek mythology meant to illustrate the loyal bond between two close friends. In various tellings, each pledges his life as a substitute for the other's, thus demonstrating what Gunn would call a "spirit" of deep trust.

CHAPTER XXIII — THE BOARDING-HOUSE FREQUENTED BY BOSTONIANS

1. the "City of Notions": a colloquial name for Boston, suggestive of this American city's reputation as a center for thinking and learning.

2. Kaffirland: South Africa.

3. (after the style of John Leech's "swells"): John Leech, 1817–1864. Popular English illustrator, whose cartoon drawings of the men and women of contemporary London's city-streets were a recurring feature of the journal *Punch*.

4. King of Castile: Alfonso X, 1221–1284. Spanish monarch popularly known as "the Wise" or "the Learned" for his great store of learning. Gunn refers to a famous quote from Alfonso (never documented), which the ruler allegedly made upon receiving a complicated explanation of the astronomer Ptolemy's mathematical formula for planetary motion: "If the Lord Almighty had consulted me before embarking on creation thus, I should have recommended something simpler."

5. the American Athens: a colloquial name for Boston, which raises the city's intellectual status to the imposing levels of the storied Greek city-state.

6. Sparta: an ancient Greek city-state, whose inhabitants organized even their everyday lives according to a strict military regimen.

7. our forthcoming park: legislative planning for New York's premier public park, Central Park, began as early 1853; the park officially opened in 1873.

8. Boston Common: central historic green of Boston, long a gathering point for the city's inhabitants—for purposes of leisure and on occasions of civic significance.

9. the view from Greenwood or Hoboken heights: founded in 1838, Brooklyn's Greenwood Cemetery recalls in its design and layout the rolling rural landscapes of the acclaimed Mount Auburn Cemetery in Cambridge, Massachusetts. In Gunn's day, Hoboken Heights was a wooded area in neighboring New Jersey, overlooking Manhattan.

10. Dorchester: at the time, a rural suburb south of Boston; the area was annexed to Boston proper in 1870, and thereafter urbanized rapidly.

Bunker Hill Monument: a hillside obelisk located just outside Boston, commemorating a famous early battle of the American Revolution. The monument opened in 1843.

11. Washington-street: a major historic thoroughfare running in and through Boston, connecting much of the metropolis.

12. Greeley, Raymond, Beecher, Chapin, Astor, Grinnell: Horace Greeley (1811–1872) and Henry Jarvis Raymond (1820–1869), prominent American newspapermen, and founding editors, respectively, of the *New York Tribune* and *New York Times*; Henry Ward Beecher (1813–1887) and Edwin Chapin (1814–1880), two of the leading New York ministers and lec-

turers of the mid-nineteenth century; and John Jacob Astor (1763–1848) and Moses H. Grinnell (1803–1877)—the former being New York's wealthiest businessman and real estate baron, the latter a prosperous merchant and sometime president of the New York Chamber of Commerce.

13. Amos Lawrence: 1786–1852. Wealthy New England industrialist, who in 1830 opened the first of his famous textile mills in Lowell, Massachusetts. Lawrence devoted much of his subsequent life to philanthropy.

14. Jenny Lind, Grisi, and Rachel: Jenny Lind (1820–1887), Giulia Grisi (1811–1869), and Elisabeth Rachel Félix (1821–1858). Lind and Grisi were contemporary sopranos—the former Swedish, the latter Italian. "Rachel," as she became known both on and off stage, was a leading French actress of the day. All three performers conducted mid-nineteenth-century tours of the United States, drawing much fanfare and large audiences in the process—particularly during their extended stays in New York.

15. Boston State House: one of Boston's most recognizable political and architectural landmarks, the city's gold-domed State House sits high atop Beacon Hill, overlooking Boston Common. In 1858, Massachusetts man of letters Oliver Wendell Holmes, Sr., expressed the local pride of many in the city when in writing he called Boston's State House the "hub of the solar system."

16. Fanny Fern: Sara Willis Parton, 1811–1872. Known by her pen name "Fanny Fern," the New England–born Parton was one of America's most popular and versatile writers before the Civil War—her work a mainstay among tens of thousands of U.S. children, newspaper readers, and fans of her several full-length novels. A former resident both of Boston and Philadelphia, Fern spent her most productive years in New York, and derived much of her literary material from the city.

17. the Academy: founded in 1833, the Boston Academy of Music was the first music school established in the United States.

18. *chaussure*: French term, for shoes.

19. the tune of "Poor Dog Tray": "My Poor Dog Tray," a popular Irish-inspired melody from the period, the sheet music of which was produced and sold by New York publishing firm J. Andrews for parlor performances in the home.

CHAPTER XXIV — THE BOARDING-HOUSE WHOSE LANDLADY IS A SOUTHERNER

1. Mason and Dixon's line: the Mason-Dixon Line, a geopolitical border completed in 1767 dividing the then-British colonies of Pennsylvania and Maryland. The Line thereafter became a convenient shorthand way to distinguish between the U.S. North and South, particularly with the approach of the Civil War.

2. Mrs. Stowe's *Aunt Ophelia*: stereotypically diligent, dutiful, and orderly New England character from U.S. author Harriet Beecher Stowe's best-selling antislavery novel, *Uncle Tom's Cabin* (1852).

3. a faro-bank: faro is a card game, popular in England and France in the eighteenth century, and revived in the American West during the next century. A "faro bank" was once a familiar phrase used to indicate a game of faro.

4. Crystal Palace Exposition of 1851: also known as the Great Exhibition, the London event marked the first of a series of subsequent international world's fairs, celebrating and exhibiting culture and industry from across the globe.

5. a very Turpin-like manner: Richard (Dick) Turpin, 1705–1739. Notorious, and violent, English highwayman, whom British authorities ultimately captured and hanged. Turpin thereafter entered popular legend through a number of nineteenth-century English ballads and plays, which together preserved his place in cultural memory.

6. port-monnaiè: *portmonnaiè*, French term, for a small carrying case normally used while traveling.

7. "Confessions of a Reformed Gambler": such "Confessions" were a mainstay of the print marketplace and lecture circuit during the middle decades of the nineteenth century. Gunn

refers here to the self-styled "Reformed Gambler" J. H. Green, whose sensational *Confessions* (1849, 2nd ed.) epitomizes the literary expression of this phenomenon.

8. Southampton and Bremen: port cities, respectively, in southwestern England and northwestern Germany; both offered transatlantic steamship crossings to and from the United States after such service began in 1838.

9. *filles-de-joie*: French term, for prostitutes.

10. *Corpus Christi*: southeastern coastal Texas town situated on the Gulf of Mexico.

11. "Old Dominion": a formally dignified phrase for the U.S. state of Virginia.

12. John Randolph and the *Tribune*, "dough face": John Randolph, 1773–1833. John Randolph was a U.S. congressional leader from Virginia, identified in his day and after as representing the slaveholding interests of the state's plantation elite. The term *dough face* was a contemporary political expression—used critically by such antislavery newspapers as the *New York Tribune*—for a person from the American North who held pro-Southern sympathies.

13. this Southern Mrs. Potiphar (not à la Curtis, but à la Genesis): in the Bible's Book of Genesis, Joseph is sold into slavery by his brothers and eventually purchased by Potiphar—whose wife in turn attempts to seduce Joseph. The other Potiphar referred to here is that of the American author and editor George William Curtis, whose collected essays from the *Potiphar Papers* of 1853 satirized New York's fashionable society.

CHAPTER XXV — THE BOARDING-HOUSE WHERE THE LANDLADY IS FROM "DOWN EAST"

1. Micawber-like: in English author Charles Dickens's novel *David Copperfield* (1850), the hapless character Wilkins Micawber eventually lands in debtor's prison after failing to meet the claims of his creditors. A "Micawber-like" life was one lived perilously close to insolvency, yet in expectation of better times to come.

2. his illustrious prototype's dealings in "coals": in Dickens's *David Copperfield* (1850), the character Wilkins Micawber at one stage embraces the coal trade as a hoped-for way to earn his living.

3. a small Ophir or Lilliputian California: Ophir is a Biblical port settlement famous for its wealth. Nearly a decade after the Gold Rush of 1849, California remained in the minds of many synonymous with the making of sudden financial fortunes; a "Lilliputian" California would be a smaller version of the same, after the miniature island nation of Lilliput in Irish author Jonathan Swift's novel *Gulliver's Travels* (1726).

4. the popular novels of "Silenus Gobb, Junior": Sylvanus Cobb, Jr., 1823–1887. A prolific, widely read American author of romantic tales and novels from the period, many of the latter of which appeared serially in Robert Bonner's *New York Ledger* story paper.

5. the High Bridge, Harlem: a brick, arched bridge spanning New York's Harlem river, which separates Manhattan from the city's northern Bronx borough. The area around the bridge (which still stands today) was a scenic, much-visited site for promenades in Gunn's time.

CHAPTER XXVI — THE BOARDING-HOUSE IN WHICH ENGLISHMEN PREDOMINATE

1. Whig ticket: in America, the Whigs were one of the nation's two principal political parties during the decades leading up to the U.S. Civil War. At once economically conservative and socially progressive, and supported largely, although not entirely, by a native-born electorate based in the northeastern United States, the Whigs ceded to their Democratic Party rivals the vast majority of the urban immigrant vote, including that of Irish Americans.

2. badger-drawings: also called badger-baiting; a rowdy popular entertainment of the English-speaking Atlantic world well into the nineteenth century, involving staged, wagered fights between untamed badgers and dogs.

3. Sandwich Islands: the present-day Hawaiian Islands.

4. comestibles: edibles.

5. cullender: a colander, or bowl-shaped strainer.

6. Collins' steamers: the first large American steamship line, offering service between the United States and England beginning in the early 1850s. The Collins line competed directly with the British Cunard Line.

7. the fate of the *Arctic*: the *Arctic* was a steamship vessel from the Collins Line, lost at sea in September 1854 when it collided with a smaller French ship in dense fog.

8. an "all-rounder" collar: familiar English phrase for a common style of shirt collar from the period, one whose versatility made it fit "all round"—that is to say, on various types of shirts, for various different occasions.

9. the *European*: short-lived New York weekly newspaper, published by H. Forbes between 1856 and 1857 and featuring European news items.

10. *Coal 'Ole, Evans'*: *Coal 'Ole* is London street dialect for "coal hole," or "coal cellar"; both *Coal 'Ole* and *Evans'* refer in this case to the names of London pubs.

11. 'Arry Widdicombe: Harry Widdicombe, stage name of a contemporary London performer; the surname Widdicombe most likely derives from the traditional English folk song, "Widdicombe Fair."

12. Mrs. Gaskell's *North and South*: Elizabeth Gaskell, 1810–1865. English author, whose novels from the period portray the different layers of her home country's social class system. Gaskell's *North and South* (1854) examines the gap between England's gritty industrial north and commercially prosperous south.

13. going to Kansas: in the mid-1850s, the newly settled American Midwest territories of Kansas and Nebraska were the site of a fierce political contest over slavery, with recently arrived inhabitants on both sides of the issue fighting to impose their views on their adopted home ground.

Joining Walker, *filibuster* republic: William Walker, 1824–1860. An American filibuster, or military adventurer, who in 1856 arbitrarily declared himself commander of Nicaragua's army and president of the Republic. The combined forces of surrounding Central American nations eventually defeated Walker and his army, with Walker himself being executed in the process.

14. Punch's "Unprotected Female": humorous one-act play appearing in the London periodical *Punch* in 1856; written by the dramatist, early staff writer, and sometime editor of *Punch* Tom Taylor (1817–1880).

15. Halliburton's Clock-maker: Thomas Chandler Haliburton, 1796–1865. One of Canada's earliest noted authors, whose serial work *The Clockmaker* (1836) enjoyed success both in the United States and throughout the British Commonwealth. "The Clockmaker" of the title refers to lead character Sam Slick, whose keen Yankee wit earned Halliburton the reputation as one of North America's leading contemporary humorists.

16. Mr. Bull: John Bull, from the early eighteenth century onward a solid, common-sensical personification of England—in both visual and literary depictions.

17. the Crampton difficulty: John F. Crampton, a sometime top British diplomat to the United States, who in May 1856 was dismissed from his post on American soil over allegations that he had committed improprieties in attempting to recruit U.S. volunteers to join England's involvement in the Crimean War.

18. Guy Fawkes: 1570–1606. One of several English Roman Catholics involved in the Gunpowder Plot, a thwarted attempt to blow up both houses of England's Parliament, kill King James I, and thus disrupt Protestant rule in the country.

CHAPTER XXVII — THE "PENSION FRANÇAISE"

1. M. Beauvallet: 1801–1873. French actor, celebrated for his mid-nineteenth-century tragic roles at Paris's Théâtre Français, or Comédie-Française.

2. *Palais Royal*: a Parisian palace and garden located opposite the north wing of the Louvre; the reference here is a humorous one, to a modest nearby restaurant of the same name.

3. bread *à discretion*: complementary bread, served in a basket at meals free of charge.

4. *sacré*: that is, to make the French exclamation *sacré*, or "sacred."

5. *The Vicar of Wakefield*: novel of 1766 by Anglo-Irish author Oliver Goldsmith, widely read well into the nineteenth century and after.

6. *Gil Blas*: a multivolume romance by French author Alain-Rene Lesage. Appearing in four parts between 1715 and 1735, Lesage's work built upon the success of his earlier *Le Diable Boiteux*. It also, despite the Spanish trappings of its setting and central character, provided a broad satirical portrait of eighteenth-century French society.

Telemaque: didactic novel of 1699 denouncing the French monarchy, written by author François Fénelon.

7. Stewart's store: Alexander Turney Stewart, 1803–1876. Successful American merchant, who in 1846 opened at the corner of New York's Chambers Street and Broadway a large dry goods store known locally as the "Marble Palace," or simply Stewart's. Many consider this establishment to be the forerunner of the first true U.S. department store.

8. escaped exiles from Cayenne: Cayenne, capital of French Guiana on the Atlantic coast of South America, remained for several centuries a destination for political prisoners exiled by the ruling French government in Paris.

9. Danton's saying: George Jacques Danton, 1759–1794. A leading participant in the early years of the French Revolution, later sent to the guillotine by his former political allies.

10. Napoleon *le Petit*: Louis-Napoléon Bonaparte, or Napoleon III, 1808–1873. Bonaparte emerged as the first democratically elected president of the French Republic in 1848, after his predecessor, Louis Philippe, was deposed in the revolution of that year. Bonaparte nevertheless employed force of arms just several years later when he seized complete control of the French government. As Emperor Napoleon III, he reigned from 1852 to 1870. The phrase "Napoleon le Petit" derives from the title of an influential political pamphlet by French author Victor Hugo, a work that denounced the "Little Napoleon" for dissolving the French Republic.

11. Reverend Abbott: the Reverend Abbott Albinus, a Catholic Church official of late seventh-/early eighth-century Canterbury who, through writing and mutual acquaintance, served as a documentary source for the Venerable Bede's seminal history of England.

12. *dejeuner*: French term, for breakfast.

13. gambogian: dirty, pale-yellow in color.

14. *le Charivari*, or *Journal Pour Rire*: *Le Charivari* was an illustrated Parisian newspaper that began circulation in 1832; it specialized in political caricature. *Journal Pour Rire*, or the "Journal for Laughs," was a similar Paris publication, running from 1848 to 1855.

15. scélérat, polisson: French terms, respectively, for criminal and rascal.

16. Count Goggleowski: Count Adam de Gurowski, 1805–1866. Son of a Polish count, the writer, reformer, and historian Gurowski led an itinerant existence among various European universities (including a stop in Paris) before emigrating to the United States in 1849. Gurowski settled in New York for several years in the 1850s, and joined the very same journalistic circles to which Gunn belonged. The playful nickname "Goggleowski"—not Gunn's invention—refers to the rather abrasive and opinionated count's conspicuous blue spectacles, by which he was widely recognized.

17. *N. Y. Picayune*: launched in early 1850, the *New-York Picyaune* was a comic weekly newspaper in Gunn's Manhattan. Gunn, in fact, contributed illustrations to the paper.

18. Beranger's songs: Pierre-Jean de Béranger, 1780–1857. Contemporary French songwriter, whose songs found special favor among the republican sympathizers of Paris in 1830.

19. *mauvais sujet*: French phrase, for a bad or wicked subject.

20. *delirium tremens*: a shaking fit or seizure, usually caused by the excessive consumption of alcohol.

CHAPTER XXVIII — THE GERMAN "GASTHAUS"

1. Castle Garden: beginning in 1824, a theater and opera house located in New York's Battery Park, at the southern tip of Manhattan. From 1855 to 1890, the site served as the first official U.S. immigrant reception center, before the opening of Ellis Island.

2. Diedrich Knickerbocker: a fictional literary persona created by New York author Washington Irving (1783–1859), and made famous as the nostalgic, less-then-reliable, Dutch-descended narrator of Irving's serio-comic *History of New York* (1809).

3. Faust: Faust is the hero of a classic German legend, involving a medieval scholar whose quest for knowledge leads him to make a pact with the devil.

Guttemburg: Johannes Gutenberg, 1400–1468. German printer, credited with launching the first modern printing press of movable type.

4. *Fliegende Blätter*: a satirical weekly German newspaper, founded in Munich in 1845.

5. execution of Blüm: Robert Blüm, 1807–1848. German activist, author, and politician, executed in Vienna, Austria, for his role in the regional push for democracy. Blüm thereafter became for many a symbol of Germany's revolutionary struggles in 1848 and after.

6. Schiller: Friedrich Schiller, 1759–1805. German man of letters, who wrote poems, plays, essays, and histories, and devoted much of his philosophical thought to the study of aesthetics.

Goethe: Johann Wolfgang von Goethe, 1749–1832. Versatile German writer, whose life and work span the transition from Classicism to Romanticism in contemporary Western culture.

Uhland: Ludwig Uhland, 1787–1862. German poet, known primarily for his lyric productions in the romantic vein.

7. Albert Dürer: Albrecht Dürer, 1471–1528. German painter and mathematician, best remembered for the sharp precision of his carefully executed engravings.

8. the "leathery" *Burschen* ditty translated in Longfellow's *Hyperion*: New England poet Henry Wadsworth Longfellow's romance novel *Hyperion* (1839) appeared early in his writing career. The "Burschen" (German, for "young men") "ditty" that appears there reflects the author's abiding interest in European languages and legend.

9. on a certain Homeric occasion, the clouds did Jupiter and Juno on Mount Ida: as the epic poet of classical Greece, Homer recorded the legendary history of antiquity, and profiled the pagan gods worshiped in the early religions of modern-day Europe's Aegean region. Jupiter is the Roman name for Zeus, king of the gods in Greek mythology; Juno is the Roman name for his wife, Hera. Gunn refers here to a passage in Homer's account of the Trojan War, the *Iliad*. In the scene alluded to, known as "The Deception of Zeus," Hera seduces her husband behind a golden cloud at the peak of Mount Ida.

10. Bull's Ferry, Fort Lee: riverside communities in New York State and New Jersey, respectively, both a ferryboat ride away from Manhattan across the Hudson.

11. Volks' Gartens: German, for the "peoples' gardens," or outdoor beer gardens, which were much-frequented by members of New York's German community at the time.

12. Bowery: the Bowery is a neighborhood in lower Manhattan, identified in Gunn's day with ethnic immigrants—Irish, mainly, but also Germans—and the working classes generally.

CHAPTER XXIX — THE IRISH IMMIGRANT BOARDING-HOUSE (AS IT WAS)

1. Blackwell's Island: a small island situated in New York's East River, used in the nineteenth century primarily as the site of various correctional and welfare institutions, including a lunatic asylum, a hospital, and a large prison. Today the island is known as Roosevelt Island.

2. the ogre-giant in *Pilgrim's Progress*: Englishman John Bunyan's Protestant allegory of 1678, *Pilgrim's Progress*, narrates the eventful journey of the aptly named central character, Christian, toward the redeeming power of God's saving grace. En route Christian encounters a number of obstacles, including a giant named Despair from whom he ultimately escapes.

3. "runners," carmen, "dock-loafers," and blackguards: foreign immigrants arriving by boat in mid-nineteenth-century New York were met by masses of men along the city's landing wharves. Some of these men merely were plying their respective trades, notably those coach drivers and baggage handlers who worked to transport immigrants to their destinations within the city. Others—including "runners" hired by boardinghouse keepers to steer the unwary to their establishments—not infrequently were petty criminals, preying on new arrivals' lack of knowledge with respect to New York's geographic layout and customs.

4. O'Connell: Daniel O'Connell, 1775–1847. Leading Irish political figure, who in the first half of the nineteenth century earned the nickname "The Liberator" as he championed the combined causes of Catholicism, small freehold farms, and the repeal of Union with Great Britain.

the vitriolically-patriotic Mitchel: John Mitchel, 1815–1875. Irish nationalist and journalist, known for his outspoken journal articles.

President Pierce: Franklin Pierce, 1804–1869. U.S. President from 1853 to 1857, who, as standard-bearer for the Democratic Party during his time in the White House, found favor among the heavily Democratic Irish American community.

"Emmett's Speech": Robert Emmet, 1778–1803. Irish nationalist and orator, sentenced to death for urging insurrection against England. Emmet delivered at his final trial a memorable speech in which he defiantly retained his faith in Irish independence.

5. a Connecticut clock: during the latter eighteenth and early nineteenth centuries, the U.S. state of Connecticut became nationally known for its clock manufactures, so much so that the phrase "Connecticut clock" became proverbial.

6. "Licensed Immigrant Boarding-House": because of rampant fraud among certain New York boardinghouse keepers who catered to immigrants, city officials instituted a licensing policy for those homes with high immigrant occupancy rates. A $10.00 annual fee earned landlords the right to operate their houses, provided they follow the rules outlined by Gunn. Although well-intentioned, such rules often were ignored.

7. frieze coats: long winter coats, traditional dress in Ireland.

brimless caubeens: an Irish soldier's hat, brimless, beret-like, and worn tilted to the side of the head.

8. Potter's field: a burial ground reserved for the poor and/or unidentified dead. New York had several such cemeteries in Gunn's day.

CHAPTER XXX — THE CHINESE BOARDING-HOUSE

1. Flowery Country: a figurative name for China, also called the "Flowery Kingdom." The name pays homage to the important place of such flowers as the Lotus blossom in Chinese arts and crafts.

2. tabard-wise: a tabard is a short, often sleeveless, coat, common among men in the Middle Ages.

3. Celestial Empire: an historical name for China; sometimes used with racist intent, as in the epithet "Moonies" to refer to the Chinese people.

4. Hue, Bayard Taylor, Ida Pfeiffer: Evariste-Régis Hue (1813–1860). French Catholic missionary whose work *A Journey Through the Chinese Empire* appeared in English translation in New York in 1855, one year after its French publication in Paris. Bayard Taylor (1825–1878) and Ida Pfeiffer (1797–1858) were contemporary travel writers—American and Austrian, respectively.

5. murderous revolution and a war with Great Britain: between 1850 and 1864, elements within China who were opposed to the ruling Qing government conducted a full-scale rebellion, known as the Taiping Rebellion. The uprising ultimately failed. Simultaneously, the Qing government engaged the imperial powers of England and France from 1856 to 1860 in the Second Opium War.

6. Charles Lamb's immortal story of the Origin of Roast Pig: Charles Lamb, 1775–1834. Popular English author of urbane essays, widely admired and imitated in England and America. Lamb's collected *Essays of Elia* (1823) includes "A Dissertation Upon Roast Pig."

7. City Hospital: a massive stone structure located along lower Broadway in Gunn's day; an attractive landscaped lawn provided a contrast to the otherwise commercial character of the immediate area, and a still sharper contrast to the Five Points slum but several blocks distant.

8. New Amsterdam cows: in his semi-satirical *History of New York* (1809), local author Washington Irving provides an imaginative account of the city's early Dutch beginnings in the seventeenth century. At one stage in his work, Irving's fictional narrator, Diedrich Knickerbocker, claims that grazing cows set free at pasture in a once-unsettled lower Manhattan took the initiative from city officials in literally clearing paths for future development.

9. that colossal edifice: in 1854, Harper and Brothers Publishers opened a sizeable new headquarters in lower Manhattan's Franklin Square, at 331 Pearl Street. The building's imposing cast-iron façade concealed a large printing complex inside.

10. Gold-street: a short north-south thoroughfare in lower Manhattan, located several blocks inland from the South Street waterfront, below Fulton Street.

CHAPTER XXXI — THE SAILORS' BOARDING-HOUSE

1. Marryat's Pacha: Captain Frederick Marryat, 1792–1848. English sailor turned novelist, credited with helping to develop the genre of the sea story. Marryat's sixth book, *The Pacha of Many Tales* (1835), features an assortment of such stories, many of them fabulous.

2. doubling the Horn: by ship, crossing and recrossing Cape Horn, at the southern tip of South America. This was a common, if dangerous, voyage for nineteenth-century sailors working the Pacific Ocean.

3. Ole Bull: 1810–1880. Norwegian virtuoso violinist, whose well-attended American tours in the mid-nineteenth century dazzled audiences with their technical display.

4. a New Zealand chief: a reference to the ritual face-painting practices of the aboriginal tribes of New Zealand and Australia.

CHAPTER XXXIII — OF DIFFERENT SORTS OF BOARDERS

1. Alexandre Dumas: 1802–1870. French novelist, made famous by his long historical novels, many of them teeming with dramatic incident.

2. Proteus: in Greek mythology, a shape-shifting god of the sea.

the Bravo of Venice: English author Matthew Gregory Lewis (1775–1818), better known as "Monk" Lewis, attracted a large transatlantic readership in his time with his innovative Gothic novels. In 1810, Lewis translated from German into English Heinrich Zschokke's (1771–1848) novel *The Bravo of Venice*, the elusive title character of which fits very much into the Gothic mold of romance and mystery.

Junius' Letters: for three consecutive years, between 1769 and 1772, the London-based political newspaper the *Public Advertiser* ran a series of letters by an anonymous author, who wrote under the Latinate pen-name "Junius." Ranging in content from the personal to the public, the "letters" attracted much attention, and encouraged speculation over their author's identity.

3. Tabernacle: a shortened name for the Presbyterian Broadway Tabernacle Church, opened in lower Manhattan in 1836; it served primarily as a congregation space for the celebrity evangelist minister Charles Grandison Finney.

4. the Rev. Mr. Splurge-on: Charles Haddon Spurgeon, 1834–1892. British Reformed Baptist minister, whose published sermons attracted readers world-wide. Gunn refers by "Splurge" to Spurgeon's emotionally powerful, plain-spoken preaching style.

5. of *Carkerish* aspect: in Charles Dickens's novel *Dombey and Son* (1848), the story's shipping firm manager Mr. Carker bears a large, gaping set of teeth, which symbolize his greed.

6. Chantrey: Francis Legatt Chantrey, 1782–1841. Respected English sculptor, who openly acknowledged that other artists' creations inspired his own works.

7. "Byles' letters": a possible reference to Mather Byles (1706–1788), a colonial-era Boston minister and author remembered on the one hand for his ready wit and puns, and on the other for his loyalty to England during the American Revolution. In Gunn's day, the *New York Tribune* newspaper regularly featured the kind of wry social commentary in which Byles earlier had excelled; much of this commentary now took the form of mock serial letters to the editor that Gunn's contemporaries (not a few of them his friends and acquaintances) penned for papers like the *Tribune*. The unidentified "Byles' letters" may refer to Byles's "Bombastic and Grubstreet Style," an essay that originally appeared in Benjamin Franklin's *American Magazine and Historical Chronicle* in January 1745, and satirized the hasty literary productions of popular periodical authors on both sides of the Atlantic some one hundred years before Gunn himself became a working journalist.

8. "Grace Poole," the twin Mystery in Jane Eyre: English author Charlotte Bronte's (1816–1855) classic work *Jane Eyre* (1847) recounts the coming-of-age of the novel's title character. Employed at one stage as a governess in a Gothic manor home, Jane crosses paths repeatedly with the mansion's secretive servant, Grace Poole.

9. Cortez, Pizarro: Hernán Cortés (1485–1547) and Francisco Pizarro (1471–1541), sixteenth-century Spanish explorers of the Americas, and conquerors, respectively, of the Aztec and Inca Empires.

CHAPTER XXXIV — RETROSPECTIVE AND VALEDICTORY

1. Job: Biblical figure, proverbially known for his righteous suffering under God.

2. Shylockian: Shakespeare's stage drama *The Merchant of Venice* (1596–1598) features a leading character by the name of Shylock, a wealthy Jewish merchant detested by townsmen for his apparent cruel selfishness.

3. Sicilian confessional: a reference to English Gothic novelist Ann Radcliffe's (1764–1823) work *A Sicilian Romance* (1790).

4. Dickens's Raven: readers of Charles Dickens's historical novel *Barnaby Rudge* (1841) encounter a talkative pet raven by the name of Grip, whose running commentary holds clues to several of the narrative's mysteries.

5. Zooloo-Kaffir: a member of the sizeable Zulu ethnic community in South Africa.

6. *Brummagem* Paris: "Brummagem" is the name used by natives for their home city of Birmingham, England, also known as the country's "Second City"—meaning that it once ranked just behind capital London in size and national importance. More generally, "Brummagem" refers to a cheap imitation.

7. "an inaptitude for social pleasures": in Charles Dickens's novel *The Life and Adventures of Martin Chuzzlewit* (1844), the title character travels to New York from England by steamship. After encountering, upon his arrival, any number of busy Americans, Martin muses that the people of the United States "had an inaptitude for social and domestic pleasure" (chapter 16).

FURTHER READING

SELECTED WORKS OF THOMAS BUTLER GUNN

Mose Among the Britishers; or, The B'hoy in London. Philadelphia: A. Hart, 1850 (held at the University of Chicago, the New York Public Library, Harvard Houghton, and Yale).

Scrapbook of Caricatures. New York? 1856 (held at the New York Public Library).

Parton, James, and Thomas Butler Gunn, eds. *The Humorous Poetry of the English Language, from Chaucer to Saxe*. New York: Mason Brothers, 1856 (held at the New York Public Library).

The Physiology of New York Boarding-Houses. New York: Mason Brothers, 1857.

"Bonner and the New-York Ledger." *The Scalpel* 40 (April 1859): 54–62 (held at the American Antiquarian Society).

Selected Southern Civil War correspondence for the *New York Tribune*, 1861–1863.

Manuscript Diaries, 21 vols., July 17, 1849–April 7, 1863 (held at the Missouri Historical Society, St. Louis, Missouri).

Selected London correspondence for the *New York Tribune*, 1863–.

PRIMARY SOURCES

Benedict, Fannie. "Boarding-House Experience in New York." *Packard's Monthly Magazine* 1, no. 1 (1869): 100–103.

"Board for a Lady." *Harper's Monthly* 13, no. 75 (August 1856): 358–359.

Briggs, Charles Frederick. *The Adventures of Harry Franco: A Tale of the Great Panic*. 2 vols. New York: F. Saunders, 1839.

Bristed, Charles Astor. "A New Theory of Bohemians." *Knickerbocker* (March 1861): 311–317.

Cummins, Maria. *The Lamplighter* [1854]. Ed. Nina Baym. New Brunswick: Rutgers University Press, 1995.

"Editorial: Home in a Boarding-House." *Lowell Offering* 3 (1842): 69–70.

"New American Writers." *Holden's Dollar Magazine* (July 1848): 421–424.

Taylor, Bayard. *John Godfrey's Fortunes; Related By Himself: A Story of American Life*. New York: G. P. Putnam, 1865.

Whitman, Walt. *Franklin Evans; or, The Inebriate; A Tale of the Times* [1842]. Ed. Jean Downey. New Haven: Yale College and University Press, 1967.

———. "The Two Vaults." In *The Uncollected Poetry and Prose of Walt Whitman*, vol. 2, ed. Emory Holloway. New York: Doubleday, Page, and Co., 1921, 92–93.

Willis, N. P. "Cheap Boarding and True Love." *New Mirror* (October 21, 1843): 33–38.

SECONDARY SOURCES

Bergmann, Hans. *God in the Street: New York Writing from the Penny Press to Melville.* Philadelphia: Temple University Press, 1995.

Blackmar, Elizabeth. *Manhattan for Rent, 1785–1850.* Ithaca: Cornell University Press, 1989.

Blumin, Stuart M. *The Emergence of the Middle Class: Social Experience in the American City, 1760–1900.* New York: Cambridge University Press, 1989.

Faflik, David. "Community, Civility, Compromise: Dr. Holmes's Boston Boardinghouse." *New England Quarterly* 78, no. 4 (December 2005): 547–569.

———. "Boardinghouse Life, Boardinghouse Letters." *Studies in the Literary Imagination* 40, no. 1 (Spring 2007): 27–43.

Gibian, Peter. *Oliver Wendell Holmes and the Culture of Conversation.* New York: Cambridge University Press, 2001.

Kelley, Wyn. *Melville's City: Literary and Urban Form in Nineteenth-Century New York.* New York: Cambridge University Press, 1996.

Klimasmith, Betsy. *At Home in the City: Urban Domesticity in American Literature and Culture, 1850–1930.* Lebanon: University Press of New England, 2005.

McDermott, John Francis. "Whitman and the Partons: Glimpses from the Diary of Thomas Butler Gunn, 1856–1860." *American Literature* 29, no. 3 (November 1957): 316–319.

Marcus, Sharon. *Apartment Stories: City and Home in Nineteenth-Century Paris and London.* Berkeley: University of California Press, 1999.

Modell, John, and Tamara K. Hareven, "Urbanization and the Malleable Household: An Examination of Boarding and Lodging in American Families." In *The American Family in Social-Historical Perspective*, 2nd ed., ed. Michael Gordon. New York: St. Martin's Press, 1978, 51–68.

Parry, Albert. *Garrets and Pretenders: A History of Bohemianism in America.* 1933; reprt. New York: Dover Publications, 1960.

Stansell, Christine. "Whitman at Pfaff's: Commercial Culture, Literary Life and New York Bohemia at Mid-Century." *Walt Whitman Quarterly Review* 10, no. 3 (Winter 1993): 107–126.

Warren, Joyce W. *Fanny Fern: An Independent Woman* (New Brunswick: Rutgers University Press, 1992).

ABOUT THE EDITOR

David Faflik is an assistant professor in the department of English at South Dakota State University. A specialist in the city in literature, he currently is completing a book project entitled *Boarding Out: Inhabiting the American Urban Literary Imagination, 1840–1860,* which addresses U.S. writers' response to the emerging metropolis during the middle decades of the nineteenth century.